MW01098259

The Joint Line: 1880-1995

A History of the Unique Cooperation among Three Railroads serving Denver and Pueblo, Colorado

—— By Robert D. Walz ——

Cover and Frontispiece: C&S 907 (E-5B 2-10-2) and AT&SF 3825 (2-10-2) lead an extra
(according to the published schedules there should be no freight trains southbound here
in the afternoon) freight, southbound at Castle Rock, Colorado, on March 29, 1930.
The train is mostly gondola loads of iron ore for CF&I at Pueblo.
–Denver Public Library; Western History collection; Otto Perry; OP-7083

The Joint Line: 1880-1995
By Robert D. Walz
Graphic design by Jonathan Signor

© 2013 The Santa Fe Railway Historical & Modeling Society Inc.
1205 S. Air Depot #101 Midwest City, OK 73110-4807
All rights reserved.
Printed in the United States of America
by AgPress, Manhattan, Kansas.

ISBN 978-1-933587-29-5

Table of Contents

Acknowledgements

ALL AUTHORS HAVE HELP in their endeavors and I am no exception. This work would not be possible without the assistance of the following. I am deeply indebted to Larry Green who provided me with Joint Line documents, corrected my misconceptions and answered all my questions. Steve Patterson, former Santa Fe Joint Line engineer, hosted my research trip to Denver, provided photos from his collection, checked locations and directions of the photographs in this work, and patiently answered my many questions about Santa Fe operations. Hol Wagner provided material on the Colorado and Southern freight operations.

Much of the research that went into this book came from two library collections in the Denver area. Coi Drummond-Gehrig at the Denver Public Library gave me access to the collections, found materials, and greatly facilitated my use of the Library's photo collection, especially the Otto Perry collection. Kenton Forrest, Archivist at the Research Library of the Colorado Railroad Museum provided me access to the materials, gave excellent advice about where to find items of interest, and answered all my questions. I am also indebted to Craig Ordner, Archivist of the Railroad & Heritage Museum in Temple, Texas, for providing the electronic version of the employee timetables. This allowed me to work from home and greatly shortened the research time for this project.

Without illustrations, a book of this type would be barren. Gary Rich, retired Rio Grande employee and photographer, provided the data on the coal trains in Chapter 6, provided excellent photos from his collection and answered my Rio Grande questions. Stuart J. Sutton has been taking photos in the Denver area for over 50 years and provided me hundreds of photos of all three railroads from the 1950s to 1995.

My wife, Merrill, patiently read and edited the text, asked questions, probed for more information and was patient with me over the course of this project. Dr. Chris Gabel, my former colleague at the Army's Command and General Staff College, is a professional historian and Pennsy fan. He read the text and provided excellent insights that have improved the work greatly.

I would like to thank the Santa Fe Railroad Historical and Modeling society for publishing this work and for the companionship and information that it and its predecessor organizations have provided me over the span of nearly 30 years. I would like to thank Eric Hiser especially for his encouragement of my writing efforts, and most especially editor John Signor for polishing the text. I would also like to thank Jonathan Signor for his page layouts and cleanup of the photographs. Despite all the help I received, I alone am responsible for all errors of fact and interpretation that might be contained in this work.

Introduction

IN 1899 THERE WERE three competing single-track railroads between Denver and Pueblo, Colorado. These railroads were: the Atchison, Topeka, and Santa Fe; the Denver and Rio Grande; and the Colorado and Southern. By 1919, these three railroads were joined together in operating a double-track railroad, the famed Colorado Joint Line, between the same two cities. This book tells the story of how this came about, of the traffic on the line, and how the three railroads operated jointly.

The primary sources for this history are the employee timetables, most notably the Denver Division Joint employee timetables of the Atchison, Topeka and Santa Fe Railway and Denver and Rio Grande Western Railway from 1919 to 1989, which are available on CD from the Robert Pounds Collection at the Railroad & Heritage Museum Archives in Temple,

Texas. The Santa Fe published passenger train consist lists which are archived on the Santa Fe Railway Historical & Modeling Society's website. These gave general guidance to employees who had to put passenger trains together. Although trains often deviated from these instructions, they give a general idea as to how the railroad intended to serve the travelling public. Unfortunately, neither the Denver & Rio Grande Western (D&RGW) nor the Colorado & Southern (C&S) published such guidance for their employees. At least none have yet come to light. Therefore to provide similar information for the D&RGW and C&S, I have used the information published in the public timetables of the two railroads. This source is perfectly acceptable for the passenger-carrying cars, but gives no information about head end traffic. Therefore where there is sufficient photographic evidence

to indicate head end cars, I have used that. Otherwise I have simply used "head end" in the consist information. For many years freight train schedules were provided in the employee timetables. However, in the later years the railroads simplified the employee timetables and left such information out. All three railroads did publish separate freight train schedules for employees and shippers, but these are not as readily available as the employee and public timetables in archived collections. I have used those that I was able to find, but coverage in Chapters Five and especially Six is incomplete at best.

D&R R R DEPOT.

Chapter One

The Early Years to 1900

ON OCTOBER 27, 1880, General William Jackson Palmer and his lifelong friend and partner, Dr. William Bell, obtained a charter for the original Denver & Rio Grande (D&RG). Construction southward from Denver began shortly thereafter. Palmer's original intent was to build south to El Paso where the route would connect to a Mexican sister railroad for the rest of the trip to Pacific Coast ports. The preferred route was south from Denver to Pueblo, then west along the Arkansas River. Having reached Salida at the other end of the Royal Gorge, the rails would turn south across Poncha Pass and stretch out through the San Luis Valley, reaching the headwaters of the Rio Grande (the river). The little railroad would then just follow the river all the way south to the border. Narrow gauge was chosen because construction costs — and equally important, construction time — were lower than standard gauge.

By October of 1871, the rails had reached what would become Colorado Springs, but the town wasn't actually there yet. It was merely a point near Colorado City, which the railroad had decided to bypass in favor of setting up its own town. The plan was to build a station point on the railway and then convince people to come settle a brand new town. Palmer's concept was this: not only did you get to sell people railway services but also land, housing, supplies, etc. He was putting people where there would be shipping for the railroad for years to come. Palmer and his partners advertised around the world, and sure enough, people came. The railroad also opened the first dining station there. So successful was this experiment — a so-called "colony town" — that it was repeated numerous times during the building of the railroad.

Denver & Rio Grande: The First Railroad Between Denver and Pueblo

The first timetable dated November 24, 1871, listed one train a day between Denver and Colorado Springs, although the line did not officially open until January 1, 1872. By the first day of 1872, regular service to the newly founded Colorado Springs had begun, and Palmer was already grading south again, expanding towards Pueblo. By mid-June 1872, rails were complete as far as Pueblo, and the railway officially opened for operation, end-to-end, complete with another dining station. The only work done the rest of that year was an extension some thirty miles west to the Florence area, in order to tap coal mines just to the south of town. The D&RG reached Cañon City in 1874. The rails reached Grand Junction in March 1883 completing a narrow gauge transcontinental link with the Rio Grande Western Railway to Salt Lake City, Utah.

Palmer had planned for the route to pass over Raton Pass in what is now northern New Mexico. But the Atchison, Topeka and Santa Fe (AT&SF) got there first. Feverish, competitive construction with the Santa Fe provoked the 1877–1880 war over rights of way in the Royal Gorge, known as the "Royal Gorge War." Both railroads hired gunslingers and bought politicians. In June 1879, the Santa Fe defended its roundhouse in Pueblo with Dodge City toughs led by Bat Masterson. On that occasion, D&RG treasurer R. F. Weitbrec paid the defenders to leave.

The signing of the "Treaty of Boston" also known as the "Tripartite Agreement" (the AT&SF, the D&RG, and the Union Pacific) in March of 1880 ended the war. The Santa Fe agreed to stay out of western Colorado and the D&RG would not go further south than 60 miles south of Conejos, Colorado, (a village in the San Luis Valley close to the Colorado and New Mexico state line). The agreement was to last ten years and put a stop to the D&RG plans for going to Mexico City. The Santa Fe won the right to Raton Pass, while the D&RG paid the Santa Fe $1.4

Opposite: A locomotive with two passenger cars pauses on tracks of the Denver and Rio Grande Railroad depot, water tank and eating house, Palmer Lake, Colorado, circa 1890. Note the dual gauge tracks. *Denver Public Library, Western History collection X-12883*

million for tracks through the Arkansas River's Royal Gorge to the mining district of Leadville, Colorado. Subsequently, the D&RG focused on exploiting the lucrative mining service opportunities to the west. The Union Pacific (UP) entered into the agreement so all three railroads could share in and control railroad traffic in Colorado.

Passenger Trains

From 1872 until 1880, the Rio Grande ran a pair of passenger trains between Denver and Pueblo on what would become the Joint Line. In 1876, No. 1 *Express* departed Denver at 2:30 PM and arrived in Pueblo at 8:30 PM where passengers continuing on had half an hour for dinner. No. 2 *Express* departed Pueblo at 1:40 PM after through passengers had lunch and arrived in Denver at 8:00 PM. Small, Class 25 (based on 25,000 pounds engine weight) 2-4-0 locomotives pulled the passenger trains until the first Class 37 4-4-0s arrived in 1876. After that, the 4-4-0 was preferred for passenger trains. The normal consist of the train was a four-wheel baggage car and two or three coaches, each with a capacity of 33 passengers.

In 1880, the Rio Grande named trains 1 and 2 the *San Juan Express* and *Denver Express*, respectively. The little trains ran between Denver and Salida with companion trains with the same names connecting at Pueblo for Alamosa. Also in 1880, two new night trains, Nos. 3 and 4, *Leadville Express* and *Eastern Express*, respectively, began running between Denver and South Arkansas. These trains, in addition to baggage and coach cars, also carried one or two elegant new Pullman Palace 10-section sleeping cars on the end of the train. For the next ten years the Rio Grande expanded, experimented and often changed passenger train schedules using names such as *Mail*, *Express*, *Accommodation*, *Local* and *Passenger* to describe their services.

In 1881[1] the Rio Grande (the Grande) added a third rail to its line from Pueblo to Denver. Although the "Tripartite Agreement" kept the AT&SF from building to Denver on its own, the dual gauging of the line was probably done for two reasons: 1) to forestall the Santa Fe from violating the agreement to build to Denver and 2) the realization that unless the line was standard gauged, little or no interchange traffic would traverse the Rockies via the Grande. Either that traffic would go around, or more likely, competitors like the AT&SF or the Chicago, Burlington and Quincy (CB&Q) would construct their own lines through the mountains, relegating the D&RG to a branch line status. Around the same time, they also added a third rail to their line up Pueblo's Minnequa Hill to the Colorado Fuel and Iron steel mill. The line between Pueblo and Denver remained dual gauge until 1902.

At the same time the line was dual gauged, the D&RG bought standard gauge locomotives to work the line. The D&RG and AT&SF entered into an adjunct agreement to the "Treaty of Boston" or "Tripartite Agreement" to provide haulage of AT&SF cars between Denver and Pueblo. The D&RG timetables carded a "Santa Fe" train. So in a roundabout way, AT&SF traffic reached Denver in 1881 without transfer to narrow gauge cars. By this time, the Rio Grande had 109 consecutively numbered locomotives – all narrow gauge. Of these four were 2-4-0s and 21 were 4-4-0s for the passenger trains.

In 1882, the Rio Grande began running railway post office (RPO) cars and by August three routes were in operation: Denver, Pueblo and Leadville; Pueblo and Durango; and Salida and Gunnison. In 1883, the first two long distance express trains entered the Rio Grande timetable. No. 7 *Pacific Express* ran from Denver to Ogden in about 41½ hours and No. 8 *Atlantic Express* used 36 hours to make the reverse trip. These were the premier narrow gauge trains on the Rio Grande. The 1882 lineup is described in Table 1-1.

In 1887, a second pair of trains between Denver and Ogden began. January 1888 was the high point of narrow gauge passenger traffic when twelve trains ran in and out of Denver. By the summer of that year the Rio Grande started carrying Missouri Pacific (MP) standard gauge passenger trains between Pueblo and Denver. The summer 1888 lineup of Rio Grande passenger trains at Denver is described in Table 1-2.

Between 1881 and 1883, the Rio Grande purchased four 4-6-0 locomotives to pull the standard gauge trains. Additional purchases of standard gauge 4-6-0 locomotives were made through 1899. The standard gauge locomotives could also pull narrow gauge passenger trains and often did. In 1889, the *Pacific Express* and *Atlantic Express* were renumbered to 1 and 2. At the end of the 1880s, the Rio Grande was running ten narrow gauge passenger trains and two standard gauge passenger trains for the MP into and out of Denver.

On January 27, 1889, the Rio Grande began service between Denver, Littleton, and Fort Logan.

Table 1-1

No.	Name	Details
1-2	*Thunderbolt Express / Denver Express*	Daytime between Denver and Leadville
3-4	*Leadville Express / Eastern Express*	Overnight with coaches and sleeping car from Denver to Pueblo, Leadville, Frisco and Red Cliff with return to Denver
7-8	*Pacific Express / Atlantic Express*	Daytime from Denver to Salt Lake City and Ogden with return to Denver

---

1. Previously published materials disagreed on dates of the dual gauging of the line between Denver and Pueblo and the rationale for the Santa Fe building its own line to Denver. The consensus was that the line was dual-gauged around 1888 in response to the Santa Fe building to Denver. The reason usually given for the Santa Fe to build to Denver was its irritation over having to transload at Pueblo. I am indebted to Larry Green of Pueblo who has thoroughly researched the primary sources that dispel much of the "conventional wisdom."

Officially listed in the timetables as *Suburban Service*, these trains soon began to be called *Uncle Sam*. Initial service was a two-car train that ran four times a day each way. By 1900 the frequency had increased to five trains a day each way.

Two years later in 1891, the Rio Grande had enough standard gauge equipment to convert most of the passenger trains to standard gauge. Schedules had changed markedly. Some daytime trains became nighttime trains and destinations changed for some train numbers. Names had changed to incorporate new terms like *Limited* and *Fast Mail*. 4-6-0 locomotives pulled all the standard gauge passenger trains. The lineup out of Denver in 1891 is found in Table 1-3.

In the summer of 1892, the names of Nos. 2 and 3 were changed to *Transcontinental Limited* and *Transcontinental Express*, respectively, thanks to the inclusion of new Pullman Palace Sleeping Cars and Tourist Cars

D&RG No. 1 *Montezuma* was the first locomotive on the Denver and Rio Grande. This little Class 25 2-4-0 is typical of the locomotives that pulled Rio Grande passenger trains between Denver and Pueblo until Class 37 4-4-0s. –*Collection of Harold K. Vollrath*

Table 1-2

No.	Name	Details
1-2	Leadville Mail / Denver Mail	Daytime between Denver and Leadville
3-4	Leadville Express / Denver Express	Overnight with coaches and sleeping car from Denver to Leadville, Aspen, Alamosa, and Durango and return to Denver
5-6	Pueblo Express	Daytime between Denver and Pueblo
7-8	Pacific Express / Atlantic Express	Morning departure from and evening arrival in Denver to and from Salt Lake City and Ogden with coaches, emigrant sleeping car and buffet sleeping car
9-10	Salt Lake Express / Eastern Express	Evening departure and morning arrival in Denver to and from Salt Lake City and Ogden with coaches, emigrant sleeping car and buffet sleeping car
11-12	St. Louis Express (Durango Passenger / Denver passenger)*	Daytime standard gauge MP cars to and from Pueblo (daytime Denver and Durango narrow gauge passenger trains)
13-14	Manitou Excursion	Daytime Sunday only between Denver and Manitou Springs

* According to Danneman, Nos. 11 and 12 in the January timetable were narrow gauge and named *Durango* and *Denver Passenger*, respectively. According to Thode, by the summer of 1888, Nos. 11 and 12 were standard gauge carrying MP passenger cars.

Table 1-3

No.	Name	Details
1-2	California Fast Mail / California and Eastern Fast Mail	Overnight standard gauge between Denver and Salt Lake City-Ogden
3-4	Pacific Coast Limited / Atlantic Coast Limited	Daytime standard gauge between Denver and Salt Lake City-Ogden
5-6	California, Colorado and New Mexico Through Express	Daytime narrow gauge carrying coaches and four sleeping cars between Denver and Grand Junction and Denver and Alamosa-Durango via Salida
7-8	Trinidad and La Veta Passenger / Pueblo and Denver Accommodation	Daytime standard gauge between Denver and southern Colorado
9-10	Pueblo and Utah Passenger and Mail / Trinidad, La Veta and Denver Passenger	Daytime standard gauge between Denver and southern Colorado
11-12	Cañon City and St. Louis Express / St. Louis and Cañon City Express	Daytime standard gauge between Denver and Cañon City with MP cars to and from Pueblo
21-28	Suburban Passenger	Four standard gauge *Uncle Sam* trains throughout the day between Denver and Fort Logan

D&RG No. 2 (Class 35 2-6-0) in switching service at Burnham shops circa 1876. Also in photo are both a four-wheel baggage car and a double-truck baggage car. –*Colorado Railroad Museum collection*

Class 106 (later T-18) No. 533 built in 1891 awaits the signal to depart Denver with a standard gauge passenger train circa 1892. –*Colorado Railroad Museum collection*

via the Burlington, Rock Island, and Missouri Pacific east of the Front Range and via Southern Pacific west of Ogden. Then the Panic of 1893 hit causing wholesale changes. Nos. 7 and 8 were terminated abruptly on July 29. Then on August 22, the last narrow gauge trains into and out of Denver, Nos. 5 and 6, were discontinued and Nos. 2 and 3 were again renamed to the less pretentious *California and New Mexico Limited* and *California and New Mexico Express*.

The next year in September, thanks to the discovery of gold in the vicinity of Cripple Creek, the Rio Grande reinstated Nos. 5 and 6 with a new name, *Colorado and New Mexico Mail and Express N. G.* These trains, with three or four narrow gauge sleeping cars in the consist, connected to the Florence and Cripple Creek Railroad at Florence, just west of Pueblo. September 1894 also marked the beginning of the recovery from the "Panic" and Nos. 1 and 2 were again grandiosely renamed *Pacific Coast Fast Mail* and *Atlantic Coast Fast Mail*, respectively. The not-so-speedy Nos. 3 and 4 were also renamed to *Pacific Coast Express* and *Atlantic Coast Express*. Stability also came to these trains as they remained so named until 1900. Nos. 11 and 12, carrying Missouri Pacific (MP) equipment between Denver and Pueblo, were also renamed *Kansas City and St. Louis Express* and *St. Louis and Kansas City Express*. These two train names lasted until 1905.

Demand for transportation to Cripple Creek continued to expand and in December 1895, two additional narrow gauge trains, Nos. 7 and 8 *Cripple Creek Express N. G.*, were added to the schedule. Narrow gauge service beyond Pueblo continued to expand and in 1896 the four narrow gauge trains were again renamed to indicate their expanded roles. Nos. 5 and 6 became the *San Juan and New Mexico Express* and Nos. 7 and 8 became the *Cripple Creek and Marshall Pass Route Express N. G.* In October 1897, Nos. 7 and 8 were removed from the schedule due to competition from the shorter, faster standard gauge trains of the Colorado Midland Railway. Nos. 5 and 6 again became the only narrow gauge trains in and out of Denver with the longest name ever assigned to Rio Grande passenger trains, the *Cripple Creek, San Juan, New Mexico, and Marshall Pass Express N. G.*

Passenger traffic continued to increase so that in August 1899, to relieve pressure of local business on Nos. 1, 2, 3 and 4, the Rio Grande instituted a pair of daytime, standard gauge local passenger trains Nos. 14 and 15 (skipping unlucky 13), *Colorado Express* and *Colorado Mail*, respectively. In October they moved to overnight runs and were renumbered to 15 and 16 and renamed *Colorado Express*. In November the railroad completed the standard gauge route to Alamosa over La Veta Pass and these two trains developed into the 20th Century maids-of-all work trains with head end cars, coaches, and sleepers for Alamosa, Salida, Leadville, Glenwood Springs and Grand Junction. Also in the final six months of 1899, the Rio Grande corrected the lack of food service on their trains by adding dining cars to the through main line trains.

The narrow gauge trains were eliminated for good in February and March 1900. Nos. 5 and 6 were given to a new standard gauge train pair between Denver and Ogden, *Chicago San Francisco Express* and *San Francisco and Chicago Limited*, respectively. The fall 1900 lineup into and out of Denver is in Table 1-4.

These trains were pulled by 33 4-6-0 locomotives of the 106 Class. These locomotives were rated for 360 tons on the line's ruling grade between Littleton and Palmer Lake. Most had 55-inch drivers and carried a boiler pressure of 160 pounds.

Freight Trains

The major disadvantage of narrow gauge trains is that the locomotives are smaller and the freight cars have smaller load capacities than standard gauge. Therefore to carry the same amount of freight, more

D&RG No. 95 *Embuda* (Class 42 4-4-0) built in 1880. These locomotives were the prime narrow gauge passenger locomotives in the 1880s. –*Colorado Railroad Museum collection*

Table 1-4

No.	Name	Details
1-2	*Pacific Coast Limited / Atlantic Coast Limited*	Daytime through trains between Denver and Salt Lake City-Ogden
3-4	*New Mexico, Utah and California Express / Atlantic Mail*	Overnight train out of Denver to Salt Lake City-Ogden and daytime train from Salt Lake City-Ogden into Denver
5-6	*Chicago San Francisco Express / San Francisco and Chicago Express*	Premier daytime train from Denver to Salt Lake City-Ogden and overnight train from Salt Lake City-Ogden into Denver
9-10	*Cañon City and Cripple Creek Passenger*	Afternoon locals between Denver and Cañon City connecting to Florence and Cripple Creek Railroad.
11-12	*Kansas City and St. Louis Express / St. Louis and Kansas City Express*	Daytime between Denver and Pueblo MP cars
15-16	*Colorado Express / Colorado and New Mexico Express*	Overnight locals between Denver and Leadville with connections at Pueblo to and from Alamosa and at Salida with narrow gauge to Grand Junction via Marshall Pass
21-30	*Suburban Passenger*	Five standard gauge *Uncle Sam* trains throughout the day (one daily except Sunday) to and from Fort Logan

trains are needed. The D&RG usually accomplished this on the line between Pueblo and Denver with two or four through freight trains daily and two way freight trains. In 1876, Nos. 3 and 4, named *Express Freight*, ran between Denver, Pueblo, and La Veta. Nos. 5 and 6 were the Denver and Pueblo *Way Freight* trains. The Rio Grande started pulling these freight

trains with Class 35 2-6-0 locomotives but in 1877 purchased its first 2-8-0, and 2-8-0s were preferred freight power after that.

By 1882, four through freight trains and two way freight trains were running between Denver and Pueblo. Two of the through freight trains ran on standard gauge rails and carried Santa Fe freight between

Above: Builder's photo of D&RG No. 88 *Ptarmigan* (Class 44 4-4-0) built in 1880. These locomotives were the prime narrow gauge passenger locomotives in the 1880s. –*Charles B. Chaney Railroad Photographs, Archives Center, National Museum of American History, Smithsonian Institution*

Left: D&RG 3 *Sho wa no,* a Class 35 2-6-0 bought in 1871 used in freight service from the earliest days of the Rio Grande. –*Collection of Harold K. Vollrath*

D&RG 608 (Class 120 later Class C-26 2-8-0) circa 1895. Built in 1890 as RGW 131. Locomotives of this class were the prime standard gauge freight locomotives on what became the Joint Line in the 1890s. The locomotive was renumbered 608 in 1924 and dismantled in 1934. –*Colorado Railroad Museum collection*

Denver and Pueblo. Two more trains, called *Stone* trains, ran between Denver and Colorado Springs. By 1884, largely due to the financial crisis of that year, the Rio Grande was running only four freight trains between Denver and Pueblo, a way freight each way and a through freight each way that continued to and from Salida. One must assume that all these were narrow gauge trains and that Santa Fe business had fallen off sufficiently so as not to warrant a dedicated standard gauge train. Locomotives were chosen for these trains from a pool of 18 2-6-0s and 56 2-8-0s.

Three years later, the Rio Grande was running a pair of Denver, Pueblo, and Leadville through freight trains, another pair between Denver, Pueblo and Grand Junction, and a pair between Denver and Pueblo. Additionally, there was a daily except Sunday pair of Denver and Pueblo way freight trains and a *Special Freight* daily except Sunday each way between Denver and Pueblo. Up until this time freight trains had been numbered consecutively between 19 and 30.

By 1888 with the publication of *Employee Timetable #1*, second-class freight trains were numbered in the 40s and third class in the 70s. Table 1-5 shows the trains running between Denver and Pueblo at that time.

This logical numbering system did not last for even two years. By 1890, any numbered train could be second- or third-class and fourteen freight trains were running over all or part of the Pueblo to Denver line. Narrow gauge trains predominated. By 1890 the Missouri Pacific had reached Pueblo and the Rio Grande ran a pair of standard gauge trains between Pueblo and Denver for this interchange traffic. The Rock Island had reached Colorado Springs by this time and interchanged traffic with the Rio Grande. The Rio Grande ran two narrow gauge trains each way between the "Springs" and Denver for this traffic. In addition by 1890, the Rio Grande was running another pair of standard gauge trains between Denver and Trinidad.

As shown in Table 1-6 by 1895 the total count of freight trains was down to twelve and only No. 69 was narrow gauge.

By 1898, Nos. 97 and 98 were gone and a counterpart to No. 69, No. 70 *Through Freight*, added a Salida to Denver narrow gauge train. In addition, the railroad added No. 65 *Through Freight* running from Denver to Grand Junction. This gave the Rio Grande five trains running between Denver and Grand Junction. By 1899, Nos. 97 and 98 both named *C.R I.&P. Freight* had been added back to the lineup giving the Rio Grande a total of 14 daily freight trains running between Denver and Pueblo, all but two of which were standard gauge. The Rio Grande had 74 Class 113 2-8-0 locomotives in the freight pool for these trains. The 113 Class rode on 46-inch drivers, carried a boiler pressure of 140 pounds, and were rated at 450 tons on the ruling grade up the Palmer Divide between Littleton and Palmer Lake.

We will now leave the Rio Grande until Chapter Three when the United States Railroad Administration (USRA) forced the Santa Fe and Rio Grande into joint operation of their parallel lines.

Santa Fe Enters Denver

The first Santa Fe locomotive arrived in Pueblo on March 7, 1876, providing the opportunity for, according to the local newspaper the *Chieftan*, the "biggest drunk of the present century." When the AT&SF reached Pueblo, the Rio Grande hoped that they would build their yard in South Pueblo next to the D&RG. A. A. Robinson, the Santa's Fe chief engineer, avoided what he saw as a Rio Grande attempt to manipulate the Santa Fe and chose to build diagonally across central Pueblo, which frustrated Rio Grande motives. The Santa Fe then turned its eyes to Denver.

Santa Fe first entered Denver in December 1878 when it leased the D&RG. The next year the Santa Fe terminated the lease of the D&RG. In 1881, as

D&RG 570 (Class 113 2-8-0) on a southbound freight is stopped behind a stalled freight at Monument, Colorado, circa 1899.
–*Colorado Railroad Museum collection*

Table 1-5

No.	Name	Details
41	*Fast Freight*	Denver to Leadville daily except Sunday. Old No. 19
42	*Fast Freight*	Leadville to Denver daily except Monday. Old No. 20
45	*Through Freight*	Denver to Grand Junction. Old No. 21
46	*Through Freight*	Grand Junction to Denver. Old No. 22
71	*Way Freight*	Denver to Pueblo daily except Sunday. Old No. 23
72	*Way Freight*	Pueblo to Denver daily except Sunday. Old No. 24
75	*Pueblo Freight*	Denver to Pueblo.
76	*Denver Freight*	Pueblo to Denver.
77	*Freight*	Denver to Pueblo daily except Sunday. Old No. 29
78	*Freight*	Pueblo to Denver daily except Sunday. Old No. 30

Table 1-6

No.	Name	Details
61	*California Fast Freight*	Denver to Grand Junction second-class
62	*Colorado Fast Freight*	Grand Junction to Denver second-class
63	*Colorado & California Fast Freight*	Denver to Grand Junction second-class
64	*California & Colorado Fast Freight*	Grand Junction to Denver second-class
66	*Freight*	Pueblo to Denver third-class
67	*Trinidad Fast Freight*	Denver to Trinidad third-class
68	*Trinidad Fast Freight*	Trinidad to Denver third-class
69	*Colorado & New Mexico Fast Freight*	Denver to Salida narrow gauge second-class
77	*Local Freight*	Denver to Pueblo third-class
78	*Local Freight*	Pueblo to Denver third-class
97	*C.R I.&P. Freight*	Colorado Springs to Denver third-class
98	*C.R I.&P. Freight*	Denver to Colorado Springs third-class

An Atchison, Topeka & Santa Fe locomotive speeds along with a passenger train south of Denver circa 1895. –*Denver Public Library; Western History collection; H. S. Poley; MCC-3176*

a result of the Santa Fe gaining trackage rights over the new third rail of the D&RG, it again entered Denver. This remained the situation until 1887, when the Missouri Pacific completed its line between Kansas and Pueblo. This drastically altered the traffic arrangements envisioned by the "Tripartite Agreement." Although the Santa Fe had access to Denver via trackage rights over the third rail on the Denver & Rio Grande, this arrangement was increasingly expensive. The Santa Fe abrogated the "Treaty of Boston," and decided to build to Denver, either through purchase of the parallel Denver and New Orleans (D&NO), or by new construction. The owners of the D&NO refused to sell at the price the Santa Fe was offering, so in March 1887 the Santa Fe formed its Denver and Santa Fe subsidiary, which built 116 miles of new railroad to the vicinity of Denver. In doing so, the alignment required that the Santa Fe cross the Rio Grande three times, at Fountain, Spruce and Sedalia. The Rio Grande was not happy with the Santa Fe building to Denver so it refused permission for the Santa Fe to cross at grade. Therefore the Santa Fe built flyovers at all three locations. The Santa Fe

then purchased the Denver Circle Railroad, an eight-mile terminal road, giving the Santa Fe strategic traffic connections.

Passenger Trains

Throughout its history up to 1971, the Santa Fe continuously tried to find the right balance of long distance trains between Denver and the east and trains that connected Denver to other trains at La Junta, Pueblo, and Colorado Springs. According to *Time Table No. 30* dated June 17, 1888, Santa Fe passenger trains began running into the 1881-built Denver Union Depot. At that time Santa Fe ran eight passenger trains, shown in Table 1-7, on what was to become the Joint Line. Four were long distance trains and four were connecting trains at Colorado Springs.

Times were slow and stops (both station and flag) were many. Pulled by 4-4-0s and 4-6-0s, Nos. 5, 6, and 7 all made the same 28 stops in the 180 miles between La Junta and Denver, inclusive, and No. 8 made only one less. For some reason, No. 8 did not stop at the Military Post station. Nos. 501 through

504, an attempt to capture the business between Denver and the mining areas around Leadville in conjunction with connections at Colorado Springs, all made 15 stops between Denver and Colorado Springs.

For the first few years the Santa Fe apparently experimented with passenger trains and schedules, trying to discover the right mix of services. For the rest of the decade, there was one constant, Nos. 5 and 6. The names occasionally changed, but this train pair remained the primary limited-stop train between Denver and Kansas City/Chicago. Only seven months after the first entry into Denver Union Station, the Santa Fe made some important changes. Nos. 21 *Colorado Express* and 22 *Atlantic Express* replaced Nos. 7 and 8. They ran between Denver and La Junta and connected with Santa Fe trains Nos. 1 and 2.

But by January 1891, Nos. 7 and 8 were back replacing Nos. 21 and 22 with new eastern terminals. No. 7 kept its old name of *Colorado Express* but ran from Chicago to Denver. It made 29 stops between La Junta and Denver. No. 8, renamed the *Missouri River Express*, ran from Denver to Kansas City, making 29 stops but with an average speed of 22.5 miles per hour. Until 1895, this train pair would be the all-stops trains between Denver and the east. Table 1-8

Table 1-7

No.	Name	Details
5-6	*Denver and Utah Express / Eastern Express*	Daytime Kansas City to Denver running from Pueblo to Denver in the morning / Denver to Chicago train running from Denver to Pueblo in the afternoon
7-8	*Colorado Express / Local Passenger*	Nighttime Pueblo to Denver from Newton to Denver / Denver to probably Dodge City
501-502	*Denver Express / Aspen Express*	Daytime Denver train to and from Colorado Springs
503-504	*Denver Express / Leadville Express*	Daytime Denver train to and from Colorado Springs

shows the consist of Nos. 7 and 8 in 1893.

In January 1891 the four Denver and Colorado Springs trains were all renumbered from 501-504 to 601-604 and the two southbound (timetable eastbound) trains were renamed *Pacific Express*, probably to carry the connotation that passengers could continue through connections all the way to the Pacific Ocean. The Santa Fe apparently found that there was insufficient business for four Colorado Springs trains because in August 1891 Nos. 601 and 602 were dropped from the timetable.

January 1891 also saw four new trains added to the timetable. Nos. 623 and 624, *Colorado Express* and *New York Express*, respectively, were relatively speedy but short-lived trains between Colorado Springs and La Junta that connected with Nos. 3 and 4 at La Junta. They were gone by August. The other new trains were a pair of Denver to Pueblo trains, Nos. 637 and 638 both named *Cañon City and Denver Express*, that connected with Nos. 625 and 626 at Pueblo to and from Cañon City. They would last longer, although in August they were renamed *Eastern Express* and *Pueblo and Denver Express* when they began running through Pueblo to and from La Junta. At that time they both

Table 1-8

Car Type	Route
Head End Car(s)	
Chair Car	Denver and Kansas City
Chair Car	Denver and Kansas City
Palace Sleeping Car	Denver and La Junta

Table 1-9

Car Type	Route
Head End Car(s)	
Chair Car	Denver and Chicago
Chair Car	Denver and Chicago
Dining Car	Denver and Pueblo
Palace Sleeping Car	Denver and Chicago
Palace Sleeping Car	Chicago and Ogden

connected from No. 628 from Cañon City and were scheduled for layovers of three hours, 35 minutes and four hours, 35 minutes in Pueblo, respectively.

The year 1892 brought some more changes. In August, Nos. 601 and 602, *Denver Express* and *Pacific Express*, were reinstated running between Denver and Colorado Springs. No. 603 became the *Atlantic Express* and was the first train to average over 30 miles per hour on the line, travelling the 74 miles to Denver at an average speed of 34 miles per hour. No. 604 was renamed *Utah and California Express* and made 10 stops as it ran from Denver to Colorado Springs at an average speed of 27.7 miles per hour.

The only notable change brought by the January 1893 timetable was the renaming of Nos. 5 and 6 to *Colorado and Utah Limited* and *Kansas City and Chicago Limited*, respectively. No. 6 also began running all the way to Chicago. Table 1-9 shows the consists of Nos. 5 and 6 in June 1893.

The August 1894 timetable saw Nos. 636 and 637 replaced by Nos. 603 and 604 and La Junta became the southern terminal instead of Pueblo. Nos. 603 and 604 also took 636 and 637's names *Pueblo and Denver Express* and *Eastern Express*, respectively. Table 1-10 shows how Santa Fe passenger trains

Table 1-10

No.	Name	Details
5-6	*Colorado and Utah Limited / Kansas City and Chicago Limited*	Limited-stop Chicago and Denver trains
7-8	*Colorado Express / Missouri River Express*	Chicago and Denver all-stops accommodation train running over the Pueblo-Denver line during hours of darkness
601-602	*Denver Express / Pacific Express*	Denver and Colorado Springs accommodation trains
603-604	*Pueblo and Denver Express / Eastern Express*	Daytime Denver and La Junta locals

looked in 1894.

1895 brought more changes. Nos. 7 and 8 were dropped and two new train pairs were added, a Denver and Pueblo pair and a second Denver and Colorado Springs pair. Nos. 605 *Denver and Pueblo Express* and 606 *Pueblo and Denver Express* added a second local train running between Denver and Pueblo. No. 604 moved to an evening schedule, No. 606 replaced it in the afternoon, and No. 605 ran in the morning. Nos. 607, *Colorado Express*, and 608, *Leadville Express*, added a second Colorado Springs and Denver round trip. This lasted until 1898 when two more trains were added. No. 8, *Kansas City and Chicago Express*, ran from Pueblo to Kansas City and No. 617, *Pueblo and Colorado Springs Express*, ran from La Junta to Colorado Springs. This schedule lasted through the remainder of the 19th Century.

Freight Trains

According to the June 1888 timetable, the Santa Fe initially ran four second-class freight trains between Denver and Pueblo, shown in Table 1-11.

Usually pulled by 4-6-0s, the freight trains ran on slow schedules and Nos. 43 and 44 probably did local work between Denver and Pueblo while Nos. 31 and 32 did local work between Pueblo and La Junta. No. 31 was the fastest, covering the 180 miles between La Junta and Denver in nine hours and 50 minutes plus 30 minutes switching in Pueblo. No. 32 spent 11 hours 50 minutes on the road and over 7 hours in Pueblo being switched. No. 43 took ten and a half hours to cover the nearly 117 miles from Pueblo to Denver while No. 44 took even longer at almost 11 and a half hours.

The year 1891 brought some major changes to freight schedules. Both 31 and 32 had their schedules shortened, 31's by an hour and 32's by almost two hours, even though it was downgraded to a third-class freight train. Nos. 43 and 44 were dropped from the schedule and two short-distance freight trains were added at this time, Nos. 605 and 606; see Table 1-12.

In August 1891, newly added Nos. 41 and 42 became the first third-class way freight trains on what was to become the Joint Line. No. 41 took over eight daylight hours to work the line from Pueblo to Denver and No. 42 took thirteen mostly daylight hours to work the line south from Denver to Pueblo. Both ran daily and in August were extended to La Junta on schedules of between 12 and 13 hours.

In August 1892 two short-distance, third-class freight trains running between Pueblo and Colorado Springs, Nos. 45 *Colorado Springs and Utah Freight* and 46 *Pueblo Freight*, were added to the schedule. Both ran daily except Sunday on a relatively fast (between two and three hours) schedule. August 1894 brought some major changes to the freight trains schedules. Nos. 41 and 42 were renumbered to 45 and 46, but continued to operate on roughly the

Table 1-11

No.	Name	Details
31	*Freight*	Kansas City to Denver running overnight Pueblo to Denver
32	*Freight*	Denver to La Junta running in the morning Denver to Pueblo
43	*Freight*	Pueblo to Denver running mid-morning into the evening
44	*Freight*	Overnight Denver to Pueblo

Table 1-12

No.	Name	Details
31	*Second Class Freight*	Kansas City to Denver running overnight Pueblo to Denver
32	*Third Class Freight*	Denver to La Junta running in the morning Denver to Pueblo
605	*Third Class Freight*	Colorado Springs to Denver on a 3½ hour schedule
606	*Third Class Utah Freight*	Denver to Colorado Springs on a 3½ hour schedule

same way freight schedules between Denver and La Junta. The two Pueblo and Colorado Springs trains that had used 45 and 46 were dropped. Nos. 605 and 606 between Denver and Colorado Springs were renumbered to 641 and 642 with 642 retaining the *Utah Freight* name. A new second-class train, No. 634 *Fruit Express*, ran from Colorado Springs to La Junta in four hours to connect with No. 34 *Fruit Express*. Table 1-13 displays the changes.

Apparently these changes were not effective. In November 1894, Nos. 634, 641, and 642 left the schedule, leaving only four freight trains: through freight trains Nos. 31 and 32 and way freight trains Nos. 45 and 46. Except for some minor schedule changes this remained the situation until 1899 when Nos. 45 and 46 were renumbered to 83 and 84, *Way Freight*, and began operating daily except Sunday on about 13-hour schedules between Denver and La Junta.

Colorado and Southern Beginnings

The Colorado and Southern Railway (reporting marks C&S, CS), formed in 1898 from an amalgam of narrow gauge and a standard gauge railroad in Col-

Table 1-13

No.	Name	Details
31	*Second Class Freight*	Kansas City to Denver running overnight Pueblo to Denver
32	*Third Class Freight*	Denver to La Junta running in the morning Denver to Pueblo
634	*Second Class Fruit Express*	Colorado Springs to La Junta connecting with No. 34 *Fruit Express*
45	*Third Class Way Freight*	La Junta to Denver daily
46	*Third Class Way Freight*	Denver to La Junta daily
641	*Third Class Freight*	Colorado Springs to Denver on a 3½ hour schedule
642	*Third Class Utah Freight*	Denver to Colorado Springs to on a 3½ hour schedule

orado and New Mexico, operated independently from 1898 to 1908. It then operated as part of the Chicago, Burlington and Quincy Railroad until it was absorbed into the Burlington Northern Railroad in 1981.

The first unit of what became the Colorado and Southern Railway Company was the Colorado and Clear Creek Railroad Company, incorporated February 9, 1865. The next year the name was changed to the Colorado and Pacific Railroad Company, and on January 14, 1868, modified again to Colorado Central Railway. The promoters were citizens of communities west of Denver. Their purpose was to promote the interests of their communities over the interests of Denver. Construction of the line began at Golden, and in September 1870 the first narrow gauge train operated between Golden and Denver.

In 1881 the controlling interests of the Colorado Central wished to extend the railroad from Georgetown to Silver Plume and Graymont. In order to obtain the necessary financial backing, they formed a new entity known as the Georgetown, Breckenridge and Leadville Railway Company, which completed the line in 1884. The outstanding feature of this extension was the serpentine "Georgetown Loop."

Another component of the Colorado and Southern was Denver, South Park and Pacific Railroad Company (DSP&P), which was chartered in June 1873 and by 1888 had completed a narrow gauge line from Denver to Gunnison and Leadville as well as several branches, a total distance of 324.54 miles. The DSP&P was sold in June 1889 to the Denver, Leadville and Gunnison Railway.

The standard gauge Denver and New Orleans (D&NO), which after becoming part of the Colorado and Southern would eventually route its trains over the Joint Line, was started by former Colorado Governor John Evans, along with railroad entrepreneur David Moffat and other associates in 1881. The company was chartered to build a railroad from Denver, Colorado, to the Gulf of Mexico. The charter was later changed from building to the Gulf of Mexico and instead called for establishing a connection with the Fort Worth and Denver City Railway (FW&DC), which was building northwest from Fort Worth, Texas.

The D&NO built from Denver to Pueblo, Colorado, through Parker, Elizabeth, Falcon and Manitou Junction, all of which were east of the Denver and Rio Grande alignment. From here it eventually connected to Colorado Springs at the end of 1882. On May 4, 1882, the D&NO entered Pueblo with a special train. Regular service began on May 11 with one daily round trip passenger train consisting of a baggage car and one or two coaches. A coal mine opened around that time at Franceville and the D&NO built a branch from Franceville Junction to Franceville. The mine provided coal for the locomotives and a source of desperately needed revenue because the D&RG actively fought the D&NO at every opportunity.

Because the "Tripartite Agreement" had divided Colorado traffic among the Union Pacific, Santa Fe, and Rio Grande, none of those three would interchange traffic with the D&NO. Nor would the CB&Q interchange with it at Denver. Thus by 1885, the D&NO, owning four passenger and four freight locomotives, was operating on a financial shoestring. But it had gained access to the Bessemer works that was to later become the Colorado Fuel and Iron Company, a huge steel-making plant in south Pueblo. And it had started a rate war, which benefited no one. Evans tried to show the company was viable by adding a second round trip between Denver and Pueblo, but traffic was minimal with freight trains averaging only 14 cars and passenger trains ran with at most three.

So on January 1, 1886, the D&NO was sold at foreclosure and reorganized as the Denver, Texas and Gulf (DT&G). The new company received all the assets of the D&NO including eight locomotives, four passenger cars, and 248 freight cars. The new company still ran a daily passenger round trip between

C&S 410 (2-8-0) is possibly at Franceville, Colorado, in early 1899. –*Colorado Railroad Museum collection*

Denver and Pueblo, Nos. 1 and 2, *Mail & Express*, pulled by 4-4-0 locomotives. The DT&G had inherited 2-6-0s for freight service and purchased more. In 1888 the company bought two light 2-8-0 Consolidations for service on the coal drags from Franceville. Then in 1889 ten more Consolidations, built to Union Pacific specifications, came from Baldwin and seven more similar engines came from Rhode Island in 1890. Together, they were the prime freight power for the road.

Evans still had the goal of reaching the Gulf of Mexico but did not have the financial backing to do so. He looked for backing anywhere he could find it, trying to work a deal with the newly created but unbuilt Colorado Midland, and then trying to sell the line to the Santa Fe. The Santa Fe was willing to buy but was unwilling to pay Evan's asking price. Meanwhile the Ft. Worth and Denver City, run by Grenville Dodge, the former chief engineer of the Union Pacific, was gradually pushing north to the Texas-New Mexico border and was still desirous of joining their rails to those of the DT&G. Finally signs of a

break occurred. The Rock Island and Missouri Pacific were about to enter Colorado Springs and Pueblo, respectively, causing the "Tripartite Agreement" to break down.

At the same time that Evans' banker continued to negotiate with the Santa Fe, Evans and Dodge worked a deal whereby a third railroad, the Denver, Texas, and Ft. Worth (DT&FW), was organized to build from Pueblo to the Texas-New Mexico border to create three railroads that would operate as one. The Union Pacific had been persuaded by Dodge, who had maintained close ties with the organization, that an outlet to the Gulf via the combined Denver to Ft. Worth railroads was a good thing and that it should offer no opposition. Even the D&RG offered no opposition and allowed the DT&FW trackage rights between Pueblo and Trinidad.

The DT&FW proceeded to build south from the DT&G at Pueblo to the Texas border. On March 14, 1888, it linked up with the FW&DC. The newly dubbed Panhandle Route began freight service immediately and on April 9, passenger trains 1 and 2, *New*

View over the Santa Fe and Colorado Midland Railway's Union Depot in Colorado Springs, Colorado, includes boxcars, water tank and storage sheds. It also shows residences, the Antlers Hotel and Pikes Peak. –*Denver Public Library, Western History collection X-14678*

Orleans & Denver Mail & Express, started running between Denver and Fort Worth on an approximately 30 hour schedule that lengthened the next year to about 36 hours. The consist included a baggage-lounge car, several coaches, and a couple of Pullman sleeping cars. On April 12 the pride of the line, the dining car *Colonnade*, was added to the consist between Trinchera and Pinon to serve dinner to southbound passengers and breakfast and dinner for northbound passengers. By July three new 4-6-0 locomotives began pulling Nos. 1 and 2.

At this time, the UP was feeling competitive pressure from the newly built transcontinental railroads. Because of the close relationship between General Dodge and the UP leadership, the DT&FW, DT&G, FW&DC, (the Panhandle Route) and Union Pacific entered into a comprehensive traffic agreement in May 1889. A merger soon followed when the Union Pacific, DT&FW and DT&G railroads combined on

April 1, 1890. Texas law did not allow the FW&DC to be merged, but the UP controlled it. The UP at the same time combined twelve controlled railroads into the Union Pacific, Denver and Gulf (UPD&G). The UPD&G, with both standard gauge and narrow gauge lines ran from Orin Junction, Wyoming, to Ft. Worth, Texas, and from Julesburg to Leadville and Gunnison, all in Colorado.

Prospects looked good for a while, with the development of the Pueblo Union Stockyard Company and the nearby Nuckolls Packing Company, together with the building of the Rocky Mountain Oil Refinery at Overton on the UPD&G. Although the Santa Fe handled the largest amount of traffic of the Pueblo Union Stockyards, the UPD&G was third behind the D&RG. During this time, the UP proceeded to upgrade the line between Denver and Pueblo with heavier rail and rebuilt bridges.

The good times did not last as the Rocky Moun-

tain Oil Refinery went bankrupt during the Panic of 1893. During 1893 and 1894 floods and fires ravaged the Denver and Pueblo line, and in 1893 the UPD&G, along with its parent company and several other railroads, declared bankruptcy. This situation was further aggravated by a ruinous rate war between the Santa Fe and the UPD&G. John Evans, still interested in the affairs of the railroad he had built, complained to the bankruptcy judge about the receivers appointed to oversee the UPD&G. Evans recommended Frank Trumbull and the judge forthwith appointed Trumbull as receiver on August 7, 1894. This appointment proved to be very fortuitous for the UPD&G and successor Colorado and Southern.

Of course the railroad continued to run. The UP had brought in several of its antiquated locomotives and moved some of the newer locomotives to other of its properties. The flagship passenger trains of the UPD&G, Nos. 1 and 2 the *Mail and Express*, often were pulled by 1867-built 4-4-0s. The normal consist of Nos. 1 and 2 differed little from that of the Panhandle Route, usually a baggage car, two coaches and a Pullman sleeper. Six other passenger trains, Nos. 3, 4, 5, 6, 7, and 8, were scheduled between Denver and Pueblo or Colorado Springs. Freight trains were usually hauled by 4-6-0s with 56-inch drivers.

In October 1897, Trumbull announced the sale of $20,000,000 in securities and that he would work out a plan of reorganization that could be implemented with a new name in about nine months. On June 1, 1898, the Franceville coal mine shut down. Production had dropped steadily from 2,885 tons in January 1898 to just 886 tons in May. Another source of revenue for the railroad was lost and the branch to the mine was taken up.

The Colorado and Southern Railway Company (C&S), led by President Frank Trumbull, was chartered on December 20, 1898, as successor to the Union Pacific, Denver and Gulf Railway and the Denver, Leadville and Gunnison Railway (DL&G).

A month previously, the reorganization committee had purchased the bankrupt property owned by the UPD&G, 749.05 miles, and the DL&G, 336.56 miles. The necessary legalities were completed and on January 11, 1899, the new company took possession of the railroad. With the property of the UPD&G, the Colorado and Southern came into possession of a controlling interest of the capital stock of the Fort Worth and Denver City Railway Company. Later, in June 1900, the C&S acquired the Leadville Mineral Belt Railway, which had built 2.99 miles of narrow gauge road within the town of Leadville; and in March 1900 the C&S purchased the Colorado Railroad Company, a standard gauge road in the vicinity of Fort Collins and Walsenburg, completing the Colorado and Southern.

The C&S wasted no time in upgrading service, especially passenger service. Previously the receiver had ordered five new locomotives and 100 new freight cars. On May 28, 1899, brand-new Pullman equipment made its debut on Nos. 1 and 2. This time the railroad was running four passenger trains. Nos. 1 and 2 *Mail and Express* ran between Denver and Fort Worth with the consist shown in Table 1-14.

Nos. 9 *Cripple Creek Express* and 10 *Denver Express* ran between Denver and Cripple Creek with head end car(s), a chair car and a Pullman Palace Sleeping Car.

But the new equipment would not run for long on the original line of the D&NO as almost immediately the officials of the C&S met with the officials of the Santa Fe to negotiate use of the Santa Fe's Denver to Pueblo line. On July 21, 1899, the two companies initialed details on the agreement and on August 1, 1900, signed the formal agreement.

The C&S had strong reasons to enter into the contract. They had an inferior line that was longer with steeper grades and more curvature than that of either the Santa Fe's or the Rio Grande's. It is less obvious why the Santa Fe was willing to sign the agree-ment, although the one reason given in the preamble to the contract tells us that the Santa Fe wanted better facilities in Denver because its then current facilities were "not sufficient to handle its business satisfactorily." The C&S facilities in Denver were superior to the Santa Fe's. The preamble went on to state that the agreement would reduce "the cost of transportation between said points," (Denver and Pueblo) provide "more satisfactory terminal facilities for both parties, and more efficient service to the public."

The Joint Line Contract

The major provisions of the contract are listed in the appendix, but the contract envisioned that the Colorado and Southern and Santa Fe truly operate the line jointly. The agreement gave the Colorado and Southern through-trains access to the Santa Fe line between Denver and Pueblo. Both companies had access to the other's customers at Denver, Pueblo, and Colorado Springs. The C&S provided terminal facilities and switching at Denver and the Santa Fe provided them at Colorado Springs and Pueblo. Only the Santa Fe could serve customers on the rest of the Joint Line. Therefore the C&S did not operate local freight trains.

It seems to have been envisioned that passenger and freight trains would be scheduled jointly and that locomotives and cars would be freely intermixed. In fact it did not work out quite that way. Each carrier maintained its own freight and passenger train schedules, but both railroads' schedules, especially passenger schedules, were carried in the public timetables of each for a while. It was not uncommon to see locomotives of one railroad on the other railroad's trains.

The two companies created joint pools for engineers, firemen, conductors and brakemen. Each company was allotted a percentage of the pool based on the amount of traffic it moved between Denver and Pueblo. The C&S enjoyed a higher percentage of the traffic and hence had a slight majority of engineers, firemen, conductors and trainmen.

Each company was allowed to set rules about the condition of the pool, such as bidding in and out. The Santa Fe allowed crew members to bid in and out to their original districts. The C&S did not, so once an employee bid the Joint Line he was stuck. If there was a downturn and layoffs occurred, Santa Fe employees could bid back to their old districts; C&S men were out of work. This attitude put a chill on C&S employees bidding for the original Joint Line. Crews on the Joint Line were always mixed. It did not matter if you were Santa Fe or Colorado and Southern, when called, you went to work with whoever was called. It seems from the first that the Colorado and Southern had decided that once one of their employees vacated a slot, the C&S would not fill the vacancy and would allow a Santa Fe employee to take it. Thus by the late 1940s or early 1950s most of the C&S spots on the roster and their employees were gone and the AT&SF solely crewed the Joint Line. In the next chapter we will see how operations under this agreement were carried out.

Table 1-14

Car Type	Route
Head End Car(s)	
Coach	Denver and Ft. Worth
Coach	Denver and Ft. Worth
Buffet-Sleeping Car	Denver and Houston via Houston and Texas Central Railroad (H&TC)

1411 & PIKES PEAK SPECIAL ON THE COLO. & SOUTHERN RY.
PHOTO BY L.C. MCCLURE, DENVER

22

Chapter Two

AT&SF/C&S Contract Operations: 1900 to mid-1918

THIS CHAPTER EXAMINES Santa Fe and Colorado and Southern operations from 1900, when the operations under the Joint Line contract began, until 1918 when, in response to World War I, the United States government nationalized the railroads and the Joint Line came under the control of the United States Railroad Administration (USRA). For the readers, there is a note of caution in that for the early years the records consulted are incomplete and contradictory. For example, the *Colorado Division Timetable No. 29* dated June 16, 1907, and the *Official Guide Of the Railways* containing the June 16, 1907, timetable do not agree on the number of trains over the line or their numbers, especially for the Colorado and Southern. Where this occurred, I have used what I considered the most reliable data, which in most cases came from the employee timetables.

In 1900, the newly created Joint Line was a part of the Santa Fe's Western Division, which ran from Dodge City, Kansas, to Denver. In June 1901 the line between Pueblo Junction and Denver split off from the Western Division to form the Colorado Division. About four months later, in November, the Colorado

Opposite: AT&SF 1440 (four-cylinder, balanced compound 4-4-2) leads C&S's Pike's Peak Special passing over a hand-cut stone culvert on Joint Line between Denver and Colorado Springs circa 1910. –Denver Public Library, Western History collection, L.C. McClure collection, MCC-1411

Division added the line between La Junta and Pueblo Junction. Between 1902 and 1906 the Santa Fe completed the installation of a manual block signaling system to supplement timetable and train order dispatching.

Edwin Hawley interests purchased control of the C&S in 1902. Then after a year of negotiation with the Chicago, Burlington and Quincy Railroad, on December 19, 1908, Hawley sold the C&S for almost $16.5 million to the Burlington. CB&Q President James J. Hill saw the C&S as a vital link between the Pacific Northwest and the Gulf of Mexico. It was ironic that one of the railroads that refused to interchange with the D&NO now owned its successor.

For the Santa Fe, train operations continued much as they had, but the big challenge was to now work Colorado and Southern passenger and freight trains into its schedules. Initially this included four passenger and two freight trains, but this number had increased to eight passenger trains and four freight trains by 1910. Many schedule changes, especially in passenger train schedules, happened in the first ten years as both railroads tried to find the right mix of long distance and local trains. We will first look at Santa Fe and C&S passenger and then freight operations.

Santa Fe Passenger Trains

In 1900, the Santa Fe ran eight passenger trains over all or parts of the newly created Joint Line as shown in Table 2-1. No dining cars were carried on Santa Fe trains until around 1938 and then the car was not a full dining car but a cafe-lounge or cafe-observation car. Palmer Lake had a Fred Harvey lunchroom until 1902 and Colorado Springs had both a Fred Harvey lunchroom and dining room until closed in 1938. Joint Line trains that ran beyond La Junta carried single-digit numbers and trains operating just between La Junta and Denver carried 600-series numbers. During the 18 years covered by this chapter, the Santa Fe always operated at least one train pair between Denver and Chicago and often a second train pair between Denver and either Chicago or Kansas City. One or two local trains each way between Denver and La Junta, connecting with main line trains at the latter location, were also the norm.

Begun in 1893, Nos. 5 and 6 were the workhorses of Santa Fe service over the Joint Line for more than 30 years. By 1905, the names were shortened to *Chicago Express* and *Colorado Express* in the public timetables, although they carried the longer names in the employee timetables for many years thereafter. They carried head end traffic including an RPO for many years, coaches, chair cars and sleeping cars from

Table 2-1

No.	Name	Details
5-6	*Colorado & Utah Express / Kansas City & Chicago Express*	Limited-stop chair and sleeping car trains between Denver and Chicago
601-602	*Pueblo & Denver Express / Pacific Express*	Denver and Pueblo local with 28* and 12 stops, respectively
603-604	*Colorado Express / California Express*	Denver and La Junta with 15 and 21 stops, respectively
605-606	*Denver Express / Pacific Express*	Denver and Colorado Springs limited-stop coach trains

* Stops include both station and flag stops and include the end terminals, usually Denver and Pueblo.

Table 2-2: 1905 Colorado Express / Chicago Express

Car Type	Route
Buffet-Smoking Car	Chicago and Denver
Chair Car	Chicago and Denver
12-1 Sleeping Car	Galveston and Denver via Newton
12-1 Sleeping Car	Houston and Denver via Newton
10-2 Sleeping Car	Chicago and Denver
10-Section Observation	Chicago and Denver

AT&SF 3518 (four-cylinder, balanced compound) heads a passenger train about to leave Denver's Union Station in 1914. –*Denver Public Library, Western History collection; Otto Perry, OP-867*

a number of different sleeping car lines. In 1900, No. 5 ran over the Joint Line in the morning averaging 28.8 miles per hour with nine stops, including a breakfast stop at Colorado Springs. No. 6 ran in the evening at an average speed of 32 miles per hour primarily because it made only four stops. A typical consist for Nos. 5 and 6 is shown in Table 2-2.

No. 601 made its run in the early afternoon accounting for the large number of stops and averaged 31.1 miles per hour in the process. No. 602 ran in the very early morning so it had fewer stops and it averaged 32.1 miles per hour. Both Nos. 603 and 604 ran in the late afternoon and early evening averaging 35.0 and 31.7 miles per hour, respectively. No. 604 had a thirty-minute dinner stop at Colorado Springs. Nos. 605 and 606 were morning and evening trains that averaged 30.6 and 31.7 mph, respectively.

Locomotive assignment records of these early years have not come to light and the photographic

evidence is skimpy at best. As a result, locomotive assignments are speculative. Motive power for these trains probably came from Santa Fe's large stable of newer ten-wheelers for 5 and 6 and older ten-wheelers and 4-4-0s for the local trains.

By June 1901, the Santa Fe had restructured local traffic on the Joint Line dropping both the Pueblo and Colorado Springs trains, adding another pair of La Junta-Denver trains and doing some renumbering and renaming in the process. No. 603 *Colorado Express* remained and No. 602 *California Express* replaced 604 as the counterpart to No. 603. These were all-stop locals on the route with No. 603 making 24 stops during its afternoon run and No. 602 making 23 during its late afternoon/early evening journey. Nos. 601, 604, 605 and 606 all were dropped from the Joint Line and Nos. 607 *Pueblo & Denver Express* and 608 *Pacific Express*, another pair of Denver-La Junta trains, were added. No. 607 was a morning/

early afternoon train making 17 stops and No. 608 was a very early morning train making 12 stops.

On June 1, 1902, the Santa Fe added another long distance train pair to a portion of the Joint Line. No. 9 the *Colorado Flyer* was originally a westbound summer season train and along with its eastbound counterpart, No. 10, the *Missouri River Flyer*, ran initially between Kansas City and Colorado Springs. By the summer of 1905 they were running between Denver and Chicago. They did not run in 1907 or 1908.

This train pair was, for many years, the luxury Santa Fe train on the Joint Line – the fastest with the fewest stops. It often carried either a sleeper-observation car or a café-observation car. The 1905 consist as shown in a Santa Fe advertising sheet is shown in Table 2-3. The lineup of Santa Fe passenger trains from 1902 through 1905 is shown in Table 2-4.

The number of stops the 600-series trains made on the Joint Line changed with great regularity dur-

A southbound AT&SF passenger train (probably *Missouri River Flyer*) on flyover of D&RG main just east of Sedalia, Colorado, circa 1907. –*Colorado Railroad Museum collection*

AT&SF 1477 (four-cylinder, balanced compound 4-4-2) is ready to take a train south at Denver Union Station in 1918. –*Colorado Railroad Museum collection*

Table 2-3: 1905 Colorado Flyer / Missouri River Flyer

Car Type	Route
Head End	
Chair Car	Chicago and Denver
Chair Car	Chicago and Denver
12-1 Sleeping Car	Chicago and Denver
12-1 Sleeping Car	Chicago and Denver

Table 2-4

No.	Name	Details
5-6	*Colorado & Utah Express / Kansas City & Chicago Express*	Limited-stop chair and sleeping car trains between Denver and Chicago
9-10	*Colorado Flyer / Missouri River Flyer*	Summer only limited-stop chair and sleeping car trains between Denver and Kansas City
602-603	*California & Chicago Express / Colorado Express*	Denver and La Junta local with a chair car and coaches making 39 stops each in 1905
607-608	*Pueblo & Denver Express / Kansas City & Chicago Express*	Denver and La Junta with chair cars making 33 and 38 stops respectively in 1905

ing the first decade of the 20th Century. Nos. 5, 9, 602, and 608 all stopped for meals at the Fred Harvey lunch and dining room in Colorado Springs. In February 1906, No. 601 *Colorado Express*, replaced No. 603 on the La Junta to Denver run. In June 1908 the Santa Fe recreated the *Colorado Flyer* with a new name and number – 609, *Colorado Flyer and Fast Mail*, making four stops on the Joint Line. At the same time No. 610, *Local Passenger*, was added making 31 stops. Both new trains stopped at Colorado Springs for meals. Both ran only during the summer and exited the timetable in November. The *Colorado Flyer* and *Missouri River Flyer* returned in June 1909 as Nos. 609 and 610. In January 1910, the *Colorado Flyer* and *Missouri River Flyer* got numbers 11 and 12, the numbers they would keep until their demise in May 1934.[2] Also in 1910, No 602 was dropped and No. 610, renamed *California & Chicago Express*, took its place operating from Denver to La Junta as a local making 29 stops including a meal stop at Colorado Springs. The lineup

at that time is shown in Table 2-5.

Beginning in 1903 and 1904, Baldwin Locomotive Works began building a large stable of high-driver, swift, compound 4-4-2s numbered between 507 and 559 as well as three classes in the 1400s. These Atlantics were probably assigned to Nos. 5/6 and 9/10 (later 11 and 12) by the latter half of the first decade. 4-4-0 and 4-6-0 types probably continued to haul the 600-series trains between Denver and La Junta.

Santa Fe Joint Line trains continued relatively unchanged until 1915 when Nos. 601 and 608 were

2. According to the employee timetables from 1911 until 1915, Nos. 11 and 12 were named the *Colorado Flyer* / *Missouri River Flyer*, respectively. However the public timetables for the same period named No. 610 on the Joint Line and No 10 east of La Junta the *Missouri River Flyer* and No. 12 was called the *Chicago Fast Mail*. The consist of No. 11, the *Colorado Flyer*, turned at Denver to No. 12, the *Missouri River Flyer*, according to the employee timetables or *Chicago Fast Mail* according to the public timetables. By 1915, the public timetables had renamed No. 12 the *Missouri River Flyer* and No 610/10 was called *The Overland*.

Head on view of AT&SF 1350 (four-cylinder, balanced compound 4-6-2) ready to leave with a passenger train from Denver in 1914. Also showing CRI&P 827, a 4-6-2. –*Denver Public Library, Western History collection; Otto Perry, OP-408*

AT&SF 526 (balanced compound 4-4-2), typical of the early balanced compound Atlantics, is stored at La Junta, Colorado, on October 26, 1921, after having pulled Joint Line passenger trains for a decade and a half. –*Denver Public Library, Western History collection; Otto Perry, OP-44*

dropped, leaving only one pair of local trains on the Joint Line. Gradually Nos. 11 and 12 added stops until in 1915 they were making seventeen and nineteen stops, respectively. Nos. 5 and 6 also added a few stops and by 1915 were making seven and six, respectively. In addition, their names were simplified in the public timetables to *Colorado Express* and *Chicago Express* even though they carried the old longer names in the employee timetables for some years more. On October 21, 1915, the *Missouri River Flyer* was renamed the *Chicago Flyer* even though it still ran only to Kansas City. In June 1918, No. 608 returned

AT&SF 1428 (four-cylinder, balanced compound 4-4-2) on a passenger train at Pueblo, Colorado, in 1915. This is a typical view of the Atlantics extensively used on Joint Line passenger trains from 1905 to around 1920. –*Denver Public Library, Western History collection; Otto Perry, OP-450*

with a new name, *California and Chicago Express*. The USRA would publish its first timetable in October 1918 so Tables 2-6 through 2-9 are a last look at the passenger trains run by the Santa Fe and their consists before that timetable.

At the same time the Atlantics began to appear so did a number of balanced compound 4-6-2 locomotives numbered in the 1200-, 1300- and 3500-number series. These were originally built to handle passenger trains in mountainous territory. By the second decade of the 20th Century, limited photographic evidence indicates that these Pacific types began to be assigned to Nos. 5, 6, 11, and 12 when these trains were more than about five or six cars long. Otherwise, Atlantics continued to be assigned. By 1918, the Pacifics predominated on Nos. 5, 6, 10, and 11 while the Atlantics handled the locals.

Table 2-5

No.	Name	Details
5-6	*Colorado & Utah Express / Kansas City & Chicago Express*	Limited-stop chair and sleeping car trains between Denver and Chicago
11-12	*Colorado Flyer / Missouri River Flyer*	Limited-stop coach, chair, and sleeping car trains between Denver and Kansas City
601-610	*Colorado Express / California & Chicago Express*	Denver and La Junta local with 30 and 29 stops, respectively, carrying head end car(s) and coaches
607-608	*Pueblo & Denver Express/ Kansas City & Chicago Express*	Denver and La Junta with 25 and 26 stops, respectively, carrying head end car(s), a coach and two 12-1 sleeping cars

Table 2-6

No.	Name	Details
5-6	*Colorado Express / Chicago Express*	Limited-stop chair and sleeping car trains between Denver and Chicago
11-12	*Colorado Flyer / Chicago Flyer*	Limited-stop chair and sleeping car trains between Denver and Kansas City
607-610	*Pueblo & Denver Express / California & Chicago Express*	Denver and La Junta locals with 38 and 41 stops, respectively, connecting to Nos. 1 and 10 at La Junta
608	*Kansas City & Chicago Express*	Denver and La Junta with 16 stops connecting with No. 8 at La Junta carrying head end car(s) and a coach

Table 2-7: 1918 Colorado/Chicago Express

Car Type	Route
Head End	
Chair Car	Chicago and Denver
Tourist Sleeper	Los Angeles and Denver via La Junta
12-1 Sleeping Car	Chicago and Denver
12-1 Sleeping Car	Denver to Trinidad (6 only) via La Junta

Table 2-8: 1918 Colorado/Chicago Flyer

Car Type	Route
Head End	
Chair Car	Kansas City and Denver
12-1 Sleeping Car	Denver to Kansas City (12 only)

Table 2-9: 1918 Nos. 607/610

Car Type	Route
Head End	
Coach	La Junta and Denver
12-1 Sleeping Car	La Junta and Denver
10-1-2 Sleeping Car	Los Angeles to Denver (607 only) thrice weekly via La Junta

AT&SF 3513 on passenger train (probably No. 5) with nine cars approaching Denver, Colorado, in June 1918. The train is heavier than called for in the consist lists. *–Denver Public Library, Western History collection; Otto Perry, OP-1667*

Colorado and Southern Passenger Trains

As a north-south railroad, the C&S flagship passenger trains ran between Denver and Ft. Worth and later Dallas. By 1910, the C&S had two train pairs between Denver and Ft. Worth. Although its core business was north-south, the C&S through the first decade of the 1900s tried, in conjunction with other railroads, to build an east-west passenger business by running through trains and through cars to Cripple Creek, Leadville, Grand Junction, Ogden and California. None of these trains were particularly successful and they were gone by 1914. The C&S also had a bewildering habit of changing train names so much that often the public and employee timetables did not agree. Thus their passenger train history in the first decade of the 20th Century is quite complex.

Initially, the C&S scheduled four passenger trains over the Joint Line as shown in Table 2-10. The numbers in parentheses are the numbers assigned to Colorado and Southern trains by the Santa Fe over the Joint Line. As the C&S was a north-south road, odd numbers were southbound and even numbers were northbound. Thus C&S trains going in the same geographical direction on the Joint Line meant just the opposite of the Santa Fe. C&S trains leaving Denver were southbound (odd) while Santa Fe trains leaving Denver were eastbound (even). Throughout the history of the Joint Line various systems were used to deal with this problem.

C&S trains only stopped at the most important towns on the Joint Line. Initially Nos. 1(618), which ran over the Joint Line in the early afternoon, and 2(619), running between 9:30 AM and about 1:00 PM, made four stops each, including Denver and Pueblo at average speeds of 35 and 34.6 miles per hour, respectively. The two intermediate stops were

C&S 320 (4-6-0) departing Denver circa 1910 with passenger train. –*Colorado Railroad Museum collection*

Table 2-10

No.	Name	Details
1-2 (618-619)	*Texas Express / Colorado Express*	Limited-stop chair and sleeping car trains between Denver Ft. Worth
9-10 (620-621)	*Cripple Creek Express / Denver Express*	Denver and Colorado Springs with cars from and to Cripple Creek on the Colorado Midland

Table 2-11

No.	Name	Details
1-2	*Colorado Express / Texas Express*	Limited-stop coach and sleeping car trains between Denver and Ft. Worth
3-4	*Denver Express / Pacific Express*	Denver and Pueblo with cars to and from the west via Denver and Rio Grande
9-10	*Denver Express / Cripple Creek Express*	Denver and Colorado Springs with cars from and to Cripple Creek on the Colorado Midland
11-12	*Denver Express / Pacific Express*	Denver and Colorado Springs with cars from and to Cripple Creek on the Colorado Midland

Colorado Springs and Palmer Lake. Nos. 9(620) and 10(621) made more stops on their shorter runs between Denver and Colorado Springs. In addition to its end points of Colorado Springs and Denver, No. 9 made a station stop at Palmer Lake and had flag stops at Littleton and South Denver averaging 29.6 miles per hour during its nocturnal trip. No. 10 did not have a flag stop at South Denver but otherwise made the same stops as No. 9 on its early morning journey. It averaged a slightly faster 31.7 miles per hour. Initially locomotives inherited from the UPD&G, usually 4-4-0s and 4-6-0s, pulled C&S passenger trains.

By June 1901, the C&S had added four passenger trains to the Joint Line and adopted the Santa Fe east-west numbering system. Two of the added trains ran the full length of the Joint Line between Denver and Pueblo and two only ran between Denver and Colorado Springs. The lineup is shown in Table 2-11.

The two new train pairs also added stops. No. 3 was an evening train out of Pueblo and had nine stops. No. 4 was a morning train out of Denver and made eleven stops. No. 11 departed from Pueblo

in early morning and stopped at eight towns while No. 12 was an evening train out of Denver and only stopped at Palmer Lake between Denver and Colorado Springs.

In late 1902 the C&S dropped Nos. 9 through 12 and added 7 and 8, *Colorado Express* and *Texas Express*, running between Denver and Ft. Worth and giving the C&S two trains with the same name each way between Denver and Ft. Worth. Starting in 1903 and for the next four years, Nos. 7 and 8 ran only in the summer time. When they came back in June 1907, Trinidad had replaced Ft. Worth as the southern terminal, but the trains ran year round.

In November 1903, No. 11, *Denver Express*, reappeared running between Colorado Springs and Denver making nine stops. In November of the next year, after No. 8, *Texas Express*, ceased its summertime only run, a different No. 8, *California Express*, appeared in the timetables as a counterpart to No. 11, *Denver Express*. This pair of trains ran between Denver and Ogden, Utah, via the Colorado Midland and Rio Grande Western. In June 1904, the C&S added three

new passenger trains to the Joint Line making a total of eleven. This gave the C&S two southbound trains from Denver to Colorado Springs and one northbound from Colorado Springs to Denver. Table 2-12 shows the way the lineup looked at that time.

In November 1905, the C&S changed No. 12, *California Express'* number to No. 16. Then in February 1906 it brought No. 12, *California Express*, back and dropped No. 13, *Denver Express*. This had the effect of reversing the frequency between Denver and Colorado Springs with one southbound and two northbound. In June 1906, the C&S hit the high point for number of passenger trains on the Joint Line with twelve by reinstating No. 13, *Denver Express*, from Colorado Springs to Denver and running Nos. 7 and 8 only in the summer. Table 2-13 has the lineup.

This did not last as the C&S soon eliminated a Denver and Pueblo train pair by dropping Nos. 14

and 15 in November. Trains were relatively short and cars were all made of wood. The consists of C&S passenger trains at this time are shown in Tables 2-14 through 2-18.

Summer 1907 saw the C&S eliminate the Denver and Colorado Springs trains by annulling Nos. 11, 12, 13, and 16, but adding a new No. 15, *Denver Special*, running from Pueblo to Denver with four stops. Nos. 11, 12, 13, and 16 reappeared in November 1907 and No. 15 was dropped at that time.

In 1902 and 1903 the C&S bought four, large ten-wheelers, Nos. 323 through 326, from Schenectady and assigned them to the two top passenger trains, Nos. 1 and 2 and 7 and 8. These locomotives had piston valves actuated by Stevenson valve gear and 67-inch drivers. The C&S was so satisfied with these that they bought three similar locomotives from Brooks in 1906 and two heavier versions from Baldwin in 1907. These nine engines, assigned in 1906 to Class C3H and C3H1[3], pulled the important passenger trains between Denver and Pueblo until 1911 when the first Pacifics arrived.

In June 1908, trains 3 and 4, which had been running between Denver and Pueblo making connections with the D&RGW, began running to and from Trinidad, necessitating a name change for No. 4 to *Trinidad Express*. Nos. 7 and 8 again ran between Denver and Ft. Worth during the summer months. The C&S schedule remained stable with Nos. 7 and 8

C&S 324 (4-6-0) has just pulled a southbound passenger train into Pueblo, Colorado, in 1905. –*Colorado Railroad Museum collection*

Table 2-12

No.	Name	Details
1-2	*Colorado Express / Texas Express*	Limited-stop coach and sleeping car trains between Denver and Ft. Worth
3-4	*Denver Express / Pacific Express*	Denver and Pueblo with cars to and from the west via Denver and Rio Grande
7-8	*Colorado Express / Texas Express*	Limited-stop coach and sleeping car trains between Denver and Ft. Worth (summer only)
11-12	*Denver Express / California Express*	Denver and Colorado Springs with cars from and to Cripple Creek on the Colorado Midland
13	*Denver Express*	Colorado Springs to Denver with cars from the Colorado Midland at Colorado Springs making 22 stops
14-15	*Pueblo Express / Denver Express*	Denver and Pueblo making 4 and 9 stops, respectively

Table 2-13

No.	Name	Details
1-2	*Colorado Express / Texas Express*	Limited-stop coach and sleeping car trains between Denver and Ft. Worth
3-4	*Denver Express / Pacific Express*	Denver and Pueblo with cars to and from the west via Denver and Rio Grande
7-8	*Colorado Express / Texas Express*	Limited stop coach and sleeping car trains between Denver and Ft. Worth (summer only)
11-12	*Denver Express / California Express*	Denver and Colorado Springs with cars from and to Cripple Creek on the Colorado Midland
13 & 16	*Denver Express / California Express*	Colorado Springs and Denver with cars from the Colorado Midland at Colorado Springs making 22 and 8 stops respectively
14-15	*Pueblo Express / Denver Express*	Denver and Pueblo making 4 and 9 stops, respectively

3. The C&S began classifying locomotives according to the ICC system in 1906. This system used a letter indicating number of lead and trailing truck wheels and a number indicating number of driver axles. For example, "C" indicates a four-wheel lead truck and no trailing truck, and "3" indicates three driving axles. The final letter indicates class differences. In this case "H" indicates the eighth different class of ten-wheelers. The last number, "1," in Class C3H1 indicates a follow-on to the class but with some slight differences. Initial letters in this system are "A" indicating no lead or trailing trucks, "B" indicating one-axle lead truck with no trailing truck, "E" indicates one-axle lead and one-axle trailing truck, and "F" indicates two-axle lead truck and one-axle trailing truck.

C&S 326 (4-6-0) on three-car passenger train on trestle over Shook's Run approaching Colorado Springs circa 1912. –*Jackson Thode collection, photographer unknown, Colorado Railroad Museum collection*

now named *Denver Express* and *Texas Express* running between Denver and Ft. Worth only during the summer until January 1910. At that time, C&S dropped Nos. 11, 12, 13, and 16 and ran Nos. 7 and 8 for the whole year.

Change again came in January 1911, when Nos. 3 and 4 were cut back to Pueblo and Denver trains, with No. 4 being renamed *Pueblo Express* while four Denver and Colorado Springs trains again reappeared, this time numbered 13 (*Denver Express*), 14 (*California Express*), 15 (*Denver Express*) and 16 (*California Express*). Nos. 7 and 8 ran during the 1911 summer season. Then in November 1911 the C&S decided to run only one pair of Denver and Colorado Springs trains, Nos. 13 and 16, *Denver Express* and *California Express*, respectively. Trains were becoming longer and with the introduction of all steel cars, heavier, necessitating heavier power. So in 1911 Baldwin delivered five F3A 4-6-2 locomotives which

thereafter hauled the longer trains with the C3H and C3H1 pulling the lighter trains. Tables 2-19 through 2-23 show how the consists for 1911 looked.

In November 1912 Trinidad became the southern terminal for Nos. 7 and 8 with a name change to *Colorado Express* and *Trinidad Express*. Nos. 13 and 16 were annulled at the same time. December 1913 recreated the situation of November 1911 with Nos. 7 and 8 again renamed *Denver Express* and *Texas Express* with an extension to Ft. Worth and Nos. 13 and 16 reinstated. Then in June 1914, the C&S gave up competing with the Rio Grande for traffic west of the Joint Line and thereafter concentrated on its north-south business by dropping Nos. 13 and 16 for good and extending 3 and 4 to Trinidad. Apparently business was not sufficient for three train pairs because in February 1915 the C&S started running two train pairs on the Joint Line, one pair between Ft. Worth and Denver and one between Trinidad and Denver,

Table 2-14: 1907 Nos. 1 & 2 Colorado Express / Texas Express

Car Type	Route
Head End	
Coach	Denver and Ft. Worth
Coach	Denver and Ft. Worth
Café Car	Denver and Ft. Worth
12-1 Sleeping Car	Denver and Ft. Worth

Table 2-15: 1907 Nos. 3 & 4 Denver Express / Pueblo Express

Car Type	Route
Head End	
First Class Coach	Denver and Pueblo
Dining Car	Denver and Pueblo
Observation Car	Denver and Cripple Creek via C&S, Midland Terminal and Colorado Springs and Cripple Creek District Railway at Colorado Springs

Table 2-16: 1907 Nos. 7 & 8 Colorado Express / Texas Express

Car Type	Route
Head End	
First Class Coach	Denver and Trinidad
First Class Coach	Denver and Trinidad
Dining Car	Denver and Pueblo
10-Section Sleeper-Observation	Denver and Trinidad

Table 2-17: 1907 Nos. 11 & 12 Denver Express / California Express

Car Type	Route
Head End	
Chair Car	Denver and Grand Junction via Colorado Midland at Colorado Springs
Tourist Sleeper	Denver and Trinidad
Café Car	Grand Junction to Denver (11) via Colorado Midland at Colorado Springs
Café Car	Colorado Springs to Grand Junction (12) via Colorado Midland
10-Section Sleeper-Observation	Denver and Ogden via Colorado Midland at Colorado Springs, D&RGW at Grand Junction

a situation that would continue up to the takeover by the USRA. Table 2-24 has how the C&S lineup looked in February 1915, and Tables 2-25 and 2-26 show their representative consists. C3H and C3H1 ten wheelers likely pulled Nos. 2 and 3 and F3A Pacific locomotives likely hauled Nos. 7 and 8 on the Joint Line.

Table 2-18: 1907 Nos. 13 & 16
Denver Express / California Express

Car Type	Route
Head End	
Coach	Grand Junction to Denver (13) via Colorado Midland at Colorado Springs
Chair Car	Denver and Grand Junction via Colorado Midland at Colorado Springs
12-1 Sleeping Car	Denver and Grand Junction via Colorado Midland at Colorado Springs
12-1 Sleeping Car	Denver and Leadville via Colorado Midland at Colorado Springs

Table 2-19: 1911 Nos. 1 & 2
Colorado Express/Texas Express

Car Type	Route
Head End	
Coach	Denver and Ft. Worth
Coach	Denver and Ft. Worth
Chair Car	Denver and Ft. Worth
Chair Car	Denver and Ft. Worth
Café Car	Denver and Ft. Worth
12-1 Sleeping Car	Denver and Ft. Worth
12-1 Sleeping Car	Denver and Ft. Worth

Table 2-20: 1911 Nos. 3 & 4
Denver Express / Pueblo Express

Car Type	Route
Head End	
First Class Coach	Denver and Pueblo
First Class Coach	Denver and Pueblo
Café Car	Denver and Pueblo
First Class Chair Car	Denver and Pueblo
First Class Chair Car	Denver and Pueblo

Table 2-21: 1911 Nos. 7 & 8
Colorado Express /Texas Express

Car Type	Route
Head End	
Coach	Denver and Ft. Worth
Coach	Denver and Ft. Worth
Chair Car	Denver and Ft. Worth
Chair Car	Denver and Ft. Worth
12-1 Sleeping Car	Denver and Ft. Worth
12-1 Sleeping Car	Denver and Ft. Worth

Table 2-22: 1911 Nos. 13 & 14
Denver Express/California Express

Car Type	Route
Head End	
Coach	Denver and Colorado Springs
Coach	Denver and Colorado Springs
Chair Car	Denver and Colorado Springs
Chair Car	Denver and Colorado Springs
12-1 Sleeping Car	Denver and Colorado Springs
12-1 Sleeping Car	Denver and Colorado Springs

Table 2-23: 1911 Nos. 15 & 16
Denver Express/California Express

Car Type	Route
Head End	
Coach	Denver and Colorado Springs
Coach	Denver and Colorado Springs
Chair Car	Denver and Colorado Springs
Chair Car	Denver and Colorado Springs
12-1 Sleeping Car	Denver and Colorado Springs
12-1 Sleeping Car	Denver and Colorado Springs

Table 2-24

No.	Name	Details
2-3	*Trinidad Express / Denver Express*	Limited-stop coach and parlor-observation trains between Denver and Trinidad making 7 and 8 stops, respectively
7-8	*Denver Express / Texas Express*	Limited-stop coach and sleeping car trains between Denver and Ft. Worth making 8 and 6 stops, respectively

C&S 134 (4-4-0) at Denver in 1918. Early in the 1900s, it and its mates would have pulled secondary C&S passenger trains over the Joint Line. –*Colorado Railroad Museum collection*

C&S 354 (4-6-2) at the engine terminal in Denver in 1915. This first batch of 4-6-2s began hauling the premier passenger trains on the C&S in 1911. –*Jackson Thode collection, photographer unknown, Colorado Railroad Museum collection*

C&S 350 (4-6-2) on passenger train (probably No. 2, *Trinidad Express*) at Denver, Colorado, 1915. –*Denver Public Library, Western History collection; Otto Perry, OP-6518*

Table 2-25: 1915 Nos. 2 &3
Trinidad Express / Denver Express

Car Type	Route
Head End	
Coach	Denver and Trinidad
Coach	Denver and Trinidad
Dining Car	Denver and Trinidad
Parlor-Observation Car	Denver and Trinidad

Table 2-26: 1915 Nos. 7 & 8
Colorado Express / Texas Express

Car Type	Route
Head End	
Coach	Denver and Ft. Worth
Coach	Denver and Ft. Worth
Dining Car	Denver and Ft. Worth
12-1 Sleeping Car	Denver and Ft. Worth
12-1 Sleeping Car	Denver and New Orleans via Sunset Central Lines at Ft. Worth
12-1 Sleeping Car	Colorado Springs and Ft. Worth
12-1 Sleeping Car	Denver and Trinidad

Santa Fe Freight Trains

Throughout the period of this chapter, the Santa Fe scheduled two through freight trains over the Joint Line each day, one each way and for most of the period the Santa Fe ran a way freight each way daily except Sunday between Denver and Pueblo. The westbound freight was usually timed for an early morning arrival in Denver and the eastbound for an early evening departure, both being convenient for Denver merchants. In 1900 No. 31, *Colorado Fast Freight*, left Pueblo westbound a minute after midnight and arrived in Denver six hours 59 minutes later at 7:00 AM. Its eastbound counterpart No. 32, *Missouri River Fast Freight*, departed Denver at 6:10 PM and arrived in Pueblo at 1:30 AM. It is interesting to note that No. 31 was a second-class train while No. 32 was a third-class train. In June 1901 the Santa Fe dropped the fancy name of No. 32 naming it just

Freight and in 1902 cut its running time to just short of six hours.

At the beginning of the 1900s, Santa Fe through freight trains were pulled by lower–drivered 4-6-0s. In 1902, the Santa Fe took delivery of 40 tandem compound 2-8-0 locomotives. These locomotives had 57-inch drivers, carried 210 pounds of steam pressure through 16 x 28 x 32 inch cylinders, and had a tractive effort of 43,226 pounds. The Santa Fe used them in through freight service in southern Colorado, including the La Junta-Pueblo line.

In June, 1903 the Santa Fe reworked the through freight train schedules. No. 31 now departed Pueblo almost five hours earlier at 7:10 PM and took over three hours longer to make the trip, still achieving an early morning arrival in Denver at 5:55 AM. No. 32 maintained its 6:10 PM departure but took about an hour longer to make the trip to Pueblo, arriving at 2:05 AM, a six hour 55 minute run. The Santa Fe

maintained this basic schedule until 1911.

After 1903, the Santa Fe had 153 Vauclain compound 2-6-2 locomotives of the 1000, 1014, and 1050 classes. Some were initially built for passenger service with 79-inch drivers but soon exchanged them for 69-inch drivers. The 69-inch drivered machines developed between 34,700 pounds when working compound mode and 45,100 pounds tractive effort when working simple mode. Many of these showed up on Joint Line freight trains.

The Prairie types were quickly replaced with 2-10-2 tandem compound locomotives of the 900 and 1600 classes and simple 2-10-2s of the 1674 class. The 900s were built in 1903 and 1904, the 1600s in 1905 and 1906, and the 1674s in 1912. These locomotives had tractive efforts between 62,560 and 63,000 pounds with 57-inch drivers. Coal burning examples pulled the heaviest Joint Line freight trains until the arrival of the 3800 class 2-10-2s.

In 1902 and 1903, the Santa Fe had taken delivery of 15 Vauclain compound 2-8-2 locomotives with extra-wide fireboxes to burn Gallup coal. They were all rebuilt in 1908 and 1909 as simple engines and several were used in Joint Line freight service after rebuilding. As rebuilt they rode on 57-inch drivers, had 24 x 32-inch cylinders, and had a tractive effort of 59, 600 pounds.

In June 1909, the Santa Fe changed the numbering system for Joint Line freight trains adding a "6" in front of 31 and 32 but making no significant changes to names or schedules. In January 1911, No. 632 became a second-class train. From this point until June 1918, when through freight trains lost their timetable rights, all Santa Fe through freight trains were second-class. No. 632 also had a minor schedule change, departing Denver a bit later at 6:45 PM. Arrival at Pueblo was the same, however, making running time seven hours 20 minutes. November 1912 brought a significant schedule change for No. 631. Now timed for an evening arrival in Denver, No. 631 left Pueblo at 8:45 AM and arrived in Denver at 7:45 PM taking 11 hours to make the trip. Apparently this schedule did not work out as in the next employee timetable, dated December 7, 1913, No. 631 returned to its previous schedule of an evening departure from Pueblo and a morning arrival in Denver. No. 632 had its Denver departure pushed back to 7:50 PM with an arrival of 2:10 AM in Pueblo. This schedule remained the same until the USRA took over in 1918. In June 1918 through freight trains began operating as extras with no timetable rights.

From 1900 to 1918, the Santa Fe operated a pair of way freight trains over the Joint Line. Although schedules did change, the Santa Fe provided daily except Sunday local freight service in competition with the Rio Grande between Pueblo and Denver. In 1900 third-class No. 87 left Pueblo at 7:50

AT&SF 1004 (2-6-2 Vauclain compound, Baldwin 1901). Locomotives like this often appeared on Joint Line freight trains in the early 1900s. –*ATSF photo, Kansas State Historical Society collection*

AT&SF 891 (2-8-2 Baldwin 1902 as Vauclain compound) on freight at Littleton, Colorado, in 1918. –*Denver Public Library; Western History collection; Otto Perry, OP-151*

AT&SF 1852, a four-cylinder balanced compound 2-6-2 leads a eastbound freight (probably way freight No. 90) near Sedalia, Colorado, in 1918. –*Denver Public Library, Western History collection; Otto Perry, OP-1372*

Left: AT&SF 1695 (Baldwin 1913) is at Denver, Colorado, in 1918. Santa Fe's early 2-10-2s served as principal freight power until the arrival of the 3800s beginning in 1919. –*Denver Public Library, Western History collection; Otto Perry, OP-538*

AM and arrived in Denver at 4:30 PM, taking eight hours 40 minutes to accomplish its work. No. 88, also a third-class train, took a bit longer to work east, leaving Denver at 7:15 AM and arriving in Pueblo at 4:30 PM. Apparently nine hours proved insufficient because in November 1901 the schedules for both Nos. 87 and 88 were significantly lengthened. No. 87 took ten and a half hours to work its way to Denver after leaving Pueblo at 4:15 AM while No. 88 took ten hours 20 minutes to reach Pueblo after leaving Denver at 4:40 AM.

Minor schedule adjustments were made from time to time, but the practice of leaving their respective terminals before dawn and arriving in mid-afternoon about 10 hours later continued until 1910. In January of that year, No. 87 began to leave Pueblo at 6:15 AM and worked the line for ten hours 45 minutes before arriving in Denver. No. 88 took even longer to get from Denver to Pueblo, departing at 7:00 AM and arriving at Pueblo eleven hours later.

June 1918, in the last timetable before the USRA published its first, saw a major change in local freight service on the Joint Line. Apparently business had grown too great for one pair of trains and Santa Fe operations personnel were also probably influenced by the USRA, which was poised to take over Santa Fe operations. So the line was split in two and one pair worked between Denver and Colorado Springs and another pair worked between Colorado Springs and Pueblo. Nos. 87 and 88 ran between Pueblo and Colorado Springs with one crew. No. 87 left Pueblo at 6:30 AM and arrived in Colorado Springs four hours later at 10:30 AM. The equipment then turned and left Colorado Springs at 11:30 AM and arrived back in Pueblo at 2:30PM. It took two crews and sets of equipment to work between Colorado Springs and Denver. No. 89 left the "Springs" at 7:45 AM and worked to Denver, arriving eight hours later. No. 90 left Denver at 6:45 AM and took seven and a half hours to work to Colorado Springs.

Power for the local trains started with 4-6-0s in the early 1900s. When the 2-6-2s were bumped from the through freight trains, they replaced the 4-6-0s on the local freight trains. In 1907 the Santa Fe received balanced compound 2-6-2s of the 1800 class. Although designed for fast freight work on the plains, they proved to be very good local freight locomotives on the Joint Line. Beginning in 1910 the early Vauclain compound 2-6-2s started to receive simple cylinders. In the teens, the compound 1800s and the simple 1000 and 1100s provided the bulk of the local freight pool.

Colorado and Southern Freight Trains

It took the Colorado and Southern a bit of time to find the right mix of through freight trains on its new route. The C&S did not operate any local freight trains on the Joint Line although it continued to operate local freight service over its original main line into the 1930s. The newly formed company also had a great need for new freight power. After experimenting with locomotives from Baldwin, Cook and Rhode Island, the C&S chose the Rhode Island design and ordered five consolidations numbered 451 through 455 that were delivered in 1900. These locomotives, classed B4P in 1906, had large, straight-top boilers, 21 x 28 inch cylinders, 56-inch drivers and carried a boiler pressure of 185 pounds, resulting in a tractive effort of 34,618 pounds. They were used mostly between Denver and Pueblo.

Even these locomotives, which were a great im-

AT&SF 1695 (2-10-2) freight (probably No. 632, *Colorado Fast Freight*) leaving Denver, Colorado, on May 19, 1918. –*Denver Public Library, Western History collection; Otto Perry, OP-1329*

provement over the older consolidations left over from the UPD&G, proved to be too light for the heavy freight service on the main between Denver and Pueblo and, a year later, the C&S ordered ten similar but heavier 2-8-0s, numbered 460 through 469 from Rhode Island. The boiler on these new locomotives was larger and the cylinders were an inch larger. They also had a newly designed cab. The C&S liked these so much they ordered 15 (470 through 484) more in 1902 from Richmond.

The first schedule using Santa Fe tracks had two third-class trains, Nos. 11 and 12 but with no names. While on the Santa Fe these two trains were numbered 642 and 643. No. 11 (642) left Denver at 7:10 PM and arrived in Pueblo at 2:30AM. No. 12 (643) left Pueblo at 7:05 PM and arrived in Denver at 4:50 AM. By June 1901, the two railroads had worked out a common numbering system, at least for the Joint Line, and the two C&S trains were renumbered 19 and 20. No. 19, old C&S 12 (643), also had a name, *Colorado Fast Freight*, and ran on the same schedule as its predecessor. No. 20, old C&S 11 (642), named *Texas Fast Freight*, moved from a nighttime operation to mostly daylight, leaving Denver at 5:50 AM and arriving in Pueblo at 1:00 PM. From the

AT&SF 457 (4-6-0) is typical of the ten-wheelers used on Joint Line in early 1900s. Built by Dickson in 1899. –*ATSF photo, Kansas State Historical Society*

names, one can assume that both these freight trains ran between Denver and Ft. Worth. In June 1902, No. 20 moved back to a nighttime journey over the Joint Line, leaving Denver at 9:00 PM and arriving at Pueblo at 4:45 AM.

The Colorado and Southern, observing the tandem compound consolidations on the Santa Fe, was so impressed that in 1903 it ordered twelve virtually identical engines from Rhode Island, numbered 520 through 531 and classified in 1906 as class B4S. The

View of C&S railroad yard in Denver, Colorado; shows Colorado and Southern Railroad box cars, circa 1910. The Santa Fe also used this yard. –*Denver Public Library, Western History collection; L.C. Mc-Clure collection, MCC-4171*

only difference was in the heating surface as the C&S did not use brick arches. These locomotives were put into heavy freight service south of Denver.

November 1903 saw another schedule change for No. 20 and the addition of another C&S southbound through freight train. No. 20 now left Denver at 4:30 AM and arrived at Pueblo at 3:10 PM, lengthening its schedule by nearly three and a half hours. The new train, No. 22 *Colorado Springs and Pueblo Merchandise*, left Denver at 12:01 AM and arrived in Pueblo at 8:30 AM. From the name it probably did not proceed beyond Pueblo. In June 1904 No. 22 had its schedule moved to a 9:40 PM departure and 6:00

AM arrival. And in June of 1905 No. 22 again moved to an earlier 8:15 PM departure and 4:45 AM arrival.

In 1906 the railroad received another 19 consolidations, this time from Brooks. The railroad then renumbered the earlier 460 through 484 locomotives to 600 through 624 and the new locomotives were numbered 625 through 643. All 44 locomotives were placed into the B4R class and this class provided the power for all through freight trains on the C&S until the delivery of 2-8-2 and 2-10-2 locomotives between 1910 and 1920. After 1920 they were downgraded to local freight and switch service.

The C&S continued to fiddle with the south-

bound schedules and in June 1907 lengthened No. 20's time on the road to ten hours 40 minutes by advancing its arrival in Pueblo to 3:10 PM while keeping its 4:30 AM departure from Denver. No. 22's departure was moved back to 9:10 PM with a 5:45 AM arrival in Pueblo.

Aside from a couple of minor changes, the C&S freight schedule remained relatively constant until 1910. At this time the *Colorado Springs and Pueblo Merchandise* got a new number, 76, but operated on essentially the same schedule as did old No. 22. At the same time No. 19, *Colorado Fast Freight*, was upgraded to second-class. In November 1912 the C&S

dropped No. 76 and in December upgraded No. 20 to second-class. From this time forward until June 1918, all C&S freight trains were second-class. After that they operated as extras as did Santa Fe freight trains.

1911 C&S 2-8-0 locomotives were supplemented in heavy freight service south of Denver by five light 2-8-2 locomotives of class E4A. The E4A locomotives had 57-inch drivers, a low boiler pressure of 170 pounds and 27 x 30 inch cylinders.

In March 1914 the C&S again added a second southbound freight train, No. 50 *Fast Freight*. This train ran beyond Pueblo at least as far as Trinidad. It left Denver at 6:50 PM and arrived in Pueblo at 1:45 AM. This was the last change to C&S freight schedules until the first USRA timetable in 1918.

By 1915 C&S had received five E5A 2-10-2 locomotives from Baldwin. This turn of events meant that most of the E4A 2-8-2s were relegated to lines north of Denver. Copies of the CB&Q class M2A, the E5A locomotives had 60-inch drivers, 30 x 32 inch cylinders and a tractive effort of 71, 500 pounds. From this time on the C&S, as did the Santa Fe, relied on the 2-10-2 as primary freight power on the Joint Line.

C&S 800 (2-8-2) Colorado Springs, Colorado, July, 1918. –*Denver Public Library, Western History collection; Otto Perry, OP-6696*

C&S 900 (2-10-2) at Denver circa 1917. This was the first of a series of 2-10-2s that formed the backbone of C&S freight service from 1915 into the 1950s. –*Denver Public Library, Western History collection; L.C. McClure collection, MCC-3428*

Chapter Three

Enter the USRA and the D&RGW: 1918 to World War II

Denver & Rio Grande Western, 1900-1918

IN 1900 GEORGE J. GOULD, who was attempting to build a transcontinental railroad to fulfill his father's (Jay Gould) dream, controlled the Rio Grande. In 1901, Gould merged the Denver and Rio Grande and the Rio Grande Western, which had long been affiliated. Gould also owned the Missouri Pacific (MP) that connected with the Rio Grande at Pueblo. He then, between 1903 and 1910, used the Rio Grande as a cash cow to finance the building of the Western Pacific (WP). Actual cost of construction of the WP reached a staggering price for that time — $79,611,410. Of this, the Rio Grande paid $31,547,000. It also eventually cost the Rio Grande almost this much to free itself from Gould. Gould favored his eastern roads at the expense of the Rio Grande by appropriating the earnings of the Rio Grande to pay dividends to the others, notably the Missouri Pacific.[4]

---

4. Robert Athearn, *Rebel of the Rockies*. New Haven, CT: Yale University Press, 1962, p. 210.

Opposite: AT&SF 3712, a coal-burning 4-8-2, is pulling No. 5, *Chicago Express*, at Palmer Lake, Colorado, on July 14, 1929. –*Denver Public Library; Western History collection; Otto Perry; OP-1716*

This had the effect of intensifying the rivalry between the Rio Grande and the Santa Fe since Gould lines served much of the same territory and customer base as the Santa Fe. When the Western Pacific went bankrupt, the D&RGW fell with it entering bankruptcy on January 26, 1918. This caused hard feelings between the MP and the Rio Grande. Friendly interchange with the MP dropped off and through St. Louis passenger service was severed. At this time the property was in sad shape. Rails were thin; ties rotten; ballast was inadequate or non-existent; and locomotives, passenger and freight cars were in disrepair. This was the railroad that the Santa Fe was ordered, in effect, to go into partnership with.

USRA Mandates Double-Track Operations

On December 26, 1917, President Woodrow Wilson signed an executive order nationalizing all the railroads in the United States. On March 21, 1918, the Railway Administration Act became law, affirming Wilson's 1917 executive order. President Wilson then appointed William G. McAdoo as director of the newly created United States Railroad Administration (USRA). The USRA issued its first passenger timetable for the Joint Line on June 2, 1918, and its first employee timetable on October 1, 1918. According to that timetable, northward trains, regardless of track ownership, were under AT&SF operating jurisdiction and southward under D&RGW operating jurisdiction between Bragdon and South Denver. To accomplish the double track operation of the Joint Line that the USRA desired, the railroads had to make connecting tracks at the flyover locations. The flyovers were then eliminated.

Most towns along the way had both a D&RGW depot and an AT&SF depot so passengers in those locations could take a train in either direction. This was the case because each depot served the riders using the track of the train bound in the direction the passengers wanted to go. Some towns only had a depot of one railroad. Thus they could only go one direction from that depot and could not return.

Under the USRA all Santa Fe train numbers changed at La Junta from east-west to north-south numbers. Trains that formerly ran from La Junta west to Denver using odd numbers now ran north using even numbers and trains formerly running east from Denver to La Junta using even numbers now ran south using odd numbers. After the USRA gave up control, the Santa Fe made this number change at Pueblo.

World War I did provide some relief to the Rio Grande. The government paid the Rio Grande for the use of its facilities and in May 1918 gave the Rio

Grande a grant of $3 million for badly needed betterments and equipment.[5] Although this did not cure all the ills of the Rio Grande it certainly helped.

Apparently the double-track operation used by the USRA worked well for both companies, so on June 29, 1920, representatives of the Santa Fe and the Rio Grande met in Denver to discuss a continued operation of the Joint Line. The minutes of this meeting constituted the agreement for operation of the line until 1936 when a written agreement was finalized. The main provisions of this agreement are in the appendix. Basically the two companies agreed to operate their respective lines as they had under the USRA. The Rio Grande agreed to ballast their track not already ballasted and install a manual block signaling system where it had not been installed already. The Santa Fe had already installed a manual block system. All facilities that served the public such as stock yards, team tracks, and station facilities except private industry tracks were included in the joint facilities and could be used by either of the companies including the C&S. The two companies also decided to establish joint facilities at Pinon, Buttes, Palmer Lake, Sedalia, Littleton, and Louviers. The later two replaced Gann and Struby.

It took some time to make all this happen. The Rio Grande was in receivership and money was tight. However it did ballast the track and on October 16, 1921, the manual block system was in place between Bragdon and South Denver on both lines. The D&RGW depot at Littleton was in use as the consolidated passenger depot by 1923. However, the Santa Fe depot was not retired and continued in use, presumably as a freight office until 1957. The water tank at Struby was out of service by January 1, 1923, but Gann and Struby were not eliminated as passenger stops until between 1936 and 1939. By 1936 additional consolidated stations were in operation at

Littleton, as mentioned above, Pinon and Kelker, all of which were Rio Grande depots. The two railroads eventually created the joint station at Palmer Lake by retiring both the D&RGW and AT&SF depots and moving the depot from Pring to Palmer Lake and adding a second operator's bay in 1938.

Some things were never accomplished. There is no evidence that joint stations were ever created at Sedalia or Buttes. It appears that this is the case as D&RGW and AT&SF stations were listed in the 1954 public timetable for both locations.

On July 31, 1921, the Rio Grande emerged from the receivership caused by its bankruptcy. However, as a result of the Depression, which caused several years of serious financial losses, coupled with the acquisition of the Denver and Salt Lake Railway and the building of the Dotsero cutoff, the D&RGW slipped into bankruptcy again on November 1, 1935. It would remain in receivership for the next twelve years. The entire railroad had been badly neglected and the trustees decided to begin an extensive modernization program. They also must have decided to formalize the relationship with the Santa Fe.

Thus on February 26, 1936, with an effective date of January 1, 1936, the Santa Fe and Rio Grande signed a formal agreement for operation of the Joint Line. While the minutes were mostly concerned with property and facilities, this agreement dealt mostly with operations. Key provisions of the agreement are in the appendix. The agents and other employees at all stations on the Joint Line were to act as the agents and employees of both parties without preference in the handling of their respective traffic, except at Colorado Springs where each party was to handle its own business. When prospective passengers did not designate the route, agents on the Joint Line, including those at the two Colorado Springs passenger stations were to sell tickets over the line of the party whose train was next scheduled to depart, unless the passenger specified a train leav-

ing at another time.

The Santa Fe was to dispatch trains moving on the tracks designated for use by northward trains and the Rio Grande was to dispatch trains moving on the tracks designated for use by southward trains, regardless of ownership.

In 1940 the Santa Fe and Colorado and Southern updated their Joint Line agreement which expired on March 1 of that year but which had been extended by letter of agreement to September 1, 1940. This accord did not substantially change the compact of 1915, which had updated the original 1900 agreement. Important provisions, which had changed, are in the appendix. Basically each company was to furnish equipment based on the freight ton-miles operated. Now let's take a look at the towns along the Joint Line from south to north.

ATSF MP 618.8 D&RGW MP 118.5 Pueblo

Although Pueblo itself is not on the Joint Line, it served as the southern terminus of the line for all three railroads using the Joint Line. For more on Pueblo, see "Pueblo, a Santa Fe Town," in the Second Quarter 2010 issue of the Santa Fe Railway Historical & Modeling Society magazine *The Warbonnet*. The major industry at Pueblo was the Colorado Fuel and Iron (CF&I) steel mill at Minnequa south of the city center. All three railroads using the Joint Line served CF&I.

ATSF MP 632.7 D&RGW MP 105.3 Pinon

Pinon is named for the Spanish piñon or pine nut. In 1918 there was both a Rio Grande depot, which served northbound trains, and an 1888-built 16 x 32 ft., later expanded with a 16 x 24 ft. addition, Santa Fe depot, which served southbound trains. In 1923 a 10 x 47 ft. agent residence was added onto the end of the depot. By 1936 passenger operations had been consolidated at the Rio Grande depot. The Santa Fe depot was retired in 1940. In 1905 the Santa Fe had built a 24 x 43 ft. standard, steel water tank

5. Ibid. p. 238.

feeding a 10–inch Otto water crane. This replaced a low, standard 24 x 16 ft. wooden tank. The D&RGW also had water facilities at Pinon, a standard wooden tank with spout. In 1919 under the USRA, Pinon was a flag stop for five of the eighteen passenger trains on the Joint Line. The southbound water stop at the Santa Fe tank was eliminated in October 1929 but northbound trains could still take water at the Rio Grande tank in Pinon. By 1930 passenger service was down to a flag stop for one northbound train, and passenger service ended on January 1, 1940. There were no significant freight customers in Pinon.

ATSF MP 650.5 D&RGW MP 87.9 Fountain

Fountain is located just ten miles south of Colorado Springs and just east of Fort Carson. Fountain is named for nearby Fountain Creek, called by early French explorers *La Fontaine qui Bouille* (the spring that boils) because of the bubbling springs at its head. In 1888 the town was nearly destroyed by the explosion of a carload of blasting powder on the Rio Grande tracks. The settlement of the claims from the explosion allowed the town to rebuild itself. In 1890, the Santa Fe built a 24 x 42 ft. standard depot there and the D&RGW also had a depot there. After the USRA started double-track operations, southbound passengers used the Santa Fe depot and northbound passengers used the Rio Grande depot. In 1906 the Santa Fe built a 24 x 43 ft. steel water tank supplying a 10–inch Otto water crane to replace a low, standard 24 x 16 ft. wooden tank. With the coming of the USRA, this tank provided water to southbound locomotives. The Rio Grande also had a water tank serving northbound locomotives. Both the Santa Fe and Rio Grande served a stockyard with four pens and fourteen-car capacity.

ATSF MP 663.2 D&RGW MP 74.9
Colorado Springs

General William Palmer founded Colorado

Above: D&RGW water tank at Pinon, CO., on May 22, 1939. –*Donald E. A. Rogers; Colorado Railroad Museum Collection*

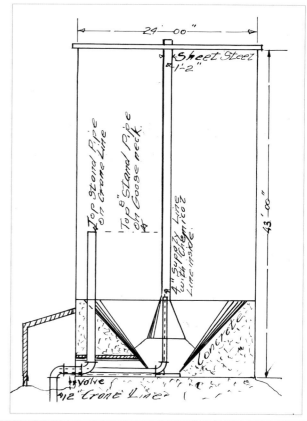

Right: Drawing of a Santa Fe standard 43 ft. water tank. The Santa Fe built 43 ft. tanks at Pueblo, Pinon, Fountain, Colorado Springs, Pring, Larkspur, Sedalia and Struby. –*R. L. Crump/ Priest Library collection*

Below: Track layout diagram of Pinon and Bragdon. –*R. L. Crump/Priest Library collection*

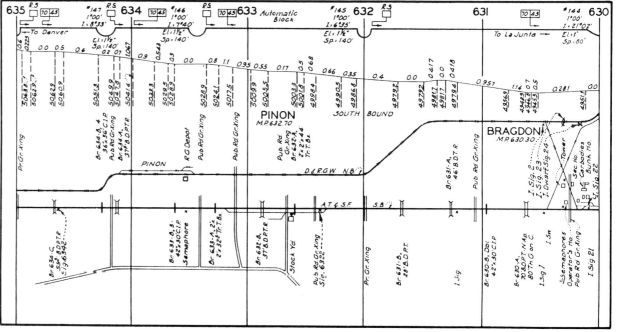

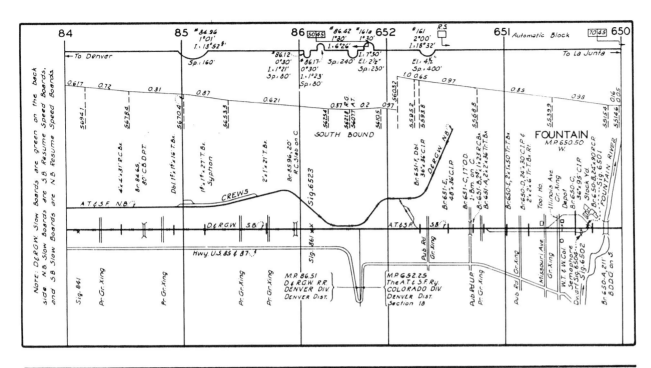

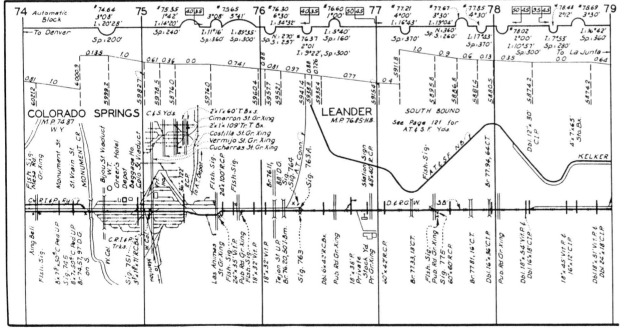

Springs on July 31, 1871, with the intention of creating a high-quality resort community. Nearby Pikes Peak and the Garden of the Gods made the city's location a natural choice.

Colorado Springs saw its first military base in 1942 shortly after Pearl Harbor was attacked. For several years the city had been trying to attract a military installation to boost its flagging economy. In 1941, the city purchased 25,000 acres (100 km²) of what is now Fort Carson to try to lure a prospective Army installation. During this time the U.S. Army established Camp Carson near the southern borders of the city in order to train and house troops in preparation for World War II. It was also during this time that the Army began using Colorado Springs Municipal Airport. It was renamed Peterson Field and used as a training base for heavy bombers. (The airport and base still share parts of the flight line.) After the Korean War, Peterson Field was renamed Peterson Air Force Base and was permanently activated. In 1954 Camp Carson became Fort Carson. Later that same year, President Dwight D. Eisenhower selected Colorado Springs, out of 300 other sites around the nation, to be the site of the United States Air Force Academy. A new and growing Army post, an Air Force Base, and the Air Force's military academy together jump-started Colorado Springs' growth so that by 1960, Colorado Springs became the second largest city in Colorado.

Colorado Springs is the most important city on the Joint Line between Pueblo and Denver. In addition to the three railroads on the Joint Line, the Rock Island also provided rail service to Colorado Springs. All passenger trains on the Joint Line stopped at Colorado Springs. In 1918 the Santa Fe replaced the 1889 stone depot and hotel with a 96 x 245 ft. brick one- and two-story depot and Harvey facility with lunch

Left: Track layout diagrams of Fountain, Colorado Springs and Leander. –*R. L. Crump/Priest Library collection*

1882-built 16 x 156 ft. Santa Fe Pinon, Colorado, combination depot. The extra 10 x 47 ft. length at the far end was the residence for the agent. Between 1918 and the depot's retirement in 1940, passengers on southbound trains used this depot. –*ATSF photo, Colorado Railroad Museum Collection*

1882-built Santa Fe Fountain, Colorado, combination depot on May 7, 1931. After the USRA, this depot served passengers on southbound trains that stopped at Fountain. –*ATSF photo, Colorado Railroad Museum collection*

and dining rooms. Northbound passengers used the Santa Fe depot and southbound passengers used the Rio Grande depot. In 1919 northbound passengers on C&S 606 and AT&SF 610 ate breakfast and lunch, respectively, at the Harvey facility. Southbound Santa Fe passengers had no facility so a scheduling consideration was to avoid meal times on southbound trains between Denver and Pueblo. The Harvey facility closed in 1938.

Santa Fe railroad facilities included a 1924-built concrete coaling tower, which replaced an earlier Hill gravity chute, a 1902-built 24 x 43 ft. standard steel water tank supplied three 8-inch Fairbanks Morse water cranes, and a freight house. Rio Grande facilities included a coaling tower and water facilities. Colorado Springs had a small stockyard with seven-car capacity served by all three railroads.

Colorado Springs had many industries that provided business to all the railroads serving the city. For example, in 1951, inbound shipments included newsprint to the Colorado Springs *Gazette-Telegraph*, cement to Transit Mix Cement Company, raw milk to four creameries, dairy products to Meadow Gold Products, lumber to six lumber yards, automobiles to

Bird's eye view of Minnequa Steel Manufacturing plant, Colorado Fuel and Iron Company, Pueblo, Colorado; shows blast furnaces, stoves, and warehouse and industrial buildings with smokestacks belching thick smoke; elevated railroad track and gondola railroad cars are on ground level track in foreground. *Denver Public Library, Western History collection, Theodore Anderson, X-10630*

PAIRED TRACK OPERATION BETWEEN DENVER AND PUEBLO

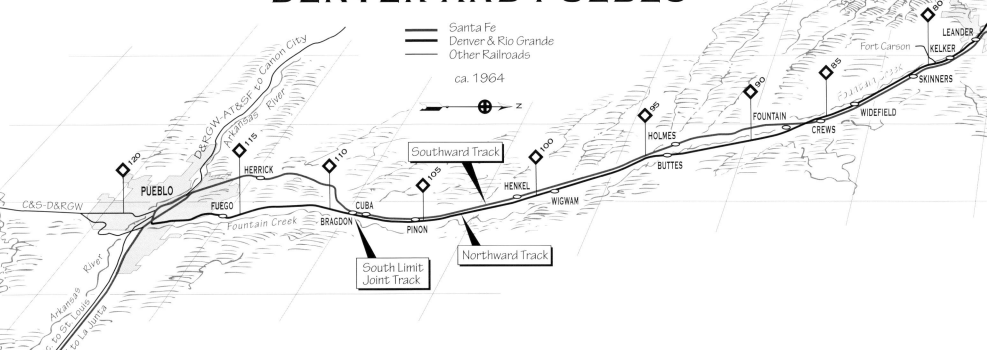

Santa Fe
Denver & Rio Grande
Other Railroads

ca. 1964

Pikes Peak 14,109 ft.

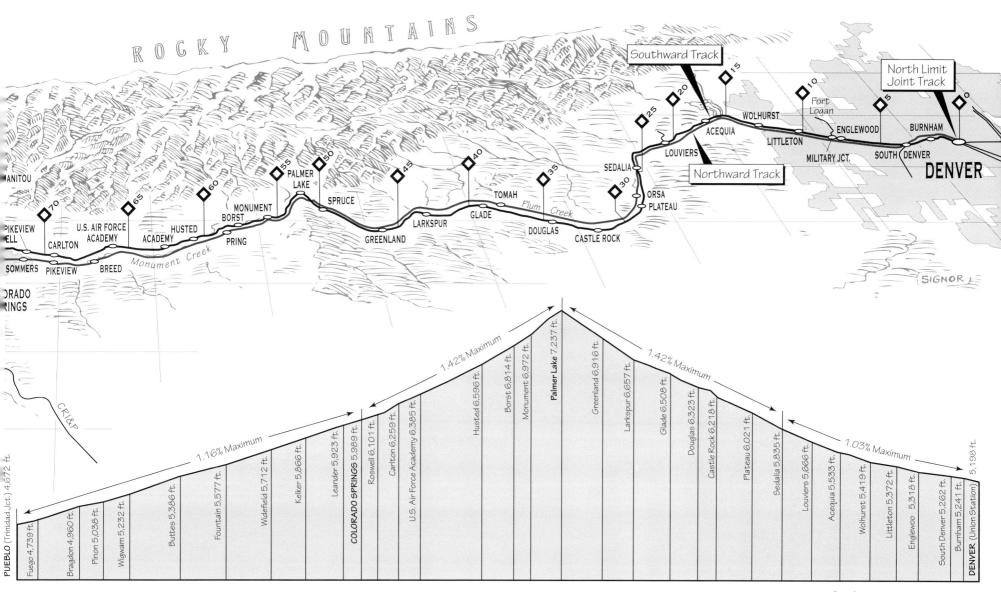

−Map by John R. Signor

1924-built 300 ton Roberts and Schaefer concrete coaling tower at Colorado Springs in 1931. –*AT&SF photo, R. L. Crump/Priest Library collection*

1889-built AT&SF depot at Colorado Springs circa 1890. Note water tank and freight house in background. –*Colorado Railroad Museum collection*

Joint freight depot AT&SF, C&S and Midland Terminal 30 x 111 ft. corrugated metal and 30 x 32 ft. stone office in Colorado Springs, Colorado, on May 7, 1931. –*R. L. Crump/Priest Library collection*

1918-built Colorado Springs Santa Fe depot circa 1920 at which northbound trains on the Joint Line stopped after 1918. The Santa Fe water tank is in the background. –*Colorado Railroad Museum collection*

two auto unloading ramps, and petroleum products to thirteen bulk dealers. In 1951 outbound shipments included embalming fluid from Decker Laboratories and meat from Smith Packing.

After 1941, when it was established after heavy lobbying by Colorado Springs interests, Camp and later Fort Carson provided regular business to both the Rio Grande and Santa Fe. Both railroads delivered government-bought goods to the Fort and after the establishment of the Army's National Training Center (NTC) in 1981, the Santa Fe shipped military equipment to the NTC.

ATSF MP 679.6 Pring

The Santa Fe arrived in Pring in 1887. There was never a Rio Grande station at Pring. The nearest Rio Grande station was Borst. When the USRA took control, the Santa Fe depot served northbound passengers only. It was a flag stop for two of the nine northbound passenger trains in 1919 and three of eleven in 1925. Passenger service ended in 1931 and the depot was boarded up. In 1938 it was moved to Palmer Lake. In 1906 the Santa Fe built a 24 x 43 ft. standard steel water tank supplying a 10–inch Otto water crane. This tank replaced a low, standard 24 x 16 ft. wooden tank. Pring continued to be a water stop to the end of steam. There was never significant freight business in Pring.

ATSF MP 682.5 D&RGW MP 55.9 Monument

Monument was established in 1874 and the Rio Grande established a station, originally called Henry, there. The town was named for a rock formation west of it. The Santa Fe arrived in 1887 and built a 24 x 42 ft. standard frame depot. With the coming of the USRA, northbound passengers stopped at the Santa Fe depot, and southbound passengers stopped at the

Right: Track layout diagram of Pring and Husted. –*R. L. Crump/ Priest Library collection*

D&RGW depot in Colorado Springs in March 1972. –*Gary A. Rich photo*

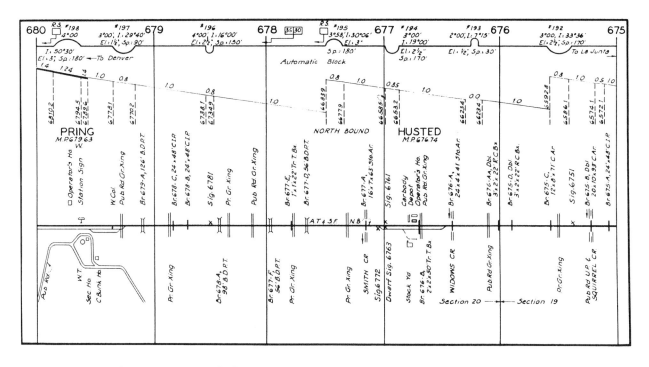

1888-built 16 x 32 ft. Santa Fe Pring, Colorado, combination depot. The depot is boarded up in this May 7, 1931, photo. In 1937 the depot was moved to Palmer Lake. –*ATSF photo, Colorado Railroad Museum collection*

1888-built 24 x 42 ft. Santa Fe combination depot at Monument, Colorado, May 7, 1931. After USRA control the depot served only northbound trains. –*ATSF photo, Colorado Railroad Museum collection*

1882-Santa Fe built 17 x 40 + 24 x 41 ft. depot at Palmer Lake, Colorado, on May 7, 1931. After USRA control, northbound trains stopped at this depot until 1938 when the little depot moved from Pring replaced it and the D&RGW depot. –*AT&SF photo, R. L. Crump/Priest Library collection*

Above: In 1938, the Santa Fe moved the 1888-built 16 x 32 ft. depot from Pring to Palmer Lake and added a second operator's bay for the Rio Grande operator. The depot then became the consolidated AT&SF/D&RGW depot. This November 1966 photo shows the AT&SF operator's bay with Santa Fe train order semaphore. To the left of the photo the D&RGW train order signal lights can be seen. –*Frank Kelly; Roger Ziegenhorn collection*

Left: D&RGW water tank and mail crane at Palmer Lake, Colorado, on May 22, 1939. –*Donald E. A. Rogers, Colorado Railroad Museum Collection*

1888-Santa Fe built 65 x 65 ft. Monument, Colorado, stockyard on May 7, 1931. After 1918, both Santa Fe and Rio Grande could serve this typical Santa Fe stock pen. –*AT&SF photo, R. L. Crump/Priest Library collection*

D&RGW depot. In 1919 Monument was a station stop for four and a flag stop for an additional four of the eighteen passenger trains on the line. In 1942, it was a flag stop for only one of fourteen passenger trains, AT&SF No. 130 to Denver. Passenger service increased after World War II with Monument being a flag stop for four of fourteen passenger trains. Passenger service ended in June 1968.

For many years a single-pen stockyard with seven-car capacity was served by the Santa Fe and after 1918, the Rio Grande. In 1951, two mercantile companies received coal and groceries.

ATSF MP 686.2 D&RGW MP 51.9 Palmer Lake

Palmer Lake is located at the crest of a long ridge called the Palmer Divide, which divides the watersheds of the Arkansas and South Platte Rivers. Trains running south have to continuously climb out of Denver with the ruling grade being 1.403% just before reaching Palmer Lake. Northbound trains have a continuous, but gentler, climb from Bragdon to the top at Palmer Lake.

Originally the settlement was called Divide Lake for the small lake that the railroad used to water steam locomotives. The Rio Grande erected a wooden water tank for that purpose. Later the town was renamed in honor of General William J. Palmer. The Santa Fe arrived in 1887 and built a wooden water tank, which also drew its supply from the lake. The Santa Fe built an 8 x 13 x 8 ft. frame pump house. A windmill or hand pump did the pumping. The water tank did not last long as Palmer Lake ceased being a water stop around 1891. In 1888 the Santa Fe built a 24 x 41 ft. depot with tower located on the east side of the lake. The depot originally had a 17 x 48 ft. Harvey dining room, but in 1915 that was converted into a residence.

Right: Track layout diagrams for Monument. –R. L. Crump/ *Priest Library collection*

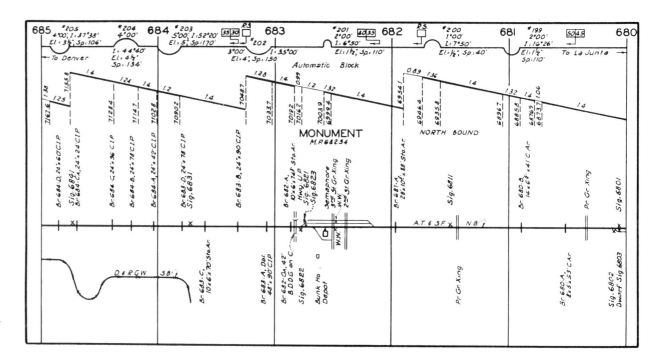

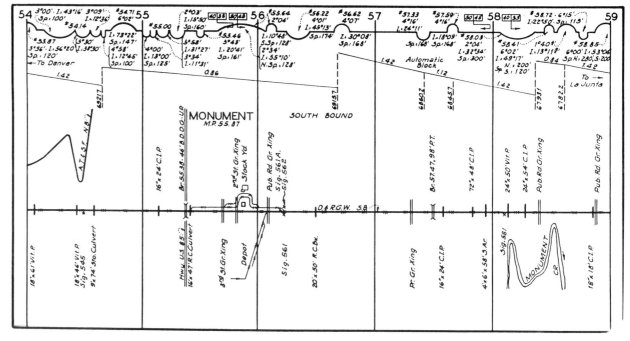

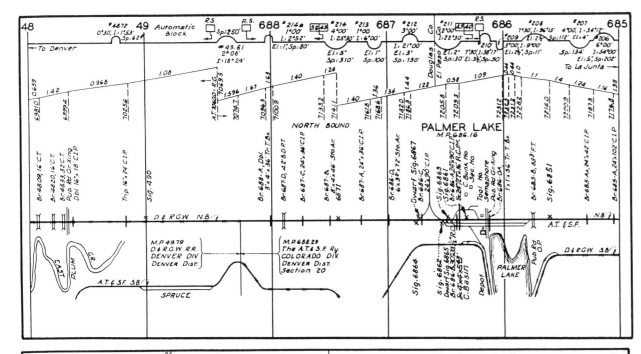

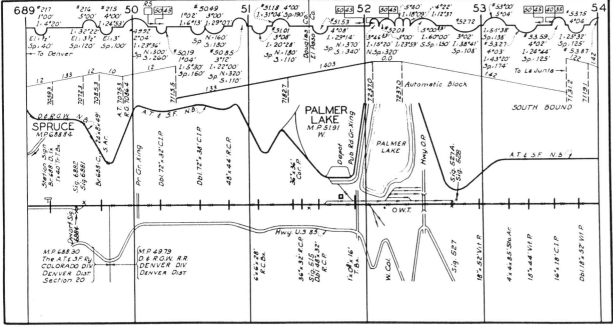

Track layout diagrams for Palmer Lake and Spruce. –R. L. Crump/Priest Library collection

In the early years up to about 1930, Palmer Lake was the most important passenger stop between Denver and Colorado Springs. The lake was a popular recreation spot and, for a long time, all passenger trains either made a station or flag stop. After 1918 northbound passenger trains stopped at the Santa Fe depot and southbound passenger trains stopped at the D&RGW depot on the west side of the lake. In 1938 the depot at Pring was moved to Palmer Lake and a second operator's bay was added. With the two operators' bays it became a union depot for both the AT&SF and D&RGW. In 1920 all eighteen passenger trains from all three railroads made station stops at Palmer Lake. The Rio Grande's depot had a lunchroom and No. 9 *Colorado Springs, Pueblo & Eastern Express* stopped for all of five minutes for lunch. In 1930 all twenty trains made a station stop at Palmer Lake. By 1935 the popularity of Palmer Lake had started to decline and of the twelve trains on the line, five made a station stop and the rest would stop if flagged. In 1938 after the depot from Pring was in place, it was a flag stop for only four of the fourteen passenger trains on the line. Palmer Lake continued to be a flag stop up to the end of passenger service on the Joint Line although the Santa Fe/Rio Grande consolidated depot was removed from the railroad property in December 1968.

Historical industries in the area included sawmills, Angora rabbit farming, and dry-land potato and grain farming. Laborers also harvested ice from Palmer Lake, and this industry continued until 1941. In 1951 there was only one business that used rail. The American Angora Rabbit Breeders Cooperative Association shipped rabbit fur from the team track.

ATSF MP 694.9 D&RGW MP 43.0 Larkspur

Larkspur is named after a beautiful flower that is poisonous to animals. The Denver and Rio Grande Railway reached Larkspur on September 21, 1871, and built a depot. The Santa Fe came to Larkspur in

1887. In 1905 the Santa Fe moved the 1888-built 14 x 38 ft. frame depot from Taylor's, Colorado, to Larkspur. In 1911 the Santa Fe built a 24 x 43 ft. steel water tank feeding a 10–inch Otto water crane to replace a wooden water tank.

After 1918, northbound trains stopped at the D&RGW depot. Southbound trains stopped at the Santa Fe depot. In 1919 four of the eighteen passenger trains on the line made station stops at Larkspur and two stopped if flagged. By 1942, three of fourteen passenger trains made station stops. In 1954 it was a flag stop for four of twelve passenger trains on the line. By 1965 Larkspur was a flag stop for three of the six passenger trains still on the line and by 1968, when only Santa Fe Nos. 191 and 200 still ran, Larkspur was a flag stop for 191.

In the 1920s Larkspur had a reputation as a health and summer resort. At that time Larkspur had one hotel, a lumber camp adjoining the town, a general mercantile store, blacksmith shop, orphanage, hardware store, grocery store, and the Frink Creamery Company, founded there in about 1900 and known for their popular Black Canyon Cheese. There was also a small two-pen stockyard built for the Rio Grande, which the Joint Line Agreement also gave access to the Santa Fe.

ATSF MP 705.2 D&RGW MP 32.5 Castle Rock

The discovery of rhyolite stone in the butte near Plum Creek put Castle Rock on the map. Castle Rock was officially founded in 1874 when the eastern Douglas County border was redrawn to its present location. Castle Rock was chosen as the county seat because of its central location. The D&RG arrived in 1871 and it was soon unloading supplies for ranchers and shipping rhyolite from the three local quarries and cheese from the dairy farms in the surrounding area.

In 1887 the Santa Fe, upon its arrival in town, built a small, non-standard 12 x 8 ft. wooden tank to which water was supplied from Plum Creek. The

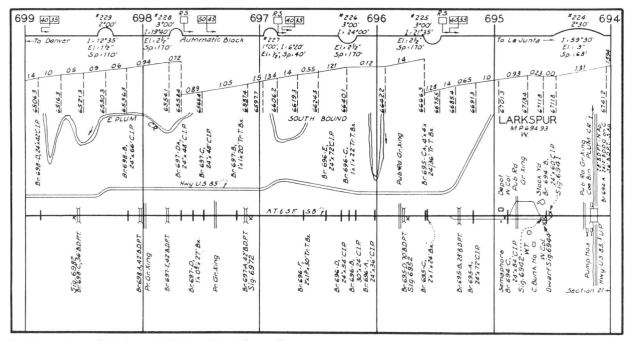

Track layout diagram for Larkspur. –R. L. Crump/Priest Library collection

water tank was retired by 1901. In 1910 the Santa Fe built a 9 x 34 ft. depot from an old boxcar with an additional boxcar functioning as the freight room. This temporary depot replaced the original that had burned. Then in 1911, the railroad built a 24 x 65 ft. standard depot.

With the coming of the USRA, northbound passengers used the D&RGW depot and southbound used the Santa Fe depot. In 1919 nine passenger trains made a regular stop at Castle Rock and six made a flag stop. In 1954 it was a station stop for Rio Grande's northbound *Royal Gorge* and a flag stop for Santa Fe's southbound No. 101. In 1968 Castle Rock was a flag stop for both Santa Fe's 191 and 200, the only two trains left on the Joint Line.

Castle Rock provided quite a bit of local traffic to both the Santa Fe and the Rio Grande. The Santa Fe, upon its arrival, began shipping stock from

1888-Santa Fe built 14 x 38 ft. clapboard depot at Larkspur, Colorado, on May 7, 1931, at which time only southbound passenger trains stopped. The depot moved to Larkspur from Taylor's, Colorado, in 1905. –*ATSF photo, Colorado Railroad Museum collection*

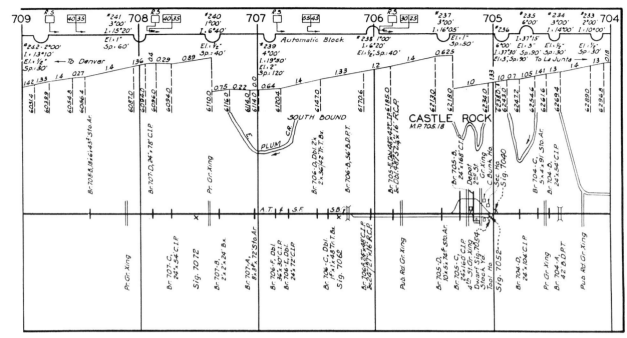

Track layout diagram for Castle Rock. –*R. L. Crump/Priest Library collection*

a stockyard with two pens and five-car capacity. After 1918, the D&RGW also gained access to the stockyard. Here is an example from 1951 of the type of traffic at Castle Rock: two hardware companies received hardware and farm implements from the team track; there was also an elevator, which shipped grain; a fuel and feed company that received coal and feed; a bulk dealer that received petroleum products; and a lumber company that received coal and lumber. In addition, the H. G. Johnson Company shipped clay from its pit on a Santa Fe spur.

ATSF MP 712.8 D&RGW MP 24.5 Sedalia

In 1865 John H. Craig founded the town that became Sedalia with the name of Round Corral. In 1870 it was sold and became Plum Station on the Denver and Rio Grande with a depot and a standard Rio Grande water tank. Later one of the original settlers named it Sedalia after his former hometown of

D&RGW cut stone Castle Rock depot on June 25, 1967. After 1918 northbound trains stopped at this depot. –*Tiv Wilkins; Colorado Railroad Museum collection*

1888-Santa Fe built 46 x 58 + 8 x 10 ft. board and batten single-story combination depot at Sedalia, Colorado, on May 7, 1931. The top of the 43 ft. water tank can be seen just to the left of the depot's chimney. Northbound passenger trains stopped at the Santa Fe's Sedalia depot after 1918. –*R. L. Crump/Priest Library collection*

Sedalia, Missouri. The Santa Fe arrived in 1887 and built a low, standard 24 x 16 ft. wooden tank that received its water from a 588-foot deep artesian well. In 1888 it built a 16 x 32 ft. frame depot. In 1899 it added a 16 x 25 ft. freight room extension. Then in 1906 the Santa Fe replaced the wooden water tank with a 24 x 43 ft. standard steel water tank feeding a 10-inch Otto water crane. Both Santa Fe and Rio Grande water tanks continued in service to the end of steam.

With the coming of the USRA, northbound passengers used the Santa Fe depot and southbound passengers used the Rio Grande depot. In 1919 Sedalia was a station for three of the eighteen passenger trains and a flag stop for five more. In 1942 it was a flag stop only for D&RGW No. 16 which stopped at the Santa Fe depot. The Santa Fe depot was retired in 1947. By 1950 passenger service had actually increased so that Sedalia was a flag stop for four Rio Grande passenger

D&RGW water tank and water crane at Sedalia, Colorado, on May 22, 1939. –*Donald E. A. Rogers, Colorado Railroad Museum Collection*

Right: Track layout diagrams for Sedalia and Orsa. –*R. L. Crump/Priest Library collection*

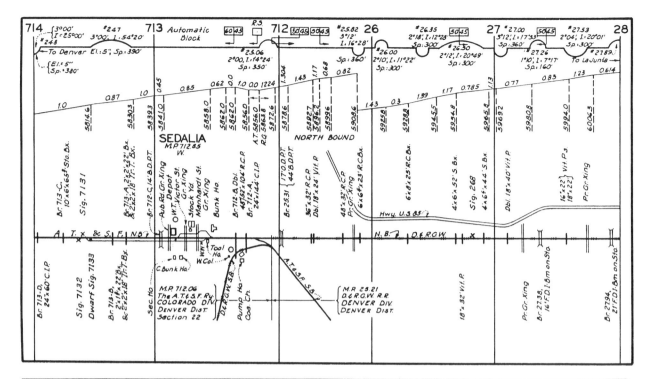

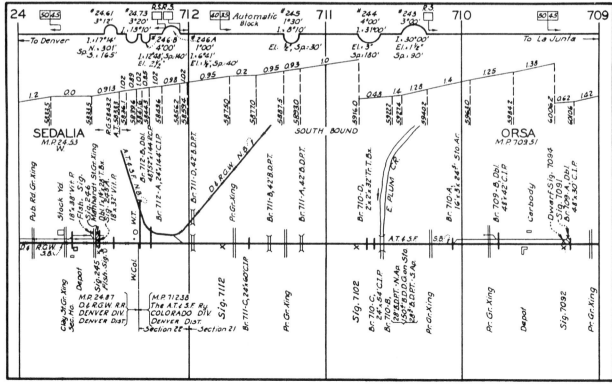

The Rio Grande Louviers depot on February 26, 1972. After June 1918 only southbound trains served this depot. The spur to the Dupont Plant took off a short distance south (left) of the depot. *–Tiv Wilkins; Colorado Railroad Museum collection*

DuPont dynamite factory in Louviers in 1958. Gable roofed sheds with ductwork are by railroad tracks. *–Denver Public Library; Western History collection; Du Pont Co. X-12156*

D&RGW depot at Littleton, Colorado, circa 1910. AT&SF depot with a large circle and cross on roof in background. By 1923, the Rio Grande depot had become the consolidated passenger stop for all three railroads in Littleton. *–Colorado Railroad Museum collection*

trains. In 1954, Rio Grande's *Royal Gorge* stopped, if flagged, both north and southbound, a situation that continued up to the end of the *Royal Gorge* in 1968.

A two-pen stockyard, built for the Rio Grande, was served by both the Santa Fe and Rio Grande at least through 1951. Also in 1951, the Santa Fe brought petroleum products for a bulk dealer while the Rio Grande received feldspar shipments from a mine and delivered coal and general merchandise to a mercantile company.

D&RGW MP 20.7 Louviers

The Rio Grande arrived and built a depot at Gann's Station in 1871. In 1908 the name was changed to Louviers after a village near the ancestral home of the E. I. DuPont family. After 1918 the de-

pot served southbound passengers. In 1919 Louviers was a station stop for one and a flag stop for another passenger train. In 1942, it was a station stop for D&RGW No. 15 only. In 1950 it was a station stop for the southbound *Royal Gorge* and a flag stop for No. 15. Passenger service ended in May 1951.

DuPont's Louviers plant, located between Denver and Colorado Springs, was one of the oldest explosives operations in the country when it closed in the early 1980s. At an altitude of 5,680 feet, Louviers was also the highest dynamite plant in the United States. In 1906 DuPont purchased 1,800 acres for the new plant at Gann's Station. Two years later the Louviers plant opened to serve the western mining, oil exploration and construction markets. The new facility included houses, stores, a school and a library for workers and

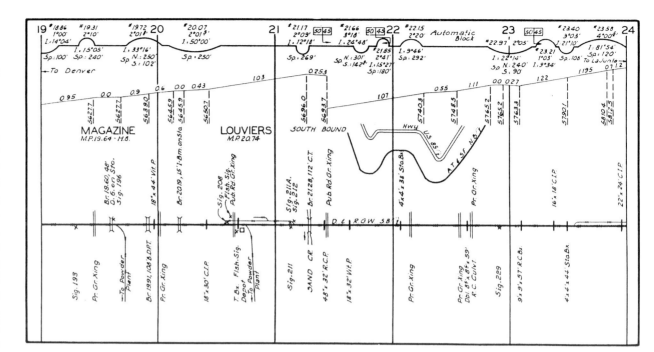

their families. It proved a lucrative source of traffic for the Rio Grande for more than 70 years.

ATSF MP 726.6 D&RGW MP 10.3 Littleton

Littleton was named for Richard Sullivan Little, an engineer from New Hampshire who made his way out west to work on irrigation systems. Little quickly fell in love with the area that is present-day Littleton and brought his wife, Angeline, out from the East in 1862. In 1867 the Littles, along with many neighbors, built the Rough and Ready Flour Mill, which provided a solid economic base in the community. In 1871, the Denver and Rio Grande arrived and built a small, attractive stone depot. The Santa Fe arrived in 1887 and in 1888 built a 24 x 42 ft. wood frame depot. In accordance with the USRA directions, Littleton's D&RGW depot served both north and southbound passengers. The Santa Fe depot then, in effect, became a freight depot and office for the agent.

Littleton provided a large amount of freight business, primarily to the Rio Grande. 1951 is an example year. The team track was busy with nine businesses receiving goods such as road machinery and supplies, home building materials, farm implements and household appliances. Flour and fire extinguishers were shipped from the team track. Next to the Rio Grande freight house there was a ramp on a three-car siding from which horses could be loaded and unloaded by the side door of express cars. A facility for unloading automobiles, trucks and tractors was adjacent to the Rio Grande freight station. This facility consisted of an unloading platform and ramp and could accommodate a single 50-foot car. Companies on Rio Grande-switched spurs shipped trucks, grain, electronics, iron and steel novelties, and rubber products. Other companies received automotive parts, coal, grain, lumber and building products, carbon black, and welding machinery.

Both the Santa Fe and the Rio Grande served a two-pen stockyard built for the Rio Grande prior to

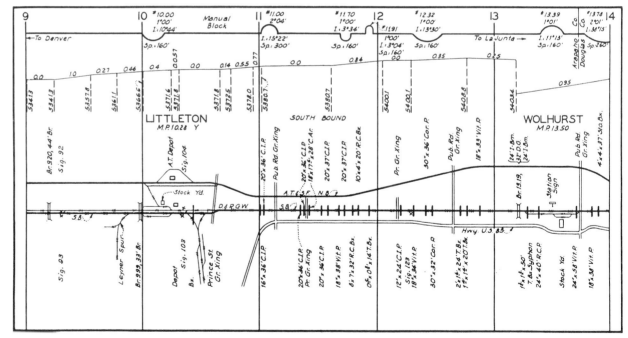

Track layout diagrams for Magazine, Louviers, Littleton and Wolhurst. –*R. L. Crump/Priest Library collection*

1915-built 22 x 75 ft. stucco on frame Santa Fe depot at Englewood, Colorado, circa 1940. At that time only Santa Fe northbound train No. 130 stopped at Englewood. –*Colorado Railroad Museum collection*

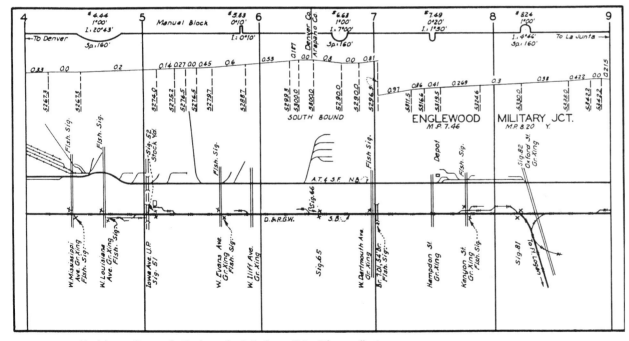

Track layout diagram for Englewood. –*R. L. Crump/Priest Library collection*

1918. In 1951 the Highland and E. G. Heckendorf Ranches shipped from the stockyard.

ATSF MP 729.4 D&RGW MP 8.0 Englewood

The history of Englewood begins when William R. Green, an early settler of the high plains, discovered gold on what came to be called Little Dry Creek in 1858. Two years later, Thomas Skerritt, considered to be the founder of the city, established a home, called Orchard Place, in the area. Four years later Skerritt himself, using his own plow, created the first road connecting Denver and Orchard Place. The Rio Grande chose not to establish a station at Orchard Place but did establish one at Military Junction a little over two miles south where the line to Ft. Logan left the main. Later the Rio Grande established a station called Petersburg, which was located 0.1 mile from where the Santa Fe depot of Englewood would be.

When the Santa Fe built its rails through the area in 1887, it established a station at a location about one mile from Orchard Place called Military Post. When the town was incorporated in 1903, the residents chose Englewood as the name, probably for the Illinois town near Chicago. In 1915, the Santa Fe retired Military Post and established a station and built a 22 x 75 ft. Mission Revival style depot at Englewood. In 1931 the Rio Grande renamed Petersburg to Englewood. In 1919 no passenger trains stopped at Petersburg but Englewood was a flag stop for one northbound Santa Fe and one northbound Rio Grande train. By 1942 Englewood was a station stop for Santa Fe train No. 130. Englewood lost all passenger service in September 1946.

The area around Petersburg/Military Junction/Englewood was a lucrative one for freight business of both the Rio Grande and the Santa Fe. Using 1951 as an example, nearly a dozen customers used the team track including two lumber dealers, a dairy products retailer, the town of Englewood, a plumbing and heating contractor, a feed dealer, two furniture

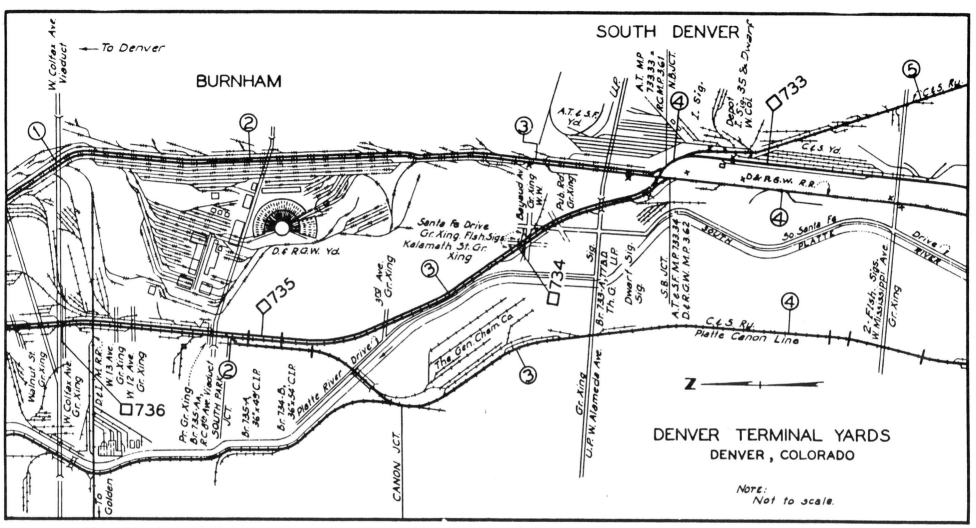

Track layout diagram for Burnham, South Denver and Denver Terminal Yards. –*R. L. Crump/Priest Library collection*

dealers, a hay dealer, a wholesale poultry dealer and a greenhouse. The Rio Grande switched a platform for unloading automobiles, trucks and tractors. It could accommodate eight 40-foot cars using either side- or end-door unloading. Four automobile dealers received their stock at this facility. The Rio Grande switched spurs for businesses that received poles, lumber and coal, petroleum products and building materials. A business on a Rio Grande Spur shipped pipe covering.

The Santa Fe switched spurs for businesses that received raw materials for making steel products and farm machinery as well as cement. Two other businesses shipped steel products and farm machinery.

ATSF MP 733.4 D&RGW MP 3.6 South Denver

South Denver Union Depot was not an important passenger stop as only No. 610 and 607 stopped if flagged in 1919. The depot was closed by 1931. However, it was important to the Colorado and Southern freight business. A Montgomery Ward's 1929-built department store and catalog warehouse, expanded in the 1930s and again in the 1940s, was located on the C&S Connors Spur, a remnant of the old D&NO main line in South Denver. In 1937, the company gained a lease from the C&S for land and constructed a new warehouse to which the C&S ran new spur tracks. Another warehouse with additional track was constructed in 1947. The entire complex was razed by 1993. Schwayder Trunk Company (later Samsonite) built a new factory in 1923 off the Connors line and the C&S continued to switch that plant.

View of Denver, Colorado, Union Station, built in Railroad Gothic style with a tower circa 1888. –*Denver Public Library; Western History collection; William H. Walker X-25177*

ATSF MP 737.3 D&RGW MP 0 Denver

Denver City was founded as a mining and supply settlement in Arapahoe County, Kansas Territory, in November of 1858. In 1861 Colorado became a territory and in 1865 Denver City became the Territorial Capital. With its newly found importance, Denver City shortened its name to just Denver. On August 1, 1876, Denver became the temporary state capital when Colorado was admitted to the Union

and became the permanent state capital in 1881. Between 1870 and 1890 the city's population increased from less than 5,000 to over 100,000. In the 1880s silver was discovered in the nearby mountains, leading Denver to a new surge of gaudiness and opulence. In 1893 financial panic swept the nation, and the silver boom collapsed. By this time, however, the city's economy was gaining a more stable base rooted in railroads, wholesale trade, manufacturing, food pro-

cessing, and servicing the growing agricultural and ranching hinterland.

All Joint Line passenger trains originated or terminated in Denver's Union Station. Both the Denver and Rio Grande and Colorado and Southern had extensive locomotive servicing facilities including roundhouse, coal, water, sand and cinder handling. The C&S's Rice Yard handled classification for both the Santa Fe and C&S. The D&RGW's major loco-

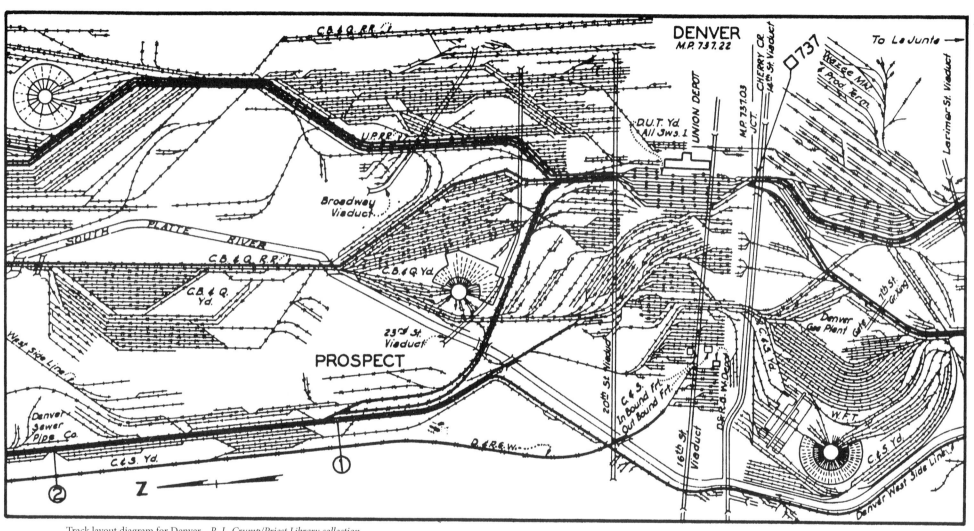

Track layout diagram for Denver. –*R. L. Crump/Priest Library collection*

motive repair shop was at Burnham.

Main products shipped from Denver were packing house products, oil and gasoline, flour and feed, fruits and vegetables, and ammunition. The primary merchandise received in Denver consisted of oil and gasoline, fruit and vegetables, livestock, rails, steel forgings, and potatoes. All three railroads had numerous customers in Denver. Among the more notable were the Gates Rubber Company, Swift, Cudahy, Tivoli Brewing Co. and Eagle Flour.

One of the more interesting customers was Wazee Market, which hosted all three railroads. The facility served as the principal wholesale and warehouse district for the city of Denver. The concept was so successful that the Union Pacific tried, without much success, to build a rival market.

Enter the USRA and the D&RGW: 1918 to World War II   59

Signaling

Train movements on the Joint Line were governed by timetable and train order. Freight trains operated as extra trains and had no timetable authority. When the USRA took control, the Santa Fe had already installed a manual block system over the entire line between Pueblo and Denver. The Rio Grande had partially installed a manual block system, which was completed in 1921. In the interim, trains entering the Rio Grande track from Santa Fe track at Colorado Springs were governed by the position of the Santa Fe order board and the Santa Fe employee in charge of the movement notified the Santa Fe operator by a telephone located at the junction. The person in charge of trains moving from the Rio Grande to the Santa Fe track had to telephone the Santa Fe operator and secure permission to occupy the block.

According to the 1927 *Santa Fe Rules and Regulations Operating Department* manual, block signals were used as train order signals and as an indication of the status of the block ahead. Operators were responsible for the operation of the block system. The operators usually worked out of a Santa Fe standard 12 x 12 ft. manual block tower or the operator's bay in the depot. The block signal was to be maintained in the stop position until the operator was notified of a train approaching his block. He would then contact the operator of the next block ahead to see if the block was clear and stop signal displayed. If so he would arrange for the operator to hold the block against all opposing trains and then set the signal to clear. The operator would then reset his block signal to stop when the rear markers of the train had passed the signal. Restricted speed signals were to be used only under special circumstances when two freight trains could occupy the same block. Passenger trains were never to accept a restricted speed block signal indication.

The manual block system continued to be used on the Joint Line long after an automatic block or

AT&SF 3719 (4-8-2) is taking water at the engine facility at C&S's Denver Rice Yard on August 4, 1940. The coal tower is in the background. *–Joe Schick; Author's collection*

centralized traffic control system had replaced it on the rest of the Santa Fe. Finally effective with *Employee Timetable No. 87*, dated June 8, 1947, an automatic block system was in place between Bragdon and South Denver. Bi-directional searchlight signals and associated electronics replaced the block operators. In the 1960s and 70s the Santa Fe and Rio Grande removed the signals facing against current of traffic.

Passenger Trains

Although the number of passenger trains usually exceeded the number of freight trains on all three carriers until the 1950s, there were never any all-Pullman Limiteds on the Joint Line. The Joint Line was a secondary operation to the Santa Fe. The trains on the Joint Line never got the latest equipment, and rarely if ever saw dining cars until the introduction of café-observation cars. Yet the Santa Fe had deeper pockets

than the other two lines and it had the Fred Harvey system and a reputation for superior service. The Joint Line was the main line for the Rio Grande until the opening of the Moffat Route on the D&RGW as well as the Colorado and Southern's main line. The passenger trains of those two roads got the latest and best equipment the railroad could afford. But neither road had deep pockets. The Rio Grande was in receivership twice in the 20th Century and the C&S was a subsidiary of the Burlington. Therefore the best they could afford was rarely better than that of the Santa Fe.

In 1919 all three roads together accounted for eighteen passenger trains plus the Rio Grande's ten suburban trains. Trains were still the primary means that people used to get from one place to another and most small communities had passenger service. Little changed during the "Roaring 20s" but improved roads had started to cut into passenger business after about 1925. The onset of the Depression began the erosion of passenger business and all three railroads struggled to adjust. Despite a slight recovery in the late 1930s, the three railroads ran only twelve passenger trains in early 1940 and the suburban trains were all gone. The Santa Fe had lost the most and was down to only one train pair daily. The C&S was still running two train pairs and the Rio Grande three.

AT&SF Passenger Operations

Passenger operations at the beginning of USRA control looked a lot like they did at the end of Santa Fe control with the exception of train numbers and the dropping of one train, No. 608. The USRA ran the Joint Line as a north-south railroad so all AT&SF even-numbered trains became odd and vice versa. North of La Junta, trains 5 and 6 became 606 and 605, respectively, and 11 and 12 became 612 and 611, respectively. Nos. 606 and 610 stopped at Colorado Springs for breakfast and lunch respectively. Table 3-1 has the lineup.

Once control returned to the Santa Fe, the railroad began to make some changes. In November 1920, the 600-series numbers were abandoned except for the Colorado and Southern trains on the Joint Line. Nos. 606 and 605, *Colorado Express / Chicago Express*, became 6 and 5 on the Joint Line and 5 and 6 for the rest of their trips between Pueblo and Chicago. Likewise Nos. 612 and 611, *Colorado Flyer / Chicago Flyer*, became 12 and 11 on the Joint Line and 11 and 12 between Pueblo and Kansas City. Nos. 607 and 610, *California & Chicago Express / Pueblo & Denver Express*, became Nos. 23 and 24, respectively, and continued to run between Denver and La Junta. Two new trains were added. No. 13, *Express*, was an overnight local carrying head end traffic, a tourist sleeper for Los Angeles and a 12-1 sleeper for El Paso, running from Denver to La Junta to connect to No. 1, *The Scout*. It made 21 stops on the Joint Line. No. 64, *Denver Express*, was a Dodge City to Denver local named *Pueblo*

Wazee Market in Denver, Colorado, circa 1939. –*Kansas State Historical Society collection*

AT&SF 1414 (4-4-2) is at Denver, Colorado, on November 22, 1921. This locomotive was used in the early 1920s on lighter trains like 23/24 and 13/64. –*Denver Public Library; Western History collection; Otto Perry; OP-446*

Enter the USRA and the D&RGW: 1918 to World War II   61

AT&SF 1347 (balanced compound 4-6-2) pulling a seven-car passenger train, probably No. 611, departing Denver, circa 1920. –*Denver Public Library; Western History collection; Otto Perry; OP-1224*

and Denver Express between Pueblo and Denver and numbered 63 between Dodge City and Pueblo. No. 64 carried head end traffic, a La Junta to Denver chair car, and a Chicago to Denver (off No. 9 *The Navajo* at La Junta) 10-section observation-sleeper. Nos. 6, 24, and 64 stopped for breakfast, lunch and dinner, respectively, at Colorado Springs. Table 3-2 summarizes the Santa Fe passenger trains at this time.

On March 15, 1925, the Santa Fe inaugurated direct Denver to El Paso service in conjunction with the Colorado and Southern. The service operated over the Joint Line at night. No. 13, *Express*, departed Denver at 10:30 PM and arrived in Pueblo at 2:25 AM. When it departed Pueblo for El Paso its name was the *El Paso Express*. Counterpart No. 14, *Denver*

Express, arrived in Pueblo from El Paso at 2:05 in the morning. Its cars for Denver were switched into C&S No. 604 also called *Denver Express* in the employee timetable but in the C&S public timetables was *Colorado Express*. No. 604 left Pueblo at 2:55 AM and arrived in Denver at 7:00 AM. For the next 20 years the Santa Fe tried various ways to provide Denver to El Paso service, but we must conclude because of the numerous different attempts to provide these services that none were terribly successful. Table 3-3 contains the initial consists of the two trains as they appeared on the Joint Line.

Nos. 6/5 and 12/11 continued to be the two Santa Fe limited-stop train pairs on the Joint Line. Gradually the number of cars and Pullman car lines

Table 3-1

No.	Name	Details
606-605	*Colorado Express / Chicago Express**	Limited-stop chair and sleeping car trains between Denver and Chicago
612-611	*Colorado Flyer / Chicago Flyer*	Limited-stop chair and sleeping car trains between Denver and Kansas City
607-610	*California & Chicago Express / Pueblo & Denver Express*	Denver and La Junta locals with 29 and 27 stops, respectively

* These trains were named *Colorado & Utah Express* and *Kansas City & Chicago Express* in the employee timetables but the simpler name was used in the public timetables for many years. I have elected to use the simpler name.

expanded throughout the 1920s. Tables 3-4 and 3-5 show the consists of the two trains in 1925 as they ran on the Joint Line.

For much of the "Roaring 20s," preferred power for passenger trains, especially Nos. 5, 6, 11 and 12, was coal-burning Pacific-type locomotives of the 1337 and 3500 classes. Both of these classes were rebuilt from four-cylinder, balanced compound locomotives to simple engines in the 1920s. As simple engines they had 73-inch driving wheels and delivered

39,650 pounds of tractive effort. Smaller 4-4-2 locomotives often pulled lighter trains. During the decade passenger train speeds gradually increased from an average of around 32 to 36 miles per hour

In March 1928, the Santa Fe dropped two passenger trains from the Joint Line and renumbered another. Dropped were Nos. 13, *Express*, and 24, *Pueblo & Denver Express*. No. 23, *California & Chicago Express*, was renumbered to 25 with no change in name or schedule.

The Depression brought a great decline in pas-

senger demand and, as a result, the Santa Fe made significant changes to all passenger schedules throughout the system. The Joint Line was no exception. The process started in August 1930 when Nos. 6 and 5 got new names in the employee timetables, *Colorado Express*, which had been used for years in the public timetables and *The Scout*, respectively. These two trains operated with similar consists and on schedules similar to their predecessors.

In February 1931 No. 13, *California & Chicago Express*, replaced No. 25 but kept 25's name and No. 14, *Denver Express*, replaced No. 64 (63) which the previous year had been renamed *Valley Express*. These two trains ran between between La Junta and Denver and connected with Nos. 4 and 3, *California Limited*, at La Junta. These two trains eventually became the new workhorses of the Santa Fe on the Joint Line. Then in November 1931, Nos. 5, renamed *Chicago Express*, and 6 *Colorado Express*, were cut back to La Junta and Denver trains connecting with Nos. 24 and 23, *Grand Canyon Limited*. Passengers on No. 6 continued to take breakfast at the Harvey facility in Colorado Springs.

No. 13 was also listed in the employee timetable as C&S No. 2 *Gulf Coast Special* and No. 6 was listed as C&S No. 1 *Colorado Special*. It is probable that C&S cars were carried between Denver and Pueblo by AT&SF Nos. 13 and 6, switched in Pueblo, and carried between Pueblo and Ft. Worth by the C&S. Table 3-6 shows the Santa Fe lineup after all these changes were made.

By April 1933, the *Colorado/Chicago Flyers* were on their last legs. They still ran between Kansas City and Denver as Nos. 11 and 12, but between Pueblo and Denver they ran with a lone chair car and whatever head end traffic there was carried by D&RGW Nos. 2 and 1, the *Scenic Limited*. For the first time since the Santa Fe arrived in Denver there were no Santa Fe through trains between Denver and Kansas City or Chicago. It would be 1940 before the rail-

Table 3-2

No.	Name	Details
6-5	*Colorado Express / Chicago Express*	Limited-stop chair and sleeping car trains between Denver and Chicago
12-11	*Colorado Flyer / Chicago Flyer*	Limited-stop chair and sleeping car trains between Denver and Kansas City
23-24	*California & Chicago Express / Pueblo & Denver Express*	Denver and La Junta locals with 29 and 27 stops, respectively
13	*Express*	Denver to La Junta overnight local with 21 stops connecting to No. 1
64	*Denver Express*	Dodge City to Denver late afternoon/evening local with 25 stops

Table 3-3: 1925 Nos. 13 & 14 (C&S 604) El Paso Express / Denver Express

Car Type	Route
Express	Chicago to Salt Lake City [14(C&S 604) only]. On No. 14/(C&S 604) La Junta to Denver.
Baggage	Denver (Pueblo) to El Paso. Only to Pueblo on No. 14.
Smoker	Denver (Pueblo) to El Paso. Only to Pueblo on No. 14.
Chair	Denver to El Paso.
12-1 Sleeper	Denver to El Paso.
Tourist Sleeper	Denver to Los Angeles. On Nos. 13 and 14/(C&S 604) Denver to Albuquerque

Table 3-4: 1925 Nos. 6 & 5 Colorado Express / Chicago Express

Car Type	Route
Express	Kansas City and Denver
Baggage	Chicago and Denver
Smoker	Chicago and Denver
Chair Car	Chicago and Denver
Tourist Sleeper	Los Angeles and Denver via La Junta
12-1 Sleeping Car	Chicago and Denver
12-1 Sleeping Car	Cleburne and Denver via Newton
12-1 Sleeping Car	Chicago to Denver [5(6)] only via No. 21 at Newton

Table 3-5: 1925 Nos. 12 & 11 Colorado Flyer / Chicago Flyer

Car Type	Route
Baggage-RPO (30')	La Junta to Denver (12 only)
Smoker	Kansas City and Denver
Chair Car	Kansas City and Denver
12-1 Sleeping Car	Galveston and Denver via Nos. 17 and 18 at Newton
12-1 Sleeping Car	San Antonio and Denver via Nos. 17 and 18 at Newton
12-1 Sleeping Car	Oklahoma City and Denver via Nos. 17 and 18 at Newton
12-1 Sleeping Car	Kansas City and Denver
12-1 Sleeping Car	Tulsa and Denver via 133/132-201/210 at Emporia
10-Section Observation	Kansas City and Denver

AT&SF 3445 (coal-burning 4-6-2) on No. 13 near Monument, Colorado, on June 10, 1934. *–Denver Public Library; Western History collection; Otto Perry; OP-1524*

Table 3-6

No.	Name	Details
5-6	*Chicago Express / Colorado Express*	Limited-stop chair and sleeping car trains between Denver and La Junta connecting with the *Grand Canyon Limited*. No. 6 merged with C&S 1 north of Pueblo.
11-12	*Chicago Flyer / Colorado Flyer*	Limited-stop chair and sleeping car trains between Denver and Kansas City.
13-14	*California & Chicago Express / Denver Express*	Denver and La Junta accommodation trains with 11 and 12 stops, respectively, connecting with the *California Limited*. No. 13 merged with C&S 2 north of Pueblo.

Table 3-7: 1933 Nos. 5 (C&S 2) & 6 (C&S 1) Chicago Express / Colorado Express

Car Type	Route
Head End	
C&S Head End	
Chair Car	Kansas City and Denver via La Junta
10-1-2 Sleeping Car	Chicago and Denver via La Junta
12-1 Sleeping Car	Albuquerque to Denver (6 only) via La Junta
12-1 Sleeping Car	Denver to San Antonio (5 only) via La Junta and Newton
C&S Coach	Denver and Ft. Worth-Dallas
C&S Coach	Denver and Ft. Worth-Dallas
C&S 10-2 Sleeping Car	Denver and New Orleans via SP at Dallas
C&S 10-Section Observation	Denver and Ft. Worth-Dallas

road again tried a through train between Kansas City and Denver. In May 1933 C&S 2 moved from being merged with No. 13 to No 5. Tables 3-7 and 3-8 show the consists of Nos. 5, 6, 13, and 14 at this time. Note that Nos. 13 and 14 are pretty skimpy but that for the first time dining service is available.

In the late 1920s, coal-burning 4-6-2 locomotives of the 3400 Class, 4-6-4 locomotives of the 3450 Class and 4-8-2 locomotives of the 3700 Class had begun to supplement the 1337 and 3500 Classes. The 3400 Class were built between 1919 and 1924.

As built, they had 73-inch drivers and a tractive effort of 40,800 pounds. The 3700 Class were built at the same time as the 3400 Class and had 69-inch drivers and a tractive effort of 54,100 pounds. Twenty of the class were built to burn coal, and it was from this group that the first 4-8-2s were assigned to Joint Line duties.

The Joint Line rarely got brand new locomotives but in 1927, at least for a while, they got some of the 3450 Class. The ten locomotives of the 3450 Class were all built in 1927 as coal burners and had 73-

inch drivers and a tractive effort of 43,300 pounds. The Santa Fe had problems with the 3450 Class with smoke and cinders drifting into the passenger cars. After attempting to remedy the situation, the railroad converted them to oil burners and began convert all passenger power to oil.

By 1933 Santa Fe had begun assigning 3751 Class 4-8-4 locomotives to heavy Joint Line passenger trains. The 3751s delivered between 1927 and 1929 had 73-inch driving wheels and a 210 pounds per square inch boiler pressure which produced a tractive effort of 66,000 pounds. Nos. 3752 through 3756 and 3764 were built as coal burners but were converted to oil in the 1930s.

By 1937 all passenger locomotives assigned to the Colorado Division burned oil. This necessitated the addition of new fuel facilities for the oil-burning locomotives at Pueblo and Denver. It must also be remembered that for the Santa Fe, the Joint Line was secondary to the transcontinental main line and so Joint Line trains often took whatever was available in the La Junta roundhouse as long as it could pull the train and keep it on schedule.

The Santa Fe made no major changes to the passenger schedule in the latter half of the 1930s except gradually increasing average speeds for all the trains by 1938 from about 36 MPH to around 40 MPH.

Passenger counts had recovered somewhat and in October 1937, the Colorado and Southern reintroduced 21 and 22 to the Joint Line (Nos. 1 and 2 south of Pueblo), again used Santa Fe 5 and 6 north of Pueblo in February 1938, and then in June 1938 permanently ran Nos. 21 and 22 on the Joint Line separate from Santa Fe Nos. 5 and 6. In February 1938 the Harvey facility in Colorado Springs closed so No. 6's stop at Colorado Springs was reduced from

thirty minutes to five minutes allowing a 43-minute earlier departure from Pueblo and a 75-minute earlier arrival in Denver. This also meant that some form of dining car (usually a café-observation or café-lounge) was in the consist of Santa Fe trains.

Tables 3-9 and 3-10 show the consists of the Santa Fe trains on the Joint Line in June 1939.

In January 1940, the Santa Fe dropped Nos. 5 and 6, leaving the Santa Fe with the lowest level of passenger service on the Joint Line up to that time. The railroad also introduced a three-digit numbering system for the Joint Line by adding a digit after the train's number used between Pueblo and La Junta. At Pueblo No. 13 became No. 130, *California & Chicago Express*, and No. 14 became No. 141, *Chicago & California Express*. The Santa Fe did not go long with only one train pair on the Joint Line. In June 1940 the railroad added Nos. 241, *Chicago Express*, and 230, *Colorado Express*, to the schedule. These were essentially a recreation of Nos. 5 and 6 except on a somewhat faster schedule. No. 241 left Denver 4½ hours earlier than No. 5 and No. 230 arrived Denver four hours later than No. 6. Connections at La Junta still were

with Nos. 23 and 24, the *Grand Canyon Limited*.

Nos. 230 and 241 did not last long as in October the Santa Fe replaced them on the Joint Line by reintroducing a through Denver and Kansas City train, *Centennial State*. Numbered 9 and 10 south of Pueblo, this train carried Nos. 90 and 101 on the Joint Line. Carrying a smoker, chair, sleeper and café-observation, this small, all air-conditioned train had all the amenities the Santa Fe was known for. It stopped only at Pueblo, Colorado Springs and Denver and averaged a fast (for the Joint Line) 45 MPH for the trip. Southbound No. 101 left Denver at 4:00 PM and arrived in Pueblo at 6:50 PM. Northbound No. 90 left Pueblo at 9:00 AM and arrived in Denver at 11:50 AM. The initial consist is shown in Table 3-11.

Table 3-8: 1933 Nos. 13 & 14 California & Chicago Express / Denver Express

Car Type	Route
Head End	
Chair Car	La Junta and Denver
10-1-2 Sleeping Car	Los Angeles to Denver (14 only)
Café-lounge	La Junta to Denver (14 only)

Table 3-9: 1939 Nos. 5 & 6 Chicago Express / Colorado Express

Car Type	Route
Storage Mail	Pueblo to Denver (6 only)
Baggage Express	Kansas City to Denver (6 only) off No. 9 at La Junta
Baggage Express Mail	Denver to Albuquerque (5 only) for No. 9 at La Junta except Sunday
Baggage Express Mail	Denver to Kansas City (5 only) for No. 10 at La Junta (Monday only)
Baggage Express	Denver to Kansas City (5 only) for No. 10 at La Junta (Monday only)
Smoker-Chair (AC)	Chicago and Denver via Nos. 9 and 10 at La Junta
Chair Car (AC)	Denver and Los Angeles via Nos. 9 and 10 at La Junta
8-1-2 Sleeping Car (AC)	Denver and Grand Canyon and Los Angeles via Nos. 9 and 10 at La Junta
10-1-2 Sleeping Car (AC)	Los Angeles to Denver (6 only) off No. 4 at La Junta
16-Sec Tourist Sleeper (AC)	Los Angeles to Denver (6 only) off No. 4 at La Junta
Café-Lounge (AC)	La Junta to Denver (6 only)
10-2 Sleeping Car (AC)	Kansas City and Denver via Nos. 9 and 10 at La Junta
10-2 Sleeping Car (AC)	Wichita and Denver via Nos. 9 and 10 at La Junta
12-1 Sleeping Car (AC)	San Angelo and Denver via Nos. 9 and 10 at La Junta

Table 3-10: 1939 Nos. 13 & 14 California & Chicago Express/Denver Express

Car Type	Route
Baggage RPO (30')	La Junta and Denver
Baggage Express	La Junta and Denver
Smoker Chair	La Junta and Denver
Chair Car (AC)	La Junta and Denver
16-Sec Tourist Sleeper (AC)	Denver to Los Angeles (13 only) for No. 3
10-1-2 Sleeping Car (AC)	Denver to Los Angeles (13 only) for No. 3
Café-Lounge (AC)	Denver to La Junta (13 only)

Table 3-11: 1940 No. 9 (90) & 10 (101) Centennial State

Car Type	Route
Baggage RPO (30')	La Junta to Denver [9(90) only]
Storage mail (Deadhead)	La Junta to Denver [9(90) only]
Baggage Express	Denver to Kansas City [10(101) only]
Smoker Chair (AC)	Kansas City and Denver
Chair Car (AC)	Kansas City and Denver
10-2 Sleeping Car (AC)	Kansas City and Denver
Café-Lounge (AC)	Dodge City and Denver

AT&SF 3751 with a new 20,000-gallon tender is pulling No. 6, *Colorado Express*, north of Littleton, Colorado, on a cold January 15, 1939. –*Denver Public Library; Western History collection; Otto Perry; OP-1814*

AT&SF Mountain-type No. 3720 is pulling No. 130 north of Littleton, Colorado, on April 6, 1941. –*Denver Public Library; Western History collection; Otto Perry; OP-1757*

Because of the speedup in passenger schedules in the late 1930s, the Santa Fe started rebuilding the 3400 and 3450 Class locomotives with disc-centered 79-inch drivers and the 3751 Class with 80-inch drivers. This allowed even higher speeds (up to 100 MPH) with only slightly lower tractive effort for all three classes. Despite the introduction of diesel locomotives on the Santa Fe in the mid-1930s and on the Colorado and Southern in early 1940, the Santa Fe was still all steam on the Joint Line.

C&S Passenger Operations

The USRA made few changes to Colorado and Southern passenger operations when they took over. Like the Santa Fe, the C&S trains got new numbers in the 600 series. No. 2 became 603, No. 7 became 604, No. 8 became 609 and No. 3 became 614. Early in the USRA tenure, Nos. 603 and 613 lost their dining cars but got them back by the end of USRA control. Without a diner, No. 614 stopped at Colorado Springs for dinner. Table 3-12 has the lineup.

In late 1918, the Colorado and Southern requested six USRA heavy 4-6-2 passenger engines, but was turned down. A bit earlier in 1918, the Burlington had received ten heavy S-3 Class Pacifics but, as it turned out, they were temporarily surplus in 1918 and so "the Q" leased three to the C&S, which numbered them 370 through 372. The C&S eventually bought them in December 1920 and classed them F3B. These locomotives had 27 x 28 inch cylinders and 74-inch drivers. In 1922 the C&S bought three similar engines, the only difference being the substitution of 69-inch drivers, making them better suited to the grades south of Denver. The C&S placed these engines in class F3C and numbered them 373 through 375. These six locomotives became the last steam passenger engines purchased by the C&S and were the principal power on trains 1, 2, 7, and 8 until the introduction of the *Texas Zephyr* in 1940. After that they continued to pull Nos. 7 and 8 into the 1950s. The 372 and 374 were in passenger protection service until 1957.

After reassuming control from the USRA in 1920, the C&S made no immediate changes and the new Joint Line timetable continued to number C&S passenger trains in the 600 series (even using the same numbers) as had the USRA. In July 1920, with passenger business apparently picking up, the C&S extended the runs of their Nos. 1 and 2 (614 and 603 on the Joint Line) to Ft. Worth and made the necessary name change of 2 (603) to *Ft. Worth Express*. The two trains also exchanged the parlor-observation on this train for a Pullman 10-section observation. The trains had also grown longer and heavier with additional sleeping cars added to both pairs. Tables 3-13 and 3-14 show how they looked in June 1921.

In November 1922, the C&S, apparently trying to differentiate the two train pairs, changed the names in the public timetables of Nos. 604(7) and 609(8) to *Colorado Express* and *Texas Fast Mail*, respectively. As had often happened, it took several years for this change to be reflected in the employee timetables. By this time all the trains except No. 604(7) stopped only at Denver, Palmer Lake, Colorado Springs and

Northbound C&S train No. 614 (1) *Denver Express* at Colorado Springs, Colorado, on June 28, 1925. *–Denver Public Library; Western History collection; Otto Perry; OP-1161*

Table 3-12

No.	Name	Details
603(2)-614(3)	*Trinidad Express / Denver Express*	Limited-stop coach and parlor-observation trains between Denver and Trinidad making 7 and 8 stops, respectively
604(7)-609(8)	*Denver Express / Texas Express*	Limited-stop coach and sleeping car trains between Denver and Ft. Worth making 8 and 6 stops, respectively

Table 3-13: 1921 Nos. 614 (1) & 603 (2) Denver Express / Ft. Worth Express

Car Type	Route
Head End	
Coach	Denver and Ft. Worth
Coach	Denver and Ft. Worth
Dining Car	Denver and Ft. Worth
12-1 Sleeping Car	Denver and San Antonio (via MKT at Ft. Worth)
12-1 Sleeping Car	Denver and New Orleans (via SP at Ft. Worth)
12-1 Sleeping Car	Denver and New Orleans (via T&P at Ft. Worth)
10-Sec Observation	Denver and Ft. Worth

Table 3-14: 1921 Nos. 604 (7) & 609 (8) Denver Express / Texas Express

Car Type	Route
Head End	
Coach	Denver and Ft. Worth
Coach	Denver and Ft. Worth
Dining Car	Denver to Ft. Worth (609 only)
12-1 Sleeping Car	Denver and Ft. Worth
12-1 Sleeping Car	Colorado Springs and Ft. Worth
12-1 Sleeping Car	Colorado Springs and Ft. Worth
12-1 Sleeping Car	Denver and Trinidad

C&S 370 (F3B Class 4-6-2) pulling No. 21, southbound *Gulf Coast Special*, leaving Larkspur, Colorado, on August 15, 1931. –*Denver Public Library; Western History collection; Otto Perry; OP-6844*

Pueblo. No. 604(7), *Colorado Express*, still made 9 stops on the Joint Line. In March 1925, No. 604 began carrying cars off Santa Fe train No. 14, *Denver Express*. Then in May of the same year, the southern terminal of C&S trains was extended to Dallas when the Fort Worth and Denver obtained trackage rights over the Rock Island. By June 1926, the names of Nos. 614(1) and 603(2) were changed in the public timetables to *Colorado Special* and *Gulf Coast Special*, respectively. As was the case previously, the old names remained in the employee timetables for some time.

In July 1928, the C&S Joint Line train numbers were rationalized by placing a 2 in front of the C&S

number used south of Pueblo. Table 3-15 shows the C&S lineup after all these changes had been made.[6]

Because of changes on the Santa Fe, Nos. 27 and 28 carried Santa Fe's El Paso traffic north of Pueblo beginning in July 1928. This lasted for about two years and then in July 1930 Santa Fe moved its northbound El Paso traffic to a Santa Fe train and a month later also moved its southbound El Paso traffic to a Santa Fe train. Gradually through the decade of the

1920s, average speeds had increased from approximately 30 to 35 miles per hour over the Joint Line. Finally in June 1930, the employee timetables began carrying the same names for C&S trains as the C&S public timetables.

As on the other two railroads on the Joint Line, the Depression caused the C&S to make adjustments in schedules and consists. Consists first shrank with Nos. 27 and 28 down to one sleeping car and no dining car by September 1931. Then in November 1931, C&S 21 and 22 shrank even further and were combined with Santa Fe trains 6 and 13 north of Pueblo. The C&S contributions to the consist at that time are

---

6. Again I have used the names as shown in the public timetables as opposed to the old names in the employee timetables.

C&S 375 (F3C Class 4-6-2) on No. 21, *Gulf Coast Limited*, south of Palmer Lake, Colorado, on June 16, 1929. –*Denver Public Library; Western History collection; Otto Perry; OP-6924*

shown in Tables 3-16 and 3-17.

In May 1933, Santa Fe No. 5 replaced No. 13 in carrying Colorado and Southern 1, *Gulf Coast Special*, cars. In 1936, Palmer Lake was dropped as a stop for Nos. 27 and 28, *Texas / Denver Express*. From this time until the end of C&S passenger service, the C&S would only serve Denver, Colorado Springs and Pueblo leaving the Santa Fe and Rio Grande to serve the smaller towns.

By June 1937, passenger traffic had recovered enough to allow the C&S to again begin running Nos. 21(1) and 22(2) north of Pueblo. At the same time, the railroad renamed all four of its passenger trains. Nos. 21(1) and 22(2) became the *Colorado Special*. Nos. 27(7) and 28(8) became the *Gulf Coast Special*, the name they would carry for the rest of their lives. Passenger loads had not rebounded in the winter season, so from February to June 1938, *Colorado Special* was again combined with Santa Fe Nos. 5 and 6. But by June 1938 *Colorado Special* was again

running north of Pueblo, this time for good. During this decade, the number of passenger cars pulled continued to increase as did passenger train speeds (from about 35 to over 41 miles per hour). The C&S also started to air-condition its cars in the late 1930s. Consists of these two trains are in Tables 3-18 and 3-19. For the winter season of 1940, *Gulf Coast Spe-*

Table 3-15

No.	Name	Details
21(1)-22(2)	*Gulf Coast Special / Colorado Special*	Limited-stop coach and sleeping car trains between Denver and Ft. Worth/Dallas making 4 and 9 stops, respectively.
27(7)-28(8)	*Texas Fast Mail / Colorado Express*	Limited-stop coach and sleeping car trains between Denver and Ft. Worth/Dallas making 4 and 9 stops, respectively. Carried Santa Fe to El Paso traffic north of Pueblo.

Table 3-16: 1931 AT&SF Nos. 13(1) & 6 (2) Gulf Coast Special/Colorado Special

Car Type	Route
Head End	
Coach	Denver and Ft. Worth-Dallas
Coach	Denver and Ft. Worth-Dallas
Dining Car	Denver and Ft. Worth-Dallas
10-Sec Observation	Denver and Ft. Worth-Dallas

Table 3-17: 1931 Nos. 27 (7) & 28 (8) Texas Fast Mail/Colorado Express*

Car Type	Route
Baggage-RPO	Denver and Amarillo?†
Baggage	Denver and Ft. Worth-Dallas
Coach	Denver and Ft. Worth-Dallas
Coach	Denver and Ft. Worth-Dallas
12-1 Sleeping Car	Denver and Ft. Worth-Dallas

* Dining facilities were opened at Trinidad, Texline, and Amarillo for meals.

† A question mark indicates uncertainty about a portion of the explanation due to limited availability of sources.

C&S 374 (F3C Class 4-6-2) on No. 28, *Colorado Express*, north of Pueblo, on Independence Day 1935. –*Denver Public Library; Western History collection; Otto Perry; OP-6904*

C&S 374 (F3C Class 4-6-2) on No. 27, *Gulf Coast Special*, south of Englewood, Colorado, on February 12, 1939. –*Western History collection; Otto Perry; OP-6909*

cial lost its sleeping cars.

June 2, 1940, was an important date for the Colorado and Southern. On this date, the C&S renamed Nos. 21(1) and 22(2) to *Advance Texas Zephyr* and assigned newly bought E5 diesel units to the train. Two sets of two-unit diesels were required. One set (C&S 9950A *Silver Racer* and 9950B *Silver Steed*) was furnished by the Colorado and Southern and one set (FW&D 9980A *Silver Chief* and 9980B *Silver Warrior*) by the Ft. Worth and Denver. The E5 by EMD was a 2,000 horsepower, streamlined locomotive with fluted sides to match Budd-built lightweight passenger cars. The *Advance Texas Zephyr* consist was similar to that of *Colorado Special* as the stainless steel cars required for the soon-to-come *Texas Zephyr* had not all been delivered. Gradually the lightweight stainless steel cars were introduced into the consist of the *Advance Texas Zephyr* until on August 22, the *Texas Zephyr* began.

Two trains sets, consisting of Budd lightweight cars and silver-painted heavyweight Pullman sleepers, were required and each participating railroad furnished one. The December 1940 consist of *Texas Zephyr* is detailed in Table 3-20.

Texas Zephyr departed Denver about one in the afternoon and averaged 52 MPH while stopping only at Colorado Springs between Denver and Pueblo and arriving around 3:30 PM. Northbound No. 22 departed Pueblo around five in the morning and arrived at Denver before 8:00 AM. It was much slower, averaging a shade under 43 miles per hour with the same stops enroute.

Table 3-18: 1939 Nos. 21(1) & 22(2) Colorado Special

Car Type	Route
Head End	
Coach (AC)	Denver and Ft. Worth-Dallas
Coach (AC)	Denver and Ft. Worth-Dallas
Chair (LW) (AC)	Denver and Ft. Worth-Dallas
10-2 Sleeping Car (AC)	Denver and Houston via SP south of Dallas
12-1 Sleeping Car	Denver to Ft Worth (21 only)
12-1 Sleeping Car	Ft. Worth to Colorado Springs (22 only)
10-Sec Observation (AC)	Denver and Ft. Worth-Dallas

Table 3-19: 1939 Nos. 27(7) & 28(8) Gulf Coast Special*

Car Type	Route
Baggage RPO	Denver and Amarillo?
Baggage	Denver and Ft. Worth-Dallas
Coach (AC)	Denver and Ft. Worth-Dallas
Coach (AC)	Denver and Ft. Worth-Dallas
Chair (LW) (AC)	Denver and Ft. Worth-Dallas
Dining Car (AC)	Denver and Ft. Worth-Dallas
12-1 Sleeping Car (AC)	Edgemont, SD, and Dallas via CB&Q north of Denver
12-1 Sleeping Car (AC)	Billings and Ft. Worth via C&S/CB&Q north of Denver

* Dining facilities were again opened at Trinidad, Texline, and Amarillo for meals.

Table 3-20: 1940 Nos. 21(1) & 22(2) Texas Zephyr

Car Type	Route
Baggage RPO (30') (LW)	Denver and Ft. Worth-Dallas
Baggage Dorm Chair (LW)	Denver and Ft. Worth-Dallas
Chair Car (52-seat) (LW)	Denver and Ft. Worth-Dallas
Chair-Dinette (LW)	Denver and Ft. Worth-Dallas
8-Sec 5-Double Bedroom Sleeping Car (HW)	Denver and Ft. Worth-Dallas
10-1-1 Sleeping Car (HW)	Denver and Ft. Worth-Dallas
Dining Lounge Observation Car (LW)	Denver and Ft. Worth-Dallas

AT&SF 3753 (4-8-4) is pulling the combined AT&SF No. 6 *Colorado Express*/C&S No. 1 *Colorado Special* near Colorado Springs, Colorado, on March 26, 1933. –*Denver Public Library; Western History collection; Otto Perry; OP-1823*

C&S 327 (C3II Class 4-6-0) C&S 370 (F3B Class 4-6-2) on No. 27, *Gulf Coast Special*, leaving Denver, Colorado, on April 21, 1936. –*Denver Public Library; Western History collection; Otto Perry; OP-6780*

Above: C&S 9950AB (E5) on train 21, *Texas Zephyr*, south of Castle Rock, Colorado, on September 8, 1940. *–Denver Public Library; Western History collection; Otto Perry; OP-7148*

Left: C&S E5 diesel 9950AB with No. 21, *Advance Texas Zephyr*, between Louviers and Sedalia, Colorado, on June 9, 1940. Note skirting over trucks of the diesel units. *–Denver Public Library; Western History collection; Otto Perry; OP-7145*

D&RGW Passenger Operations

Until the opening of the Dotsero Cutoff, the Rio Grande ran more passenger trains than either the Santa Fe or the Colorado and Southern on the Joint Line. In fact during much of the 1930s the Rio Grande ran as many passenger trains as the other two combined. When the USRA took over, the Rio Grande passenger service was focused on serving its own territory and making connections to the west via the Western Pacific (WP) and Southern Pacific (SP). This was largely due to the Rio Grande's resentment of the Missouri Pacific (MP) for its role in aiding Gould in bankrupting the Rio Grande. Gradually the Rio Grande added through cars to the east until in 1926, a complete Denver to St. Louis train was inaugurated.

In 1919 passenger trains speeds for the eight trains on the Joint Line averaged around 30 miles per hour. Over the next decade, as trains got heavier, passenger train speeds also improved to around 34 miles per hour due to better track, fewer stops, and improved locomotives. Table 3-21 shows the lineup of Rio Grande passenger trains when the USRA assumed control.

The premier passenger trains of the Rio Grande were Nos. 1 and 2. The trains began on April 15, 1915, as a combined, MP, D&RGW, and WP operation between St. Louis, Denver, and San Francisco. Denver and St. Louis sections were combined and broken up in Pueblo. By 1918, the St. Louis section had been scrapped. In the public timetables, the train used the name *Scenic Limited* for both Nos. 1 and 2, but the operating department continued to use the old names, *Pacific Coast Limited* and *Atlantic Coast Limited*, for another eight years. The name *Scenic Limited* does not appear in the employee timetables until 1924. No. 1 departed Denver around 8:00 in the morning and No. 2 arrived in Denver around 8:00 in the evening. The consist over the Joint Line as

D&RGW 1707 (M64 Class 4-8-4) on the *Panoramic Limited* at Denver Union Station on June 16, 1929. *–Denver Public Library; Western History collection; Otto Perry; OP-10458*

Table 3-21

No.	Name	Details
1-2	*Pacific Coast Limited / Atlantic Coast Limited* (*Scenic Limited* in passenger timetable)	Limited-stop coach and sleeping car trains between Denver and Ogden with San Francisco sleeping cars making 7 and 3 stops, respectively.
3-4	*Salt Lake San Francisco Express / Denver & Eastern Express*	Limited-stop coach and sleeping car trains between Denver and Ogden making 8 and 6 stops, respectively.
9-10	*Colorado Springs Pueblo & Eastern Express / Colorado Springs & Denver Express*	Local. No. 9 coach train between Denver and Pueblo making 23 stops with 5-minute meal stop at Palmer Lake. No. 10 has St. Louis to Denver sleeping car and makes 25 stops.
15-16	*Colorado & New Mexico Express*	Coach and sleeping car train between Denver and Alamosa making 6 and 16 stops, respectively.
21-29	*Suburban Passenger*	Denver and Ft. Logan coach-only commuter trains.

it appeared in 1919 is detailed in Table 3-22.

Nos. 3 and 4 over the next ten years would have their function change markedly from the secondary train on the Denver-Salt Lake City/Ogden run to the primary train on the Denver-St. Louis route. In 1919 these two trains were named *Salt Lake San Francisco Express* and *Denver & Eastern Express*, respectively.

Operating on a schedule nearly opposite that of 1 and 2, No. 3 departed Denver about 5:00 in the evening and No. 4 arrived in Denver around 1 in the afternoon. Table 3-23 shows the consists of these two trains as they looked in 1919.

Nos. 9 and 10, *Colorado Springs, Pueblo & Eastern Express / Colorado Springs & Denver Express*, served as the local, running with head end traffic, coaches and a sleeper from St. Louis for Denver on No. 10. Both trains ran over the Joint Line in daylight hours with No. 9 leaving Denver around 11 AM and No. 10 arriving in Denver around 5 PM.

Nos. 15 and 16, *Colorado & New Mexico Express*, and their extensions to the south, 315/115 and 316/116, were the workhorse trains between Denver and Salida, Grand Junction and Alamosa. At Pueblo Nos. 115/315 headed for Alamosa via Walsenburg and No. 15 continued on to Grand Junction via Salida. On the return journey Nos. 16 and 116/316 combined at Pueblo. Unlike other Rio Grande trains on the Joint Line, although they officially lost their names in 1925, they changed neither numbers nor function until they were discontinued in the 1950s, a remarkably stable run. Normally they were long, heavy trains on the Joint Line. No. 15 left Denver around 7:30 in the evening and No. 16 arrived in Denver around 8:00 in the morning. The 1919 consist for the train is shown in Table 3-24.

On October 1, 1918, the day the USRA took over operation of the Rio Grande, there were still five Uncle Sam trains a day between Denver, Littleton and Fort Logan. But patronage was declining and less than a year later, on April 15, 1919, one train each way was eliminated. Patronage continued to decline and on April 15, 1923, Sunday operation of the service ceased. Finally service ceased altogether on April 30, 1924.

The Rio Grande made very few changes to its schedule during the first few years after regaining control of operations from the USRA. In June 1923 the Rio Grande added a third local train to the Joint Line. In the timetable between June and October only, No. 8, *Colorado Springs and Denver Express*, ran from Pueblo to Denver on a four-hour schedule departing Pueblo at 7:15 AM making 30 stops along its way. Then on June 1, 1924, the Rio Grande originated Nos. 7 and 8, *Panoramic Special*, a summer season

only, all-Pullman train running between Denver and Salt Lake City with a consist of sleeper-observation, sleeping cars and Rio Grande dining car. In 1926, a lounge-observation, rebuilt by the Burnham shop forces from buffet-library cars, replaced the Pullman sleeper-observation. In 1928, the consist of the then-named *Panoramic* is as detailed in Table 3-25.

In 1925, all passenger trains except *Scenic Limited* and *Panoramic Special* lost their names and were listed as just *Passenger* in the employee timetables. The public timetables also listed them by number only. In January 1926, the schedules of Nos. 9 and 10 were rearranged to connect with Missouri Pacific 11 and 12 from and to St. Louis. In the process these trains changed from mostly coach locals to full service trains with coaches, chair cars, diner, sleepers and a sleeper observation. The consist is shown in Table 3-26.

In June 1926, the Rio Grande added another train pair with the name *The Westerner* in the public timetables. Nos. 17 and 18 ran at night as a summer train only connecting with the Missouri Pacific at Pueblo. Though short lived, the name would live on later when applied to Nos. 3 and 4. Thus, at the end of the decade, the Rio Grande's passenger lineup on the Joint Line looked very much like it did at the beginning of the decade except for the loss of the Uncle Sam trains and the addition of the summer only *Panoramic*, as shown in Table 3-27.

In 1919, the Rio Grande had a number of obsolescent ten-wheelers of several classes, T-29 being the most used on the Joint Line, and six relatively modern Pacific locomotives to haul their passenger trains. The ten-wheelers had been built between 1896 and 1909 and the Pacifics were built in 1913. The ten-wheelers

Table 3-22: 1919 Nos. 1 & 2 *Scenic Limited*

Car Type	Route
Head End	
Coach	Denver and Ogden
Coach	Denver and Ogden
Tourist Sleeper	Denver and San Francisco via WP at Salt Lake City
Dining Car	Denver and Salt Lake City
12-1 Sleeping Car	Denver and San Francisco via WP at Salt Lake City
10-Sec Observation	Denver and Ogden

Table 3-23: 1919 Nos. 3 & 4 *Salt Lake San Francisco Express / Denver & Eastern Express*

Car Type	Route
Head End	
Coach	Denver and Ogden
Coach	Denver and Ogden
Tourist Sleeper	Denver and San Francisco via SP at Ogden
12-1 Sleeping Car	Denver and San Francisco via SP at Ogden

Table 3-24: 1919 Nos. 15 & 16 *Colorado & New Mexico Express*

Car Type	Route
Head End	
Coach	Denver and Creede
Coach	Denver and Alamosa
Coach	Denver and Leadville
Coach	Denver and Grand Junction via Leadville
16-Sec Sleeping Car	Denver and Alamosa
16-Sec Sleeping Car	Denver and Salida
16-Sec Sleeping Car	Denver and Grand Junction

Table 3-25: 1928 Nos. 7/8 *Panoramic*

Car Type	Route
Head End	
12-1 Sleeping Car	Chicago and Salt Lake City via CB&Q 3 and 2, WP 1 and 2
12-1 Sleeping Car	Denver and Salt Lake City
Dining Car	Denver and Salt Lake City
10-1-2 Sleeping Car	Denver and Salt Lake City
Lounge Observation	Denver and Salt Lake City

rode on 63- or 67-inch drivers and had tractive efforts ranging from 26,000 to 29,000 pounds. The P-44[7] class Pacifics had 67-inch drivers and 44,594 pounds tractive effort.

Both the C&S and the Santa Fe were using newer and more modern locomotives and it was clear to the receivers of the Rio Grande that they too needed new passenger power. So from 1924 to 1926 the railroad bought several classes of 4-8-2 locomotives. The first were 63-inch drivered dual-service locomotives in the M-67 Class. Although powerful, the 63-inch drivers were more useful in heavier mountain territory than afforded by the Joint Line. The first truly modern passenger locomotives bought by the Rio Grande were ten 1926-bought M-75 three-cylinder 4-8-2s riding on 67-inch drivers. While successful, the Rio Grande wanted still faster but yet powerful passenger locomotives and they made a real hit in 1929 by buying fourteen M-64 4-8-4 locomotives. While the tractive effort of these was not as great as the M-75, they had 70-inch drivers, which allowed greater speed. These locomotives pulled all principal Rio Grande passenger trains on the Joint Line up to 1937. All of the M-64 locomotives made it into the 1950s still pulling passenger trains.

Responding to the Depression, the Rio Grande in 1930 began making changes to its schedule. The first trains to go were Nos. 9 and 10 in June 1930. This would have left the MP without a connection to Denver, so the Rio Grande in effect merged 9 and 10 into 3 and 4 and in the public timetable called Nos. 3 and 4, *The Westerner*. While *The Westerner* ran between Denver and Ogden it carried cars for the Missouri Pacific between Pueblo and Denver. Its consist is detailed in Table 3-28.

D&RGW 1706 (M-64 Class 4-6-4) No. 3, *The Westerner*, has departed Palmer Lake, Colorado, on October 1, 1932. –*Denver Public Library; Western History collection; Otto Perry; OP-10447*

Table 3-26: 1926 Nos. 9 & 10 Passenger

Car Type	Route
Head End	
Chair Car	Denver and St. Louis via MP at Pueblo
Coach	Denver and Pueblo
Coach	Denver and Pueblo
Dining Car	Denver and St. Louis via MP at Pueblo
10-1-2 Sleeping Car	St. Louis via MP at Pueblo
10-Sec Observation	St. Louis via MP at Pueblo

This required that the schedules of Nos. 3 and 4 and probably MP's connecting train be adjusted. What the railroad did was move the departure of No. 3 and arrival of No. 4 at Denver about halfway between the former times of Nos. 3 and 4 and Nos. 9 and 10. No. 3 had its Denver departure moved from 5:00 PM to 2:00 PM and No. 4 had its Denver arrival moved from 11:00 AM to 2:15 PM. Similar adjustments were made at Pueblo.

Table 3-27

No.	Name	Details
1-2	Scenic Limited	Limited-stop coach and sleeping car trains between Denver and Ogden with Chicago-San Francisco sleeping cars making 4 stops
3-4	Passenger	Limited-stop coach and sleeping car trains between Denver and Ogden making 8 and 6 stops, respectively
7-8	Panoramic	Summer only coach and sleeper train between Denver and Salt lake City making four stops
9-10	Passenger	Denver and Pueblo limited-stop coach and sleeping car train connecting with MP at Pueblo with cars for St. Louis making 7 and 6 stops, respectively
15-16	Passenger	Coach and sleeping car train between Denver and Grand Junction making 4 and 11 stops, respectively

---

7. In 1926, the Rio Grande adopted a new system of classifying steam locomotives using a letter to denote wheel arrangement and a number to denote tractive effort in thousands of pounds. I will use this system from here on even though it was not yet in existence when the P-44 locomotives were built.

D&RGW 1712 (M-64 Class 4-8-4) on No. 1, *Scenic Limited*, at Wolhurst, Colorado, in the early 1930s. *–George L. Beam; Colorado Railroad Museum collection*

Table 3-28: 1930 Nos. 3 & 4 The Westerner

Car Type	Route
Head End	
Coach	Denver and Ogden
Coach	Denver and Ogden
Dining Car	Denver and Ogden
12-1 Sleeping Car	Denver and Ogden
16-Sec Sleeping Car	Grand Junction to Denver (4 only)
12-1 Sleeping Car	Denver to Grand Junction (3 only)
14-Sec Sleeping Car	Denver and St. Louis via MP at Pueblo
12-1 Sleeping Car	Denver and St. Louis via MP at Pueblo
Sun-Room Lounge Car	Denver and St. Louis via MP at Pueblo

Table 3-29: 1932 Nos. 3 & 4 The Westerner

Car Type	Route
Head End	
Chair Car	Denver and St. Louis via MP at Pueblo
Dining Car	Denver and St. Louis via MP at Pueblo
10-1-2 Sleeping Car	Denver and St. Louis via MP at Pueblo
10-Sec Observation	Denver and St. Louis via MP at Pueblo

The Depression also caused *Panoramic* to lose patrons and it made its last run on the Joint Line on September 6, 1931. In November 1932 Nos. 3 and 4 were cut back to Denver-Pueblo trains connecting with the MP for St. Louis at Pueblo. It was a much shorter train and the fastest train on the Joint Line, running at an average of over 41 miles per hour. Table 3-29 shows how it looked.

In June 1935 the 10-Section observation and dining car were replaced with a diner-lounge and in September of that year, Nos. 3 and 4 lost their name in the public timetables.

1934 saw the completion of the Dotsero Cutoff, an event that would eventually change Rio Grande passenger train operation on the Joint Line from pre-eminent to secondary. Almost immediately, *Scenic Limited* lost its status as the flagship train of the Rio

Grande to first *Panoramic* and then *Exposition Flyer*, both of which ran via the Dotsero Cutoff. Table 3-30 shows its consist during this time.

By 1936, with passenger business on the rise, the Rio Grande introduced a Second Nos. 1 and 4. These two trains ran between Denver and Pueblo with Second No. 1 handling coaches, and an overflow Pullman switched into No. 1 before it left Pueblo. Second No. 4 was coach only and provided a convenient after-lunch run from Pueblo to Denver. In June 1937 these two trains were renumbered to 7 and 8. No. 7, with coaches only, left Denver before the *Scenic Limited* and handled local work at six stops. No. 8 made seven stops and carried a diner, coaches and sleepers from the Missouri Pacific. Nos. 7 and 8 ran in the summer seasons of 1937, 1938 and 1940.

In the late 1930s Nos. 3 and 4 became heavier.

The Rio Grande added a diner and a lounge as well as a tourist-sleeper to both trains. No. 3 also got two more sleeping cars.

Throughout the 1930s the *Scenic Limited* continued to provide service between Denver and Ogden, although there were consist changes and a gradual increase in average speed to around 41 miles per hour in 1940.

The same could be said for workhorse Nos. 15 and 16 whose average speed in 1940 was about 37 miles per hour. During the decade its western terminal changed from Grand Junction to Salida to Minturn.

In 1940 Nos. 3 and 4 were still the fastest train pair on the Joint Line and their average speed had increased to over 45 miles per hour. Table 3-31 has the lineup of Rio Grande passenger trains on the Joint Line in the summer of 1940.

In 1937, the Rio Grande bought M-68 Class

Table 3-30: Nos. 1 & 2 Scenic Limited

Car Type	Route
Head End	
Coach	Denver and Ogden
Dining Car	Denver and Salt Lake City?
Tourist Sleeper	Chicago and San Francisco tri-weekly via CB&Q and WP
10-1-2 Sleeping Car	Chicago and Salt Lake City via CB&Q
Lounge Observation	Denver and Ogden

Table 3-31

No.	Name	Details
1-2	Scenic Limited	Limited-stop coach and sleeping car trains between Denver and Ogden making 3 and 4 stops, respectively; carried Chicago-San Francisco sleeping cars.
3-4	Passenger	Limited-stop coach and sleeping car trains between Denver and St. Louis making 3 stops.
7-8	Passenger	Summer only coach and sleeper (8 only) train between Denver and Pueblo making 7 and 6 stops, respectively.
15-16	Passenger	Coach and sleeping car train between Denver and Minturn making 5 and 11 stops, respectively.

4-8-4 locomotives from Baldwin. These locomotives featured 73-inch disc-centered drivers and a boiler pressure of 285 pounds per square inch, giving them a tractive effort of 67,200 pounds. These six locomotives were the acme of Rio Grande steam passenger power and usually were assigned to the *Scenic Limited* and then its post war replacement, *Royal Gorge*, until diesel locomotives replaced them.

Right: D&RGW 777 (T-29 Class 4-6-0) on a section of a passenger train at Castle Rock, Colorado, on September 11, 1936. –*Collection of Harold K. Vollrath*

D&RGW 1804 (M-68 Class 4-8-4) arriving at Denver with No. 16, *Colorado-New Mexico Express*, with ten cars at 10 MPH on March 13, 1938. –*R. H. Kindig, Colorado Railroad Museum collection*

Enter the USRA and the D&RGW: 1918 to World War II   77

Above: D&RGW 784 (T-29 Class 4-6-0) on No. 8, *Passenger,* near Castle Rock, Colorado, on June 25, 1938. *–Denver Public Library, Western History collection, Otto Perry, OP-10014*

Left: D&RGW 1804 (M-68 Class 4-8-4) No.16, *Colorado-New Mexico Express,* 9 cars, 10 MPH. Photographed at Santa Fe depot Littleton, Colorado, July 9, 1939. *–Denver Public Library, Western History collection, Otto Perry, OP-10601*

Freight Trains

Denver was the largest city on both the Rio Grande and the Colorado and Southern and one of the five largest on the Santa Fe. Thus the needs of Denver customers loomed large in the design of freight schedules for all three railroads. An early morning arrival, especially for perishable traffic was desirable and an early evening departure after the close of the business day was also desirable. The schedules of all three roads into the 1950s consistently accommodated this. The Santa Fe, as the largest railroad, also had to consider the needs of customers in Wichita, Kansas City, and Chicago in designing Joint Line schedules. The needs of merchants in the other large city on the C&S, Ft. Worth, also played a role in the design of that railroad's schedules. The Rio Grande had to take the desires of its main connections, the Missouri Pacific, Santa Fe, C&S in Pueblo, Western Pacific in Salt Lake City, and Southern Pacific in Ogden into account. Between 1918 and 1940, freight trains gradually moved faster over the Joint Line, from an average of around nine hours to around five hours over the same distance.

Both the Rio Grande and Santa Fe operated local freight trains but the C&S did not as the Joint Line served as a bridge line for the C&S. Until 1937, when the Santa Fe completed its line between La Junta and Amarillo, the C&S had the only line between Denver and west Texas and carried all traffic moving between those points. Until the completion of the Dotsero Cutoff, the Joint Line was the primary freight line for the Rio Grande with traffic moving to and from the east over the MP, to and from the west over Tennessee Pass, and to and from Alamosa. The Santa Fe continued to receive from and forward to points east and west at La Junta. Usually the predominant amount of traffic was eastbound. Gradually between 1918 and 1937 freight trains lost their descriptive names on the Joint Line and became just *Fast Freight*. The one ex-

AT&SF 3114 (2-8-2) on probably No. 631 leaving Denver, Colorado, circa 1920. Note the gondolas, probably loaded with iron ore for CF&I at the front of the train. *–Denver Public Library; Western History collection; Otto Perry; OP-14181*

ception to this was the Rio Grande's *Rocket*.

By the time of the USRA, all freight trains on the C&S and Santa Fe had no timetable rights and operated as extra trains. D&RGW freights had timetable rights, until the completion of its manual block system in 1921.

AT&SF Freight Operations

In October 1918, the USRA continued the Santa Fe's freight train schedule of one eastbound and one westbound through freight train daily but, in line with the change of the Joint Line to a north-south railroad from Santa Fe's east-west, reversed the numbers. The focus of the schedule was to and from the east. Little traffic came from or went to the west. Ta-

ble 3-32 shows how Santa Fe freight schedules looked under the USRA.

No. 631, *Freight*, provided an early evening departure from Denver, which allowed for pickup of outbound traffic from Denver customers following the close of the business day. Taking a little over nine hours to get to Pueblo, No. 631 connected to No. 32 for Emporia at La Junta. Arrival of No. 632, *Colorado Fast Freight*, that connected with No. 31 from Kansas City at La Junta was scheduled for an early morning arrival to accommodate delivery to customers before the beginning of the business day. It was not particularly fast as it took well over ten hours to make the trip from Pueblo.

Way freight operations were very important in 1918, as railroads were the preferred mode of trans-

Table 3-32

No.	Name	Details
631	*Freight*	Denver to La Junta connecting to No. 32 at La Junta for Emporia
632	*Colorado Fast Freight*	La Junta to Denver with traffic off No. 31 from Kansas City at La Junta
687-688	*Way Freight*	Daily except Sunday Pueblo and Colorado Springs turn taking 3 and 4 hours, respectively
689	*Way Freight*	Daily except Sunday Denver to Colorado Springs on a 7½ hour schedule
690	*Way Freight*	Daily except Sunday Colorado Springs to Denver on an 8 hour schedule

AT&SF 1854 is ready to take a local to Denver at Colorado Springs, Colorado, on May 30, 1929. *–Denver Public Library; Western History collection; Otto Perry; OP-584*

port for delivery and pickup of all freight at the towns between Denver and Pueblo. Roads were bad and trucks were small. Over the next 22 years as roads improved and trucks got bigger, they provided effective competition for local freight traffic and the importance of the way freight declined. In 1918, the USRA added a "6" in front of and reversed the Santa Fe numbers. It operated Santa Fe way freight trains daily except Sunday each way between Denver and Colorado Springs (No. 689 southbound and No. 690 northbound) and between Colorado Springs and Pueblo (No. 687 southbound and No. 688 northbound). Nos. 687 and 688 worked as a turn. No. 688 went north in the early morning taking four hours. No. 687 must not have done too much work on the return as its schedule only took three hours in the early afternoon. Nos. 689 and 690 required two sets of equipment and each departed in the morning and took seven and a half hours and eight hours, respectively, to accomplish their work.

In 1919 the Santa Fe began taking delivery of the 3800 Class 2-10-2 locomotives, the prime through freight locomotive on the Joint Line for the next thirty years. Eleven of the 29 built in 1919 were coal burners and assigned to the Colorado and New Mexico Divisions to work north to Denver and south to Albuquerque, respectively. In 1923 six more coal burners were built to supplement the first eleven. The 3800s rode on 63-inch drivers, had 30-inch cylinders by 32-inch stroke and their boilers worked at 195 pounds pressure when new. They were equipped with Walschaerts valve gear and those not built with an Elesco feedwater heater had it added during shopping. As built they developed 75,700 pounds of tractive effort. Later the boiler pressure was raised to 220 pounds increasing tractive effort to 85,360 pounds.

During the USRA tenure, no changes were made in freight schedules, both through and way freight operations remained constant. After the Santa Fe resumed responsibility for their traffic on the Joint

Line, they made only minor schedule changes until 1926. In October 1921 the schedule of No. 631 was tightened a bit, cutting 10 minutes. But at the same time No. 632 had its Pueblo to Denver schedule lengthened an hour and 25 minutes to a full 12 hours. In January 1926, No. 641, *Freight*, replaced No. 631, *Freight*. This train ran on a much faster schedule than No. 631 connecting to No. 42 that ran from La Junta to Newton. Departing Denver 10 minutes earlier, it arrived in Pueblo a full three hours earlier than No. 631 had. Then in June 1926, No. 632 departed Pueblo an hour and 45 minutes later resulting in a ten hour 15 minute schedule to Denver.

In November 1926, the Santa Fe, probably in response to increased truck competition, cut the days of operation of the way freight trains more than in half. No. 687 and 688 ran between Colorado Springs to Pueblo only as needed. No. 689 ran from Denver to Colorado Springs on Monday, Wednesday and Friday, and No. 690 returned the next day.

In March 1928 the Santa Fe dramatically cut schedules of Nos. 632 and 641 by changing departure times but leaving arrival times the same. No. 632 departed Pueblo earlier in the evening and still arrived in Denver in the early morning a little over 9 hours later, a cut of over an hour. No. 641 saw an even more dramatic cut with an evening departure and early morning arrival in Pueblo cutting 2½ hours from the previous schedule. In July 1928 the Santa Fe finally dropped the numeral "6" from all freight train numbers.

In June 1930 the Santa Fe added a new through freight to the schedule. No. 46, *Fast Freight*, connected from new No. 45, *Fast Freight*, at La Junta and replaced No. 32 for the early morning arrival in Denver, departing Pueblo at 12:05 AM with a 6:00 AM arrival in Denver, a journey of just under six hours. No. 32 moved to an early afternoon departure from Pueblo with a late evening arrival in Denver.

Finally in February 1931, the Santa Fe finished tinkering with the schedules for a while by changing the number of *Colorado Fast Freight* from No. 32 to No. 36, connecting from No. 35 at La Junta. No. 36 also operated on a different schedule than had No. 32, departing Pueblo at 7:00 AM and arriving in Denver at 3:00 PM. The railroad also further tightened the schedule of No. 41 which now left Denver two hours and 20 minutes later and arrived in Pueblo an hour later for a saving of 20 minutes. At the same time the Santa Fe, continuing to respond to the increased competition from trucks and the Depression, changed the way freight operation to a tri-weekly Denver to Pueblo operation. New No. 97 was scheduled to leave Denver at 8:30 AM on Monday, Wednesday and Friday to arrive in Pueblo 8½ hours later. The next day, No. 98 was scheduled to leave Pueblo at 8:00 AM to use 8½ hours to work back to Denver.

Preferred power for the way freight trains throughout the 1920s was the 1800 Class Prairie-type locomotive. During the first half of the decade, these locomotives were four-cylinder balanced compounds but from late 1925 through 1928, the railroad converted them to simple expansion. These locomotives had 69-inch drivers and as compounds developed more than 37,500 pounds tractive effort. After being converted to simple expansion, they de-

AT&SF 3810 (2-10-2) on northbound (probably No. 36) freight near Breed, Colorado, on March 8, 1931. –*Denver Public Library; Western History collection; Otto Perry; OP-1960*

veloped 43,200 pounds tractive effort. Table 3-33 shows what the Santa Fe freight operations on the Joint Line looked like at the beginning of the 1930s.

The decade of the 1930s brought very few changes to Santa Fe freight operations. In November 1931 the Santa Fe, desiring an earlier arrival in Denver, pushed No. 46 back to an evening departure from Pueblo with a two hour earlier arrival in Denver at 4:00 AM, slightly lengthening the schedule in the process. In August 1932, based on more than a year's experience, the railroad cut the way freight operations back to a Colorado Springs to Denver operation, leaving towns between Pueblo and Colorado Springs without local freight service. Apparently the through

Table 3-33

No.	Name	Details
36	Colorado Fast Freight	Pueblo to Denver with traffic off No. 35 from the east at Pueblo. Scheduled for a mid-afternoon arrival in Denver.
41	Freight	Denver to Pueblo connecting to No. 42 at Pueblo for Newton. Late evening departure from Denver.
46	Fast Freight	Pueblo to Denver with traffic off No. 45 from the east at Pueblo. Scheduled for a mid-afternoon arrival in Denver.
97	Way Freight	Denver to Pueblo on an 8½ hour schedule, Mon., Wed. and Fri.
98	Way Freight	Pueblo to Denver on an 8½ hour schedule Tues., Thurs., and Sat.

AT&SF 3813 (2-10-2) on southbound freight (probably No. 31) south of Louviers, Colorado, on February 28, 1937. –*Denver Public Library; Western History collection; Otto Perry; OP-1970*

AT&SF 3815 (2-10-2), C&S 913 (E5C Class 2-10-2) on southbound freight south of Sedalia, Colorado, on January 21, 1940. Based on published schedules it is most likely that this is Santa Fe No. 31 although it is possible it could be a late running C&S 75. –*Denver Public Library; Western History collection; Otto Perry; OP-1978*

freight trains could handle whatever local business remained. On Monday, Wednesday and Friday, No. 97 was scheduled to leave Denver ½ hour before noon and arrive at Colorado Springs five hours later. A day later No. 98's schedule called for a 5:00 PM departure from Colorado Springs and an arrival at Denver 4½ hours later.

The Depression finally caught up with the Santa Fe's through freight schedules forcing the railroad to drop No. 46 in April 1933. This moved No. 36's schedule to accommodate the early morning (4:00 AM) arrival in Denver. Both Nos. 41 and 36 operated on a five hour Denver to Pueblo timing with No. 36 departing Denver at 12:30 AM. This gave the C&S Denver switch crews more than enough time to collect outgoing freight after the close of business day. Later in June 1935, No. 41's departure from Denver was moved back 2½ hours to 10:00 PM. This still gave the C&S switch crews plenty of time to collect outgoing traffic after the close of the business day. Arrival in Pueblo was a bit over 4½ hours later. In May 1936, No. 41 became *Fast Freight*, a belated acknowledgement of its then five-hour schedule

The Santa Fe made no further changes until January 1937 when business had recovered enough to reinstitute another through freight. This time, however, it was a southbound and not the northbound that had been dropped four years earlier. This was due in part to the completion of a line between La Junta and Amarillo and the new train was to carry traffic for west Texas the Santa Fe hoped to siphon off the C&S. New No. 31, *Fast Freight*, replaced what had been a joint Santa Fe/Colorado and Southern train C&S No. 73. It had a noon departure from Denver and, like the other two through freight trains, operated on a five-hour schedule. Later that year No. 36 had its name changed to *Fast Freight*.

Although the Santa Fe made a few minor schedule adjustments in the next three years, the next significant changes occurred in 1940. In January No. 36

Table 3-34

No.	Name	Details
31	Fast Freight	Denver to Pueblo with traffic for No. 32 for the east at Pueblo. Scheduled for a mid-morning departure from Denver.
36	Fast Freight	Pueblo to Denver with traffic off No. 35 from the east at Pueblo. Scheduled for a early-morning arrival in Denver.
41	Fast Freight	Denver to Pueblo connects to No. 42 at Pueblo for Newton. Scheduled for an evening departure from Denver.
97	Way Freight	Denver to Colorado Springs on a five-hour schedule, Mon., Wed. and Fri.
98	Way Freight	Colorado Springs to Denver on an 4½ hour schedule Tues., Thurs., and Sat.

had its schedule shifted to an earlier departure from Pueblo and a two-hour earlier arrival in Denver at 2:00 AM. This gave C&S switch crews a seven-hour window to deliver traffic to Denver customers. Then in June No. 31 moved to a two-hour earlier departure from Denver at 10:00 AM and had 30 minutes cut from its previous five-hour schedule. In 1940, the two way freight trains were still operating as they had since 1932. Table 3-34 shows how Santa Fe freight operations looked at the end of 1940.

C&S Freight Operations

When the USRA took over operations of the Colorado and Southern, it made no changes except to change numbers by adding a "6" and changing odd numbers to even and vice versa. With the shortest route by far, the C&S had a practical monopoly on traffic moving between Denver and Amarillo. As such its through freight trains reflected this advantage. Table 3-35 shows how it looked.

No. 619 left Denver before dawn and took ten hours to make the trip to Pueblo. No. 622, after a nine-hour trip from Pueblo, arrived at 6:00 AM to allow for delivery in Denver before the beginning of the business day. No. 651 was the late afternoon de-

C&S 906 (E5B Class 2-10-2) on northbound freight (probably No. 78, *Colorado Fast Freight*) north of Littleton, Colorado, on May 15, 1935. The train contains a cut of stock cars for Denver Stockyards on the head end. –*Denver Public Library, Western History collection, Otto Perry, OP-7076*

parture from Denver allowing pickup at Denver customers around the close of the business day.

Due to the success of the first five 2-10-2 types and because of the increase in traffic caused by World War I, the Colorado and Southern was allocated five USRA heavy 2-10-2s in April 1918. These E5B locomotives arrived on the property in mid-1919. They came with 63-inch drivers, Southern valve gear, and developed 77,710 pounds of tractive effort.

Shortly after the USRA gave back control of operations to the railroads, the C&S in October 1921 moved the departure of No. 651 to an hour later and cut more than an hour from the schedule to Pueblo. Similarly the C&S moved No. 622's arrival in Denver two hours later, which barely gave switch crews time to deliver traffic to customers before the start of the

Table 3-35

No.	Name	Details
619	Texas Fast Freight	Scheduled early morning departure Denver to Ft. Worth through freight train.
622	Colorado Fast Freight	Ft. Worth to Denver through freight. Scheduled for a morning arrival at Denver.
651	Fast Freight	Scheduled evening Denver departure for Trinidad?

business day. The railroad also cut 45 minutes from the time it took to get to Denver from Pueblo.

In October 1922, the last new steam power for the C&S, in the form of five E5C 2-10-2s, arrived on the property. These five locomotives were heavier and more modern versions of the 1915-built E5As. The

C&S 909 (E5B Class 2-10-2) on southbound freight (probably C&S No. 53, *Texas Fast Freight*) near Palmer Lake, Colorado, on July 14, 1929. Note the brakeman is riding the car tops in place to apply hand brakes. –*Denver Public Library, Western History collection, Otto Perry, OP-7094*

last two engines, 913 and 914, came with feedwater heaters, Worthington on the 913 and Elesco on the 914. Two years later the shop forces added Worthington feedwater heaters to the other three locomotives in the class and over the next few years added feedwater heaters to all of the 2-10-2 types.

After a few minor schedule changes reducing over-the-road time between Denver and Pueblo, the C&S, as did the Santa Fe, in July 1928 changed the numbers of its freight trains to two-digit numbers. No. 619 became No. 53, No. 651 became No. 51

and No. 622 became 52 – all on the same schedules as their predecessors. Then in May 1929, the C&S made some significant changes to its freight schedules. No. 49, *Fast Freight*, replaced No. 51 with the same name on a similar schedule but with a slightly later departure. A new southbound train No. 77, *Fast Freight*, was added. This train connected with a Burlington train that carried Great Northern (GN) and Northern Pacific (NP) traffic to Denver and beyond for Texas. It left Denver shortly before midnight and arrived in Pueblo at 6:00 AM before continuing on to

Texas. These moves gave the C&S three southbound trains and only one northbound train on the Joint Line. Table 3-36 is how it lined up.

Between May 1929 and February 1931, the C&S made only one schedule change, putting No. 77 on an hour faster schedule that arrived in Pueblo an hour earlier. However, due to lower traffic levels caused by the Depression, the C&S made two changes in February 1931. The railroad dropped one of the three Denver departures, No. 49 *Fast Freight*, from the schedule and adjusted the schedule of No. 77. No. 77 was now

Table 3-36

No.	Name	Details
49	Fast Freight	Scheduled evening Denver departure for Pueblo and south.
52	Colorado Fast Freight	Ft. Worth to Denver through freight. Scheduled for a morning arrival at Denver.
53	Texas Fast Freight	Scheduled early morning departure Denver to Ft. Worth through freight train.
77	Fast Freight	Seattle freight connects from GN/NP via CB&Q at Denver with traffic destined south of Pueblo. Near midnight departure from Denver.

scheduled to leave Denver almost three hours earlier at 8:45 PM and arrive in Pueblo a bit less than six hours later. Later that year, in May, almost an hour was cut from No. 77's schedule giving it an over-the-road time of five hours after its 8:45 PM departure from Denver. Still later in November 1931, the C&S made even more changes, cutting another Denver departure, No. 53 *Texas Fast Freight*. Thus, in less than a year, the C&S went from three freight trains departing Denver to one. The railroad also changed the number of *Colorado Fast Freight* from No. 52 to No. 78 and put it on a new, much faster schedule. After departing Pueblo at 4:30 PM, No. 78 took only five hours to make it to Denver, a cut of 3¼ hours.

The C&S was apparently satisfied with the two daily freight trains on the Joint Line because it made only one change over the next four years. In August 1932, it moved the departure of No. 77 from Pueblo up two hours, keeping the same five-hour over-the-road time to Denver. Then in June 1935, the C&S added two more freight trains to the schedule, one northbound and one southbound both on a five-hour schedule between Denver and Pueblo. No. 72 *Fast Freight* left Pueblo at 1:00 AM and arrived in Denver in time for delivery prior to the start of the business day. No. 73 *Fast Freight* left Denver at 8:00 AM and, after being switched in Pueblo, left for Trinidad. Thus

C&S 900 (E5A Class 2-10-2) with southbound freight (probably No. 75) near Castle Rock, Colorado, on May 9, 1938. *–Denver Public Library, Western History collection, Otto Perry, OP-7028*

C&S 911 (E5C Class 2-10-2) on northbound freight arriving Denver, Colorado, on April 6, 1939. The first several cars are Santa Fe so this might be a Santa Fe train. *–Denver Public Library, Western History collection, Otto Perry, OP-7109*

C&S 235 (0-6-0) is ready to switch for both the C&S and AT&SF at Denver on September 1, 1940. –*Jim Ehrenberger collection, photographer unknown, Colorado Railroad Museum collection*

Table 3-37

No.	Name	Details
72	*Fast Freight*	Mid-afternoon departure from Pueblo with an early evening arrival in Denver.
73	*Fast Freight*	Scheduled midnight departure from Denver for Ft. Worth freight train.
75	*Fast Freight*	Mid-morning departure from Denver for Pueblo.
76	*Fast Freight*	Ft. Worth to Denver through freight. Scheduled for an early morning arrival at Denver.

Table 3-38

No.	Name	Details
52	*California Fast Freight*	Salt Lake City to Denver on 9-hour schedule over the Joint Line.
65	*California Fast Freight*	Denver to Salt Lake City on 8-hour schedule over the Joint Line.
86	*Missouri Pacific Fast Freight*	Pueblo to Denver for early morning delivery with traffic received off MP at Pueblo on a 10-hour schedule.
80	*Way Freight*	Daily except Sunday Pueblo to Denver on a 12-hour schedule.
81	*Way Freight*	Daily except Sunday Denver to Pueblo on a 12-hour schedule.

with business starting to recover, the C&S at mid-decade had a balanced schedule of four through freight trains, all taking five hours to transit the Joint Line.

The C&S made a one-hour later adjustment to No. 73's schedule in January 1936 and then in May, No. 73 became a joint Santa Fe and C&S freight train. This lasted only until January 1937 when 73 again became C&S only. At the same time the C&S renumbered 77 and 78 to 75 and 76 and adjusted both schedules. No. 75 *Fast Freight* left Denver at 8:00 AM, 45 minutes earlier than old No. 77 and arrived in Pueblo 4¾ hours later, breaking the five hour schedule for the first time. No. 76 *Colorado Fast Freight* replaced No. 72 as the early morning arrival in Denver, arriving at 4:00 AM after a five-hour trip over the Joint Line. This gave the switch crews two hours longer to make delivery before the start of the business day and moved No. 72 to an early evening 7:30 arrival in Denver after its five-hour trip on the Joint Line. By this time all trains were named *Fast Freight* in the employee timetables.

In February 1938, the two southbound trains out of Denver had their schedules adjusted with No. 73 leaving one hour later and No. 75 leaving two hours later. Arrival in Pueblo was equally adjusted. In January 1940 No. 73's Denver departure was moved from 11:00 PM to 1:00 AM. Then in June 1940 the railroad made the last schedule change before the outbreak of World War II. Leaving No. 72 alone, schedulers changed the other three trains. No. 73 moved to a midnight departure from Denver with arrival in Pueblo six hours later. No. 75 departed at 9:00 AM with an arrival in Pueblo 4½ hours later. No. 76 departed Pueblo two hours earlier with arrival in Denver at 2:00 AM after the traditional five hours in transit. Switch crews now had seven hours to make delivery to Denver businesses before the start of the day. Table 3-37 shows how it all looked.

D&RGW Freight Operations

When the USRA took over operations in 1918, the Rio Grande was running three through freight trains daily and two way freight trains daily except Sunday. After the USRA gave control back to the railroads during the 1920s, the Rio Grande seemed to change train numbers for no apparent reason. Within five years the numbers of all three through freight trains had changed. Table 3-38 includes information about all D&RGW freight trains in 1918.

No. 52, *California Fast Freight*, the Salt Lake City to Denver train, handled traffic received from the Western Pacific at Salt Lake City, picked up additional cars at Pueblo and arrived in Denver in mid-afternoon after a nine-hour journey from Pueblo.

D&RGW 1000 (C-41 Class 2-8-0) on way freight southbound (possibly No. 71) south of Denver, Colorado, in the 1920s. *–Denver Public Library, Western History collection, Otto Perry, OP-10091*

No. 65 *California Fast Freight* was the Denver to Salt Lake City through freight. It handled all classes of traffic received from Denver customers and connected to the Western Pacific at Salt Lake City. It departed Denver in the evening allowing for pick up from customers after the close of the business day and took eight hours to get to Pueblo.

No. 86, *Missouri Pacific Fast Freight* ran between Pueblo and Denver, receiving traffic off the Missouri Pacific slated for an early morning delivery in Denver. It operated on a leisurely ten-hour schedule from

Pueblo.

The USRA also operated a pair of Rio Grande way freights over the entire Joint Line daily except Sunday. No. 80 departed Pueblo before dawn and took twelve hours to work its way to Denver. Working south from Denver No. 81 departed at 5:00 AM and also took twelve hours to work to Pueblo.

Although many different classes[8] of Rio Grande locomotives could be seen on their Joint Line freight trains as the locomotives worked to and from Denver's Burnham shops for servicing, the principal

freight locomotives on the Joint Line under the USRA were the C-41 and C-48 Class 2-8-0s for local freight trains and the F-81 Class 2-10-2s for through freight trains. The C-48 Class locomotives were built in 1906 and 1908 and rode on 57-inch drivers, developing 48,100 pounds of tractive effort. The F-81

8. As mentioned before, the system of identifying classes that I am using in this chapter and beyond did not come into being until 1926, but in the interest of clarity, I have chosen to apply the 1926 class designations.

D&RGW 1141, 1516 (C-48 Class 2-8-0, M-78 Class 4-8-2) on southbound 90-car freight (probably No. 61, *California Fast Freight*), leaving Denver, Colorado, on May 15, 1927. *–Denver Public Library, Western History collection, Otto Perry, OP-10125*

Class 2-10-2s were built in 1917 and rode on 63-inch driving wheels. They developed 81,200 pounds tractive effort but, with exceptionally small (10,000-gallon) tenders for so large a locomotive, proved to be more useful in the more mountainous areas of the Rio Grande and did not last long on the Joint Line.

Unlike the Santa Fe and Colorado and Southern which settled on the 2-10-2 type for through freight, the Rio Grande tried several types of wheel arrangements on its freight trains. In 1922, the Rio Grande began receiving what would prove to be the most often used freight locomotives on the Joint Line, the 30

dual service M-67 and M-78 Class 4-8-2 locomotives in the 1500 number series. Both classes rode on 63-inch drivers and had 210-pound boiler pressure. The difference in the two classes was that the M-78s had a trailing truck booster which, when cut in, developed a total tractive effort of 78,967 pounds. The non-booster equipped M-67s developed 66,640 pounds tractive effort.

In November 1920, a year after the last USRA timetable, the Rio Grande replaced No. 52 with No. 62 on a different schedule but with the same name, *California Fast Freight*. Moving from a morning de-

parture from Pueblo to an early afternoon departure, the train arrived in Denver around midnight.

In June 1923 the Rio Grande added another Denver to Salt Lake City through freight. The new train carried number 61 and got 65's name, *California Fast Freight*. It left Denver at 9:00 AM and arrived in Pueblo eight hours later. No. 65 retained its schedule but got a new name, *Utah Fast Freight*. Three months later, the Rio Grande changed No. 86 to No. 66 on the same schedule with the same name. In March 1925 the Rio Grande made minor schedule adjustments and changed the name of No. 65 to *Colorado Fast Freight*, possibly reflecting a route change carrying traffic for Colorado points south and or west of Pueblo.

In November 1920, the Rio Grande reduced the time way freight trains Nos. 80 and 81 had taken under the USRA. No. 80 still left Pueblo at 4:00 AM but was scheduled for only 9½ hours to get to Denver. No. 81 had 3½ hours lopped off its schedule from Denver to Pueblo. Then two years later, the Rio Grande changed the numbers of the way freights to Nos. 70 and 71 and moved departure times from Pueblo and Denver to 6:00 and 7:00 AM, respectively. Both trains were scheduled to make their trips in 9½ hours. In March 1925 No. 70 became No. 72 and two months later both trains were cut to tri-weekly. No. 71 left Denver on Tuesday, Thursday and Saturday, and arrived in Pueblo 9½ hours later. No. 72 left Pueblo at 5:00 AM on Monday, Wednesday and Friday and was scheduled to take slightly less than 9½ hours to work to Denver.

From the 1920s through the early 1950s, C-41 and C-48 Class 2-8-0s were the locomotives of choice for way freight trains. Baldwin built the C-41s in 1902 as compound locomotives. By the 1920s they had been rebuilt as simple locomotives with 55-inch drivers and 40,893 pounds of tractive effort. After all these changes, Table 3-39 shows how the Rio Grande freight service on the Joint Line looked in 1925.

The Rio Grande continued to make schedule adjustments as traffic and motive power warranted. No. 66's name changed to *Fast Freight*, but it continued to connect from the MP at Pueblo on the same basic schedule. No. 68, *Fast Freight* replaced No. 62. No. 68 was a daytime Pueblo to Denver train receiving traffic from the San Luis Valley and the Missouri Pacific departing in mid-morning and covering the Joint Line in 9½ hours. By May 1929 No. 61, after several schedule changes, was making the Denver to Pueblo run in 6¾ hours arriving in Pueblo shortly after noon. In October 1929 the Rio Grande replaced No. 61 with No. 77, keeping the same name,

D&RGW 3608 (L-131 Class 2-8-8-2) on a northbound freight (probably No. 68, now called *Fast Freight*) at Palmer Lake, Colorado, on June 10, 1934. –*Denver Public Library, Western History collection, Otto Perry, OP-10720*

D&RGW 1513, 1501 (M-78 and M-67 Classes 4-8-2s) on a southbound freight (probably No. 61) north of Larkspur, Colorado, on August 19, 1934. –*Denver Public Library, Western History collection, Otto Perry, OP-10267*

California Fast Freight, on a new schedule with a late morning departure and a half hour shorter time on the Joint Line. No. 77 did not last long as No. 61 returned in June 1930 with the *California Fast Freight* name leaving Denver shortly after midnight, arriving in Pueblo in the early morning after a bit more than 6¾ hours travel time.

In 1927 the Alco Brooks Works delivered the L-131 class 2-8-8-2 locomotives, and in 1930 the similar L-132 class 2-8-8-2 locomotives came from Alco's Schenectady Works. Both rode on 63-inch drivers and developed 131,800 pounds tractive effort. These locomotives pulled heavier freight trains on the Joint Line.

1929 provided some changes to the way freight trains also. In May, No. 72 began running on Sunday instead of Monday. Then in October it moved to a 5:30 AM Pueblo departure. In June 1932 Nos. 71 and 72 began running in the afternoon and at night. No. 71 left Denver at 8:00 PM and was scheduled for 8½ hours to work down to Pueblo. No. 72 left Pueblo at 1:00 in the afternoon and the schedule called for a 10:30 PM arrival in Denver.

The Depression had started to affect the Rio Grande's freight traffic by August 1930 when No. 65, *Colorado Fast Freight*, began running tri-weekly. However, traffic to Salt Lake City for connection with the Western Pacific must have held up quite well as in May 1931, the Rio Grande added a second *California Fast Freight*, No. 77, departing Denver at 10:15 AM and arriving in Pueblo 6¼ hours later. No. 77's schedule was adjusted four months later to an 11:00 AM departure and an even six hours running time to Pueblo. No. 77 lasted only a little over a year as it was dropped from the schedule in June 1932. Table 3-40 shows how the Rio Grande's freight schedule looked just prior to the completion of the Dotsero Cutoff.

In 1924 when the bankrupt Denver and Salt Lake (D&SL) started on the Moffat Tunnel, the road immediately started buying land along what became the Dotsero Cutoff. Soon a battle would erupt between the D&SL and its rival, the Rio Grande. The Rio Grande, itself near bankruptcy, feared losing all freight traffic from Denver if the D&SL built the connection to the Rio Grande, so they threatened to not allow any D&SL trains onto their tracks. On the

other hand, the State of Colorado, the main creditor to the bankrupt D&SL, was afraid the D&SL would never be able to pay back its debts if it did not have a connection to the west.

The Rio Grande tried to slow down construction of the cutoff and filed a protest with the ICC (Interstate Commerce Commission). Several court battles followed and eventually the Rio Grande won. The Rio Grande would build the cutoff and the D&SL would have to allow Rio Grande freight trains onto their rails for a price.

In 1931 surveyors of the Rio Grande began the task of determining the route and ended up with a route three miles shorter than what the D&SL had planned (a fact in which the railroad took great pride). In autumn of 1932 construction started and the route was completed on June 15, 1934.

The completion of the cutoff eventually changed Rio Grande manifest freight traffic patterns on the Joint Line. The line became a bridge for the two terminals of Denver and Pueblo. Westbound traffic from Denver for stations beyond Glenwood Springs, which had travelled over Tennessee Pass via the Joint Line, now moved via Moffat Tunnel and the cutoff. Eastbound traffic for Denver likewise moved via the cutoff instead of Tennessee Pass and the Joint Line. The immediate result was the removal of the two tri-weekly way freight trains from the Joint Line and a restructuring of the remaining through freight trains. The Rio Grande's local business was now handled in through freight trains and as-needed extras. Joint Line traffic now contained Denver traffic to and from the MP at Pueblo, Colorado Fuel and Iron (CF&I) traffic, traffic routed to or from Tennessee Pass stations short of Glenwood Springs, and Denver traffic to and from the San Luis Valley.

With the June 17, 1934, timetable, the remaining trains were Nos. 61, 65, 66, and 68. No. 61 was cut back to a Denver to Pueblo routing on a relatively fast 5½ hour schedule. It also lost its name to

Table 3-39

No.	Name	Details
61	*California Fast Freight*	Denver to Salt Lake City on about a 7½-hour schedule over Joint Line.
62	*California Fast Freight*	Salt Lake City to Denver on about 9½-hour schedule over the Joint Line.
65	*Colorado Fast Freight*	Denver to Pueblo with traffic for MP and San Luis Valley on a slightly-over 8-hour schedule via the Joint Line.
66	*Missouri Pacific Fast Freight*	Pueblo to Denver for early morning delivery with traffic received off MP at Pueblo on a slightly greater than 9½-hour schedule.
71	*Way Freight*	Denver to Pueblo on a 9½-hour schedule Tuesday, Thursday, Saturday.
72	*Way Freight*	Pueblo to Denver on about a 9½-hour schedule Monday, Wednesday, Friday.

Table 3-40

No.	Name	Details
61	*California Fast Freight*	Denver to Salt Lake City on about a 6½-hour schedule over Joint Line.
65	*Colorado Fast Freight*	Denver to Pueblo with traffic for the MP and San Luis Valley on an 8-hour schedule on Monday, Wednesday and Friday.
66	*Fast Freight*	Pueblo to Denver for early morning delivery with traffic received off MP at Pueblo on a 9-hour schedule.
68	*Fast Freight*	Pueblo to Denver with traffic from San Luis Valley and MP on a 5½-hour schedule.
71	*Way Freight*	Denver to Pueblo on an 8-hour schedule Tuesday, Thursday, Saturday.
72	*Way Freight*	Pueblo to Denver on a 9½-hour schedule Wednesday, Friday, Sunday.

MP 1404, 1422 (2-8-2s) on northbound freight train (probably No. 68) near Littleton, Colorado, on September 26, 1937. –*Denver Public Library, Western History collection, Otto Perry, OP-13068*

No. 78, which operated over the Moffat line. Then in September 1934 it was dropped from the schedule. No. 65, *Colorado Fast Freight*, began running daily again and forwarded traffic from Denver to the Missouri Pacific at Pueblo and handled CF&I traffic not handled in extra trains. It left Denver at 8:30 PM and arrived in Pueblo at 4:30 AM. No. 66, *Fast Freight*, left Pueblo at 8:00 PM, arrived in Denver at 3:30 AM, and continued to handle Missouri Pacific business needing early morning delivery in Denver. No. 68, *Fast Freight*, also continued to connect from the Missouri Pacific at Pueblo as well as forward traffic from the San Luis Valley. It left Pueblo at 6:00 AM and arrived in Denver at 11:30 AM. It connected with Rio Grande No. 75 to Salt Lake City via the Moffat Tunnel once a week with Nuckolls Packing Company meat.

Inaugurated January 29, 1936, No. 35, *The Rocket*, was designed to compete with trucks in the movement of LCL business from Denver to Colorado points with a delivery in the early morning, except in the San Juan basin. It departed Denver in the early evening and made a fast 4¼-hour run to Pueblo where it was switched into two parts. One part was switched into passenger train 115 for Alamosa. The rest of No. 35 continued on to Salida where cars were forwarded to Gunnison, Montrose, and other western slope points.

Also in January 1936 No. 65's schedule was shortened to six hours. Although the way freight was formally gone from the schedules, photographic evidence indicates that the Rio Grande continued to operate a local, probably on an as-needed basis, between Denver and Sedalia. After the changes ne-

cessitated by the opening of the Moffat route, Table 3-41 shows the way Rio Grande freight traffic looked on the Joint Line.

In October 1937, *The Rocket*'s Denver to Pueblo schedule was shortened to 3¾ hours. The Rio Grande also shortened the schedules of the three other trains to 5¾ hours. In January 1940, another schedule adjustment had No. 66 making the Pueblo to Denver run in five hours.

In 1938, the Rio Grande had Baldwin build some superb 4-6-6-4s for freight service. Riding on 70-inch drivers, these locomotives developed 105,000 pounds tractive effort and were fast to boot. Some of these would be assigned to Joint Line freights. Late in the decade dual service 4-8-4s of the M-64 and later M-65 Classes were used in freight service.

The beginning of dieselization gives an oppor-

D&RGW 1512 (M-78 Class 4-8-2) on a southbound freight (probably No. 61) heading for Pueblo yard on August 12, 1940.
–Collection of Harold K. Vollrath

Table 3-41

No.	Name	Details
35	*The Rocket*	Denver to Alamosa/Salida with LCL daily except Sunday on a 4¼-hour schedule.
65	*Colorado Fast Freight*	Denver to Pueblo with perishable traffic for the MP on a 6-hour schedule over the Joint Line.
66	*Fast Freight*	Pueblo to Denver for early morning delivery with traffic received off MP at Pueblo on a 6-hour schedule.
68	*Fast Freight*	Pueblo to Denver with traffic from MP and San Luis Valley on a 6½-hour schedule
(Unscheduled)	Local Freight	Denver-Sedalia turn?

tunity to offer a quick comparison of motive power practice of the three roads under nearly identical operation conditions, the only difference being the length and weight of the trains pulled over the same tracks. The Santa Fe did not design locomotives for the specific territory of the Joint Line while the other two roads included the Joint Line in their design criteria. The Santa Fe designed their locomotives for a broad, more generic territory like mountains and assumed that if a locomotive performed well over Cajon and Tehachapi it would perform well on the Palmer Divide. As such, in the early 1920s, the Santa Fe assigned the 3800 Class 2-10-2s to Joint Line freight service and stuck with them to the end of steam. Similarly the C&S also assigned 2-10-2s to the same territory. The Rio Grande on the other hand bought husky 4-8-2s as the primary freight locomotive in the 1920s but by the mid 1930s decided to modernize freight service with 4-6-6-4s and dual service 4-8-4s.

The Santa Fe used several different types of passenger engines on the Joint Line, all bought for regions other than the Joint Line. As such, there was a progression from light 4-6-2s to 4-8-2s to heavy 4-6-2s to 4-8-4s. The later 4-6-2s and the 4-8-4s were completely rebuilt with larger disc drivers late in the 1930s. The Colorado and Southern with shorter, lighter passenger trains bought fairly light 4-6-2s and, except for adding feedwater heaters, stuck with them into the 1950s. The Rio Grande started with old and worn out locomotives, tried 3-cylinder 4-8-2s and dual service 4-8-2s before finally deciding on the 4-8-4 in 1929. The later M-68 4-8-4s were thoroughly modern locomotives and the newest used on the Joint Line by any of the railroads.

The twenty-three years from 1918 through 1940 saw some major changes to the Joint Line. USRA control forced the Santa Fe and Rio Grande to operate their respective lines as double track and it proved so successful that the two continued the operation. The 1920s saw an increase in long distance passenger traffic and the beginnings of a diminution of local passenger traffic. The Depression caused both passenger and freight traffic to fall off. By the end of the decade both freight and passenger traffic on the Joint Line had started to recover but had not reached pre-Depression levels. On a positive note, thanks to better track and signaling, heavier and faster passenger locomotives and improvements to freight locomotives, both passenger and freight trains were much faster in 1940 than they were in 1918. Finally, the Colorado and Southern had introduced diesel power to the Joint Line, the development of which we will examine in the next chapter.

Above: Less than three months old, D&RGW 3700 (L-105 Class 4-6-6-4) is on a northbound freight leaving Colorado Springs, Colorado, on April 10, 1938. –*Denver Public Library, Western History collection, Otto Perry, OP-10785*

Right: D&RGW 1700 (M-64 Class 4-8-4) is on a southbound freight at Louviers, Colorado, on December 5, 1938. –*Denver Public Library, Western History collection, Otto Perry, OP-10340*

94

Chapter Four
Diesels Supplant Steam: World War II to 1955

TWO IMPORTANT FACTORS figure prominently in the history of the next fifteen years on the Joint Line: the coming of the diesel and World War II. The war brought both passenger and freight traffic back from Depression-era levels. Diesel locomotives held out the promise of greater operating efficiencies and, especially when pulling streamlined passenger trains, greater appeal to potential passengers. The increased passenger and freight traffic caused by these two factors convinced the railroads that the passengers were back and that freight traffic would hold steady. They were right with respect to freight holding steady but terribly wrong with respect to the passenger train.

The first railroad on the Joint Line to use diesels was the Colorado and Southern when it received EMD Model E5 diesels 9950A *Silver Racer* and 9950B *Silver Steed* in early 1940 for the *Texas Zephyr*. This began an approximately 15-year process in which diesel power gradually supplanted steam on the Joint Line. Although the C&S operated the first diesels on the Joint Line, it also operated the last steam locomotives in Denver switch service in 1959.

Opposite: AT&SF 197 (FT) on southbound freight (probably No. 31) south of Castle Rock, Colorado, on July 19, 1951. –*Denver Public Library, Western History collection, Otto Perry, OP-2236*

The Rio Grande received its first diesel, an NW2 switch engine, in January 1941. It operated steam locomotives on the Joint Line at least up to the fall of 1955. The Santa Fe had begun to buy diesels in the 1930s but they did not appear on the Joint Line until 1950. Santa Fe completed the transition to diesels faster than did the other two railroads on the Joint Line as operations were completely in the hands of diesels by November of 1953.

In 1941, only the C&S was operating diesels on the Joint Line and that was on just two trains, the north and southbound *Texas Zephyr*. The number of diesels would double in 1942 with the inauguration of the *Colorado Eagle* by the MP and the Rio Grande. Both the Santa Fe and Rio Grande received FT diesels during the war. The Rio Grande did use their FTs on Joint Line freights but the Santa Fe did not, concentrating them west of Winslow, Arizona. To handle the tremendous increase in traffic, all three railroads carried military personnel in their regularly scheduled trains and ran numerous passenger extras, especially to and from the newly established Camp Carson near Colorado Springs. Only the Santa Fe added an additional scheduled freight train but most of the additional freight traffic resulted in longer freight trains and extras.

Emerging from receivership in 1947, the Rio Grande merged with the Denver and Salt Lake in 1947, gaining control of the "Moffat Road" through the Moffat Tunnel and a branch line from Bond to Craig, Colorado. From that time on, the Rio Grande remained a strong and prosperous road.

Passenger Operations

In 1941 World War II was just around the corner and passenger operations on the Joint Line were recovering from the Great Depression. The Santa Fe was again running two trains a day each way as was the Colorado and Southern. The Rio Grande, despite the opening of the Moffat Tunnel route, was operating three trains a day each way. These fourteen trains, supplemented by second sections and troop trains, would prove sufficient to handle wartime traffic. The increased wartime traffic gave all three railroads hope that the passenger train was back. That hope proved to be short-lived as increased competition from airlines and the automobile started a slow decline in the number of passengers riding trains. The new trend was evident by 1955 to all three railroads.

AT&SF Passenger Trains

The Santa Fe continued to operate its two pairs of passenger trains, Nos. 130 and 141 and the *Centennial State*, Nos. 90 (9 east of Pueblo) and 101 (10

AT&SF 1363, 3764 (4-6-2, 4-8-4) on No. 130 northbound at Englewood, Colorado, on July 6, 1946. –*John W. Maxwell, Colorado Railroad Museum collection*

east of Pueblo), throughout World War II. Nos. 130 and 141 carried names in the employe timetables, *California and Chicago Express* and *Chicago and California Express,* respectively, but were not named in the public timetables. They ran between La Junta and Denver connecting to main line Nos. 3 and 4, *California Limited*, at La Junta. Throughout the 1940s, No. 141 left Denver just after supper and arrived in Pueblo some three hours later while No. 130 left Pueblo around 4:30 AM and arrived in Denver about 8:00 AM. The trains averaged a bit over 40 miles per hour on the Joint Line in 1941. Speeds on the Joint Line declined slightly to just under 40 miles per hour during the war. The consists of Nos. 130 and 141 are shown in Table 4-1.

The *Centennial State* ran between Kansas City and Denver on a faster schedule over the Joint Line than did Nos. 130 and 141, averaging a shade over

Table 4-1: 1941 No. 130 & 141 California & Chicago Express / Chicago & California Express

Car Type	Route
Mail Express	KC to Denver (130 only) off No. 3
Baggage RPO (30')	Denver to La Junta (141 only)
Baggage Express Mail	Denver to Albuquerque (141 only) for No. 3
Baggage Express Mail	Denver to Kansas City (141 only) for No. 4
Baggage Express Mail	Denver to Newton (141 only) for No. 4 on Monday
Smoker Chair (AC)	Chicago and Denver via Nos. 3 and 4
16-Sec Tourist Sleeper (AC)	Denver and Los Angeles via Nos. 3 and 4
10-1-2 Sleeping Car (AC)	Denver and Los Angeles via Nos. 3 and 4
Chair Car (AC)	Denver and Los Angeles via Nos. 3 and 4
Lounge Diner (AC)	Denver and La Junta
10-Sec Lounge (AC)	Oklahoma City and Denver via Nos. 3 and 4

45 miles per hour with fewer stops. Speed for the *Centennial State* on the Joint Line remained relatively constant during the war. In 1947, the eastern terminal was cut back to Newton, restored to Kansas City in 1949 and, in 1950, permanently cut back to La Junta. These changes affected the timetable on the Joint Line. Throughout the war and until 1947 No. 101 left Denver in the mid-afternoon and arrived in Pueblo around dinnertime. No. 90 left Pueblo mid-morning and arrived in Denver around noon. The consists of the *Centennial State* in 1946 are shown in Table 4-2.

In 1947 No. 101 left Denver about two hours earlier and No. 90 arrived in Denver about two hours later. 1949 saw a major schedule change with No. 101 (now No. 2 east of Pueblo) leaving Denver around noon and newly renumbered No. 102 (now No. 1 east of Pueblo) arriving in Denver in the mid-afternoon.

During both World War II and the Korean War, the Santa Fe also operated numerous troop trains especially to and from the newly established Camp Carson near Colorado Springs. Preferred power for passenger trains after 1941 and until the diesels arrived were rebuilt 3751 Class 4-8-4s. 3400 Class Pacifics and 3700 Class Mountains supplemented the 3751 class. Because of its shorter consist, *Centennial State* often got the 3400s while the 3700s were most often seen on troop trains.

Table 4-2: 1941 Nos. 9 (90) & 10 (101) Centennial State

Car Type	Route
Baggage RPO (30')	La Junta and Denver
Storage Mail	Denver to La Junta [10(101) only]
Baggage Express	Denver to Kansas City [10(101) only]
Smoker Chair (AC)	Kansas City and Denver
Chair Car (AC)	Kansas City and Denver
12-1 Sleeping Car (AC)	Kansas City and Denver
Café-Observation (AC)	Dodge City and Denver

AT&SF 3762 (4-8-4) southbound at Palmer Lake with *Centennial State* in the late 1940s. –*Ross B. Grenard, Jr., Colorado Railroad Museum collection*

AT&SF 3764 (3751 Class 4-8-4) on train No. 130 south of Littleton, Colorado, on July 27, 1947. –*Denver Public Library, Western History collection, Otto Perry, OP-1903*

Santa Fe heavy Pacific 3440 is on No. 90, *Centennial State*, north of Littleton, Colorado, on March 31, 1941. The consist is typical for that nice little train, two head end cars, two chair cars, a sleeper and the café-observation. –*Denver Public Library, Western History collection, Otto Perry, OP-1502*

The two hallmarks of Santa Fe diesel passenger service, the warbonnet-painted diesels and streamliners were late arrivals to the Joint Line. It was not until February 1950 when diesels from the transcontinental pool, which were cut in and out at La Junta, arrived to power the two passenger trains on the Joint Line.

In April 1950 the Santa Fe, responding to increased competition from the automobile, cut back Nos. 101 (2) and 102 (1) to Denver and La Junta trains. These trains connected to Nos. 123 and 124, the northern section of *Grand Canyon Limited* at La Junta. Although the name *Centennial State* continued to appear in the employee timetables for several years, no names for the pair were in the public timetables. At the same time the railroad increased the number of stops to six each way and reduced the average speed to around 42 miles per hour. On the other hand, the

Table 4-3: 1954 No. 130 & 141 California & Chicago Express / Chicago & California Express

Car Type	Route
Storage Mail	La Junta and Denver
Baggage Express Mail	Kansas City to Denver (130 only) off No. 7
Storage Mail	Los Angeles to Denver (130 only) off No. 124
Baggage Express Mail	Denver to Albuquerque (141 only) for No. 123
Baggage Express Mail	Denver to Los Angeles (141 only) for No. 124
Mail Express	Denver to Kansas City (141 only) for No. 8
30-40 ft. Combination	Denver to La Junta (141 only) except Sunday
Smoker Chair (AC)	La Junta and Denver
Chair Car (AC)	Denver and Los Angeles via Nos. 123 and 124
6-6-4 Sleeping Car (AC)	Denver and Los Angeles via Nos. 123 and 124
Café-Observation (AC)	Pueblo and Denver

Santa Fe reduced the number of stops for Nos. 130 and 141 to three and increased their average speed to around 46 miles per hour. After Nos. 3 and 4 were diverted to the southern main line, the connection for this pair became Nos. 7, 8, 123, and 124.

Steam returned for a curtain call from June until November 1950 at which time four-unit F3/7s and an occasional Alco PA yet again replaced steam power. Steam continued to power some Korean War troop trains until November 1953.

Even though diesels were in charge, schedules did not change markedly. No. 141 left Denver before midnight and arrived at Pueblo in the very early morning hours. No. 130 left Pueblo about 8:00 PM and arrived at Denver between 10:00 and 11:00 PM. No. 101 left Denver in the early afternoon and arrived in Pueblo before dinner. No. 102 left Pueblo mid-morning and arrived in Denver shortly after lunch. Consists for the two train pairs in 1954 are shown in Table 4-3 and 4-4. Head end traffic had increased since World War II, passenger-carrying cars had decreased, and lightweight cars had started to appear.

In the fall of 1954, the Santa Fe, as a part of its reworking of the *Grand Canyon* trains, reestablished Kansas City and Denver service. Nos. 223 and 224 were created to relieve Nos. 123 and 124 of Kansas and Colorado traffic. North of Pueblo No. 223 became 102 and 224 became No. 101. Nos. 101 and 102 still carried the *Centennial State* name in the employee timetables. The schedule on the Joint Line was similar to what Nos. 101 and 102 had been using. No. 101 left Denver at 6:45 PM and arrived in Pueblo at 9:20 PM. Northbound No. 102 left Pueblo at 11:35 AM and arrived at Denver at 2:20 PM. This lasted only one year until, in September 1955, 223 (102) and 224 (101) were cut back to a Denver and La Junta routing ending forever Santa Fe through passenger service between Denver and points east of La Junta. Table 4-5 shows the consist.

C&S and Santa Fe Pacifics pull a 12-car No. 101, *Centennial State*, at Spruce, north of Palmer Lake, Colorado, on December 13, 1942. The consist is swollen due to WW II. –*Denver Public Library, Western History collection, Otto Perry, OP-6881*

Table 4-4: 1954 Nos. 1(102) & 2 (101) Centennial State

Car Type	Route
Baggage Mail Express	Kansas City to Denver (102 only) off No. 123
Baggage Mail Express	Los Angeles to Denver (102 only) off No. 8
Storage Mail	Albuquerque to Denver (102 only) off No. 8 except Monday
30-40 ft. Combination	La Junta to Denver (102 only)
Storage Mail	Denver to Kansas City (101 only) for No. 124
Baggage Express	Denver to Kansas City (101 only) for No. 124
Chair Car (AC)	Kansas City and Denver
6-6-4 Sleeping Car (AC)	Kansas City and Denver
Café-Observation (AC)	La Junta and Denver

Table 4-5: 1954 Nos. 223(102) & 224 (101)

Car Type	Route
Baggage Mail Express	Kansas City to Denver (223/102 only)
Mail Express	Los Angeles to Denver (223/102 only) off No. 8
30-40 ft. Combination	La Junta to Denver (223/102 only) except Monday
Baggage Express	Denver to Kansas City (224/101 only)
Chair Car (AC)	La Junta and Denver
Chair Car (AC)	La Junta and Denver
6-6-4 Sleeping Car (AC)	Denver to Los Angeles (224/101 only) for No. 19 at La Junta
Café-Observation (AC)	La Junta and Denver

AT&SF 35LABC (F3 ABBA) on No. 21, *El Capitan*, detouring at 50 mph at Palmer Lake because of flooding near Kansas City on July 17, 1951. –*Collection of Harold K. Vollrath*

AT&SF 3745 (4-8-2) with bell ringing is leaving Denver Union Terminal with No. 101, *Centennial State*, on May 29, 1949. –*Bob Andrews photo; Tom Klinger collection*

AT&SF 311LAB (F7 ABB) on 1st No. 102, *Centennial State*, has crested Palmer Lake, Colorado, on July 19, 1951. –*Collection of Harold K. Vollrath*

Although the Fairbanks-Morse Erie-builts rarely appeared on the Joint Line, here are 90LAC on train No. 101, *Centennial State*, leaving Denver, Colorado, on February 22, 1951. –*Denver Public Library, Western History collection, Otto Perry, OP-2207*

C&S Passenger Trains

Having settled on both a diesel-powered streamliner and a steam heavyweight train between Denver and Ft. Worth/Dallas, the Colorado and Southern maintained the same two train pairs for the next fifteen years. Both trains only made three stops, Denver, Colorado Springs, and Pueblo, a practice the C&S would continue to the end of passenger operations. In 1940, Nos. 27 and 28, *Gulf Coast Special*, departed Denver about 8:00 PM and Pueblo around 5:30 PM and arrived in Pueblo near 11:00 PM and Denver around 8:30 PM, respectively. Although departure and arrival times would fluctuate some during the war, the two trains would average just under 43 miles per hour. Throughout the war, *Texas Zephyr* also maintained its Denver departure just after lunch and Denver arrival just after breakfast. The consists of both trains would expand during the war with the *Zephyr* adding another sleeper to its initial consist. Tables 4-6 and 4-7 show typical World War II consists of both trains.

After the war and until 1950, the C&S made very few changes to the *Texas Zephyr* consist or schedule except to add or subtract sleeping cars, depending on the season. In that year the C&S added a full dining car to the consist and used the tail car as a buffet-lounge-observation. This lasted less than a year before the consist went back to using the tail car as the dining car for first class passengers. *Gulf Coast Special* underwent gradual schedule changes with the departure from Denver remaining about 7:00 PM until 1956, but arrival times in Denver gradually moved earlier (from 10:00 PM to 6:30 PM) between 1945 and 1955. Consists remained remarkably constant. From 1949 to early 1953, the train carried only one coach or chair car, but two sleepers returned around 1952. Starting in 1953 the C&S added a second coach. The two coaches gave way to two chair cars in early 1954 and a dining-lounge car replaced the diner in mid-1954. Between early 1951 and mid 1952, No. 27 ran without its sleeping car.

C&S 9951A and a Burlington E8 are southbound at Palmer Lake on November 20, 1955, with No. 21, *Texas Zephyr*, with a mostly heavyweight consist. *–Denver Public Library, Western History collection, Otto Perry, OP-10954*

Table 4-6: 1944 Nos. 21 (1) & 22 (2) Texas Zephyr

Car Type	Route
Baggage RPO (30') (LW)	Denver and Ft. Worth-Dallas
Baggage Dorm Chair (LW)	Denver and Ft. Worth-Dallas
Chair Car (52 seat) (LW)	Denver and Ft. Worth-Dallas
Chair Dinette (LW)	Denver and Ft. Worth-Dallas
8-Sec 5-DB Sleeping Car (HW)	Denver and Ft. Worth-Dallas
10-1-1 Sleeping Car (HW)	Denver and Ft. Worth-Dallas
12-1 Sleeping Car (HW)	Denver and Ft. Worth-Dallas
Dining Lounge Observation Car (LW)	Denver and Ft. Worth-Dallas

Table 4-7: 1944 Nos. 27 (7) & 28 (8) Gulf Coast Special

Car Type	Route
Baggage RPO	Denver and Amarillo?
Baggage	Denver and Ft. Worth-Dallas
Coach	Denver and Ft. Worth-Dallas
Coach	Denver and Ft. Worth-Dallas
Dining Car	Denver and Ft. Worth-Dallas
12-1 Sleeping Car (AC)	Denver to Amarillo (27 only)

C&S 374 (F3C Class 4-6-2) pulling No. 27, *Gulf Coast Special*, leaving Denver, Colorado, on June 29, 1952. It appears that the last car is a troop sleeper, possibly ferrying GIs back to Fort Carson.
–*Denver Public Library, Western History collection, Otto Perry, OP-6921*

C&S 372 (F3B Class 4-6-2) on a southbound passenger extra is about to pass the D&RGW water tank at Palmer Lake on August 13, 1949. From photographic evidence, the C&S ran several passenger specials using lightweight equipment and steam power in the late 1940s and early 1950s.
–*Colorado Railroad Museum collection*

C&S 375 (F3C Class 4-6-2) is on a northbound passenger special running as 2nd No. 102 at Sedalia on August 19, 1950. The photo shows Santa Fe steel 43 ft. water tank in background and water crane beside the mainline. –*Colorado Railroad Museum collection*

C&S 9950AB (E5) lead C&S No. 21, *Texas Zephyr*, leaving Denver, Colorado, on January 4, 1942 after a snowstorm. 9950 is flying green flags for a following section. –*Denver Public Library, Western History collection, Otto Perry, OP-7150*

C&S 9950AB *Silver Racer* and *Silver Steed* lead No. 22, *Texas Zephyr*, south of Littleton, Colorado, on April 12, 1950. –*Denver Public Library, Western History collection, Otto Perry, OP-7154*

Diesels Supplant Steam: World War II to 1955   103

D&RGW Passenger Trains

The Rio Grande entered 1941 running three pairs of passenger trains. In the summer of 1941, the last year the Rio Grande ran a summer-only train, the Rio Grande also ran Nos. 9 and 10, replacing the previous summer's Nos. 7 and 8. Although it was no longer the flagship train, *Scenic Limited* still was a fine train with coaches, sleeping cars, a dining car and the signature lounge observation. Nos. 3 and 4, the former *Westerner*, connected with Missouri Pacific passenger trains at Pueblo with coaches and sleepers, a diner, and lounge. Finally, workhorse Nos. 15/115 and 16/116 provided coach and sleeping car service to Salida and Alamosa with Nos. 15/16 running between Pueblo and Salida and Nos. 115/116 running between Pueblo and Alamosa. The Rio Grande preferred to use 4-8-4 locomotives of the M-64 and M-68 Classes for its passenger trains through World War II.

In November 1941 *Scenic Limited* lost its dining car and in July 1942, it had its lounge observation replaced with a 10-section observation. It had become quite a short train with much of its patronage going to trains on the Dotsero Cutoff. During the war, No. 1 normally left Denver in the morning and No. 2 arrived in Denver in the evening, averaging about

D&RGW 1803 (M-68 4-8-4) leads No. 1, *Scenic Limited*, at Louviers, Colorado, on October 29, 1944. *–Denver Public Library, Western History collection, Otto Perry, OP-10584*

Table 4-8: 1942 Nos. 1 & 2 Scenic Limited

Car Type	Route
Head End	
Chair Car	Chicago to San Francisco via CB&Q and WP (1 only)
Chair Car	Denver and Ogden
16-Sec Tourist Sleeper	Chicago to San Francisco via CB&Q and WP (1 only)
16-Sec Tourist Sleeper	San Francisco to Denver via WP (2 only)
10-1-1 Sleeping Car	Chicago to San Francisco via CB&Q and WP (1 only)
10-Sec Observation	Denver and Ogden

42 miles an hour on the Joint Line. Table 4-8 is a representative consist.

Although the Rio Grande bought its first diesel in 1941, it was the diesels of another road, the Missouri Pacific, that graced the head end of the first Rio Grande streamlined, diesel-hauled passenger train on the Joint Line. In July 1942 the MP inaugurated the streamlined *Colorado Eagle*, Nos. 3 and 4 on the Joint Line replacing the old D&RGW Pueblo-Denver train. *The Eagle*, the last streamlined train in the U.S. before the end of World War II, ran between Denver and St. Louis and used MP equipment for its entire route. On the Joint Line it averaged around 50 miles an hour with No. 3 leaving Denver in the late afternoon and No. 4 arriving in Denver mid-morning. The blue and gray streamlined consist pulled by matching EMD-built E6 diesel locomotives is shown in Table 4-9.

Averaging only around 36 miles an hour on the Joint Line, No. 15 left Denver in the early evening and No. 16 arrived in Denver around breakfast time. Table 4-10 is a representative war years consist.

Table 4-9: 1942 Nos. 3 & 4 Colorado Eagle

Car Type	Route
Baggage	Denver and St. Louis via MP
Baggage Mail	Denver and St. Louis via MP
Chair Car (56-seat)	Denver and St. Louis via MP
Chair Car (56-seat)	Denver and St. Louis via MP
Chair Grill (48-seat)	Denver and St. Louis via MP
Diner-Lounge	Denver and St. Louis via MP
6-6-4 Sleeping Car	Denver and St. Louis via MP
6-6-4 Sleeping Car	Denver and St. Louis via MP
8-1-3 Sleeping Car (HW)	Denver and St. Louis via MP, when necessary

Table 4-11 is a summary of Rio Grande passenger operations during World War II.

Shortly after the war ended on June 2, 1946, the Rio Grande gave Nos. 1 and 2 a new name, *Royal Gorge*. The new name capitalized on the scenic highlight of the run between Denver and Salt Lake City. *Royal Gorge* operated an about the same schedule as had *Scenic Limited*, with No. 1 leaving Denver at 8:40 AM and No. 2 arriving in Denver at 6:50 PM.

Table 4-10: 1942 Nos. 15/115 & 16/116 Passenger

Car Type	Route
Head End	Denver and Alamosa ?
Coach	Denver and Alamosa
12-1 Sleeping Car	Denver and Alamosa

Table 4-11

No.	Name	Details
1-2	*Scenic Limited*	Limited-stop coach and sleeping car trains between Denver and Ogden with Chicago-San Francisco sleeping cars with 4 stops
3-4	*Colorado Eagle*	Limited-stop streamlined MP coach and sleeping car trains between Denver and St. Louis with 3 stops
15-16	*Passenger*	Coach and sleeping car train between Denver and Alamosa making 6 and 11 stops, respectively

The train averaged about 41 miles per hour on the Joint Line with four stops. The initial consist of *Royal Gorge* was about the same as *Scenic Limited* except that it eliminated through cars from the WP and CB&Q and restored a dining car. As was the case with *Scenic Limited*, 4-8-4 locomotives of the M-68 Class were the preferred power. Table 4-12 is how it looked in early 1947.

In 1948, a 10-1-2 sleeping car and a lounge observation replaced the 10-section observation on *Royal Gorge* and the next year the train got another sleeping car, an 8-1-2. In March 1951, the Rio Grande added a lightweight Budd-built Vista-Dome chair car and a grill lounge replaced the lounge observation and dining car. The schedule remained relatively constant until 1950 when No. 2 was scheduled into Denver at 3:30 PM, more than three hours earlier than before. Average speed over the Joint Line gradually increased to around 43 miles an hour until 1950 when Nos. 1 and 2 were making twelve and ten stops, respectively. From there speeds gradually decreased to

MP 7003 (E6) on Train 4, *Colorado Eagle*, near Wolhurst, Colorado, on April 8, 1945. Note the lettering for both D&RGW and MP on the nose. –*Denver Public Library, Western History collection, Otto Perry, OP-13188*

D&RGW 1800 (M-68 4-8-4) on No. 1, *Royal Gorge*, near Acequia, Colorado, on July 23, 1947. –*Denver Public Library, Western History collection, Otto Perry, OP-10535*

A publicity photo of the *Colorado Eagle* with a Vista-Dome in its consist circa 1948. *–Colorado Railroad Museum collection*

D&RGW 1708, 1703 (both 4-8-4s) on No. 1, *Royal Gorge*, on August 27, 1949, at Englewood, Colorado. *–S. L. Logue, Colorado Railroad Museum collection*

Table 4-12: 1947 Nos. 1 & 2 Royal Gorge

Car Type	Route
Head End	Denver and Ogden ?
Chair Car	Denver and Ogden
Dining Car	Denver and Ogden
10-Sec Observation	Denver and Ogden

Table 4-13: 1951 Nos. 1 & 2 Royal Gorge

Car Type	Route
Head End	Denver and Grand Junction?
Chair Car	Denver and Salt Lake City via Nos. 7 and 8 at Grand Junction
Vista Dome Chair Car	Denver and Salt Lake City via Nos. 7 and 8 at Grand Junction
Grill Lounge	Denver and Grand Junction
10-1-2 Sleeping Car	Denver and Salt Lake City via Nos. 7 and 8 at Grand Junction

around 42 miles an hour.

The Rio Grande had received one FT passenger locomotive in 1944. It first appeared on *Royal Gorge* in 1949 and by 1951 diesels were the regular power with either the FT or 1946-built F3s. In 1949, the Rio Grande began receiving both passenger and freight F7s. (A bit later, the Rio Grande in the early 1950s determined that the freight gearing of 62:15 allowed passenger train operations at 70 MPH so after that all Rio Grande F units were geared at 62:15.) In February 1950, *Royal Gorge* ceased to run west of Grand Junction and its Salt Lake City cars were consolidated with Nos. 7 and 8, *Prospector*, which ran over the Moffat Route. A representative consist for 1951 is shown in Table 4-13.

The schedule and consists remained remarkably constant for the next five years. By 1955, F7s had also appeared on *Royal Gorge*.

For the five years following World War II, the schedules and consists of *Colorado Eagle* remained quite consistent. In 1948, a Budd-built dome car, called a Planetarium chair car by the MP, replaced a chair car, and 14-roomette 4-double bedroom sleep-

Table 4-14: 1955 Nos. 3 & 4 Colorado Eagle

Car Type	Route
Baggage RPO (30')	Denver and St. Louis via MP
Baggage	Denver and St. Louis via MP
Planetarium Chair Car	Denver and St. Louis via MP
Chair Car	Denver and St. Louis via MP
Chair Car	Denver and St. Louis via MP
Chair Car	Denver and St. Louis via MP
Diner-Lounge	Denver and St. Louis via MP
8-1-3 Sleeping Car (HW)	Denver and Wichita via MP
6-6-4 Sleeping Car	Denver and St. Louis via MP
10-6 Sleeping Car	Denver and St. Louis via MP

ers replaced the 6-section, 6-roomette, 4-double bedroom sleepers. In 1951, a chair car replaced the chair grill car and another chair car or two was added when necessary. The heavyweight 8-section, 1 drawing room, 3 double bedroom sleeper continued to be assigned mostly during the summer season into the mid-1950s. In the late 1940s EMD-built E7 locomotives supplemented by Alco PAs replaced the E6s.

For the next five years sleeping car assignments, in addition to the 8-1-3, seemed to be some combination of 6-6-4, 14-4, 1948-built 14-roomette, 1 drawing room, 2 double bedroom and 1949-Budd-built 10-roomette, 6 double bedroom cars. In 1955 No. 3 still left Denver at 4:00 PM and No. 4 arrived in Denver at 2:50 PM, a remarkably consistent schedule for over ten years. A consist from mid-1955 is shown in Table 4-14.

After the war Nos. 15 and 16 continued to provide local passenger service on the Joint Line, southwest to Alamosa, and west to Minturn on the same basic schedule for a while. In 1947, the route was cut back to Glenwood Springs, but No. 15 continued to leave Denver after dinner and arrive in Denver in time for breakfast until May 1951 when Nos. 15 and 16 left the Joint Line. The Rio Grande was down to just two passenger trains with *Royal Gorge* acting as the daytime local.

D&RGW 5534 + 1 (F3, PB) lead No. 1, *Royal Gorge*, south near Palmer Lake, Colorado, on July 19, 1951. –*Collection of Harold K. Vollrath*

D&RGW 5531 (F3AB) on Train 1, *Royal Gorge*, south of Sedalia, Colorado, on September 23, 1955. –*Denver Public Library, Western History collection, Otto Perry, OP-10909*

AT&SF 3817 (2-10-2) on southbound freight (probably No. 31) south of Littleton, Colorado, on June 6, 1943. No. 3817 is one of only a few Santa Fe locomotives to have an Elesco feedwater heater mounted on top of the smokebox rather than on the pilot deck. –*Denver Public Library, Western History collection, Otto Perry, OP-1981*

Freight Operations

World War II brought a huge increase in freight traffic to the Joint Line. The building of Camp (later Fort) Carson and its associated Peterson Army Airfield outside of Colorado Springs added much to the increase. In addition there were two arsenals, Rocky Mountain in Denver and Pueblo east of its namesake city that also added traffic to the Joint Line. The three railroads adopted different strategies to deal with the war. The Santa Fe added a second southbound (eastbound east of Pueblo) train giving it two scheduled freight trains a day each way. The C&S actually dropped two of its four scheduled freight trains in 1942, and the Rio Grande did not make any significant changes to its scheduled freight trains until late in the war when, in 1945, it dropped *Rocket*. Following the war traffic dropped off somewhat but was still above pre-war levels. The railroads made few schedule changes but by 1955 all freight trains were diesel-powered.

AT&SF Freight Operations

The Santa Fe started 1941 with two through freight trains departing Denver, one in the mid-morning and one in the evening. One Santa Fe through freight arrived in Denver in the early morning. The three trains typically took between 4½ and 5 hours to make the trip between Denver and Pueblo. The tri-weekly way freight trains continued to run between Denver and Colorado Springs. In November 1942, the Santa Fe added a second Denver-bound through freight, No. 40 *Fast Freight*, thanks to World War II military traffic, primarily to newly opened Camp Carson. No. 40 was an extension of Emporia to Pueblo No. 41 and arrived in Denver at 3:00 AM after a 5¾-hour trip from Pueblo, replacing No. 36 in the early morning time slot. No. 36 had a major schedule change. It departed Pueblo at 1:00 AM and arrived in Denver at 8:00 AM, taking two hours longer in the process. Table 4-15 shows Santa Fe freight service on the Joint Line during World War II.

These schedules remained in place until May 1945 when, with the war nearly over, the Santa Fe annulled No. 40 and its connection at Pueblo, No. 41. This left the Santa Fe without an early morning arrival in Denver and until November apparently tried to deliver Denver business traffic from No. 36. This allowed for only an hour to make delivery by 9:00 AM if No. 36 arrived on time. Apparently this did not work because in November No. 36 took over No. 40's old schedule, arriving in Denver at 3:00 AM after a 5½-hour trip from Pueblo. At the same time, the Santa Fe again put on a second northbound through freight train, No. 46 *Fast Freight*. No. 46 ran on exactly the same schedule as No. 36, departing Pueblo at 9:30 PM and arriving in Denver at 3:00 AM. No. 46 connected from No. 45 from La Junta at Pueblo, which ran on exactly the same schedule as No. 35. I am not sure why the Santa Fe did this but it continued until February 1949.

In late March 1948 three-unit FT diesel freight locomotives were assigned to Nos. 35 (36 on the Joint Line) between Newton and Denver and 42 between La Junta and Kansas City. Three units had difficulty with the constant climb from Newton so, within a year, four units were assigned westbound. This resulted in a diesel pool that worked from Kansas City to Denver on No. 35, then on to Amarillo and Sweetwater, then back to La Junta and finally back to Kansas City on No. 42.

In February 1949, the Santa Fe split the schedules of Nos. 36 and 46. No. 46 continued to run on the same schedule while No. 36 moved to a 4:30 PM departure from Pueblo with arrival in Denver at 9:00 PM. In November 1948 No. 31 began operating on a new schedule for the first time since June 1940. It left Denver after noon at 1:30 PM but continued to take

AT&SF 1855 (1800 Class 2-6-2) leads southbound way freight No. 97 through the siding at Palmer Lake on August 24, 1949. –*Bob Andrews photo, Tom Klinger collection*

Table 4-15

No.	Name	Details
31	*Fast Freight*	Denver to Pueblo with traffic for No. 32 east at La Junta. Scheduled for a mid-morning departure from Denver.
36	*Fast Freight*	Pueblo to Denver with traffic off No. 35 from the east at La Junta. Scheduled for a morning arrival in Denver.
40	*Fast Freight*	Pueblo to Denver with traffic off No. 41 from the east at Pueblo. Scheduled for an early morning arrival in Denver.
41	*Fast Freight*	Denver to Pueblo connecting to No. 42 at Pueblo for Newton. Scheduled for an evening departure from Denver.
97	*Way Freight*	Denver to Colorado Springs on a five-hour schedule, Monday, Wednesday and Friday.
98	*Way Freight*	Colorado Springs to Denver on a 4½-hour schedule Tuesday, Thursday and Saturday.

4½ hours for its trip to Pueblo. In January 1951, No. 41 had its schedule moved back an hour so that it arrived in Denver at 4:00 AM. In March 1953, FT diesels replaced steam on the remaining through freight trains on the Joint Line. Steam was used until the end of the year if diesels were unavailable.

However the replacement of steam with diesels did not have a notable effect on over-the-road time on the Joint Line. It still took between 4½ and 5 hours to make the trip between Denver and Pueblo.

In May 1953 the schedules of both Nos. 31 and 41 were adjusted. No. 31 had its Denver departure moved up an hour to 12:30 PM. Arrival in Pueblo was still 4½ hours later. No. 41 had its Denver departure moved back an hour to 12:01 AM with arrival in Pueblo a minute short of its previous 5-hour timing. May 1953 also had the schedules of the way freight trains Nos. 97 and 98 adjusted. No. 97 and 98 began their trips an hour earlier but the over-road timings remained the same. No more changes to freight train schedules occurred through 1955, at which time they no longer appeared in the employee timetables. Table 4-16 shows Santa Fe freight operations at the end of 1955.

Top-left: An oil-burning 4-8-2 and 2-10-2, having replaced their coal-burning brethren on the Joint Line, lead a freight train southbound (probably No. 31) at Littleton on September 13, 1952. –*Bob Andrews photo, Tom Klinger collection*

Left: AT&SF 2105 (RSD4) on way freight south of Denver, Colorado, circa 1951-52. –*Denver Public Library, Western History collection, Otto Perry, OP-2248*

Table 4-16

No.	Name	Details
31	*Fast Freight*	Denver to Pueblo with traffic for No. 32 east at La Junta. Scheduled for a shortly after noon departure from Denver.
36	*Fast Freight*	Pueblo to Denver with traffic off No. 35 from the east at La Junta. Scheduled for an evening arrival in Denver.
41	*Fast Freight*	Denver to Pueblo connecting to No. 42 at Pueblo for Newton. Scheduled for midnight departure from Denver.
46	*Fast Freight*	Pueblo to Denver with traffic off No. 45 from La Junta at Pueblo. Scheduled for an early morning arrival in Denver.
97	*Way Freight*	Denver to Colorado Springs on a 5-hour schedule, Monday, Wednesday and Friday.
98	*Way Freight*	Colorado Springs to Denver on a 4½-hour schedule Tuesday, Thursday and Saturday.

Top-right: AT&SF 3826 (2-10-2) on 30-car northbound freight at Monument, Colorado, on July 2, 1948. Because of its rather circuitous route into Denver from both California and Chicago, Santa Fe's business on the Joint Line north of Colorado Springs was not as heavy as the tonnage moved into Pueblo and Colorado Springs. –*Colorado Railroad Museum collection*

Right: AT&SF 3870 (2-10-2) on southbound freight (probably No. 31) near Wolhurst on September 14, 1947. –*Richard H. Kindig photo; Tom Klinger collection*

CB&Q 6304 (USRA heavy 2-10-2) leads a C&S freight train past the D&RGW Palmer Lake water tank on December 24 (Christmas Eve) 1950. Parent CB&Q loaned power to the C&S when necessary. *–Bob Andrews photo, Tom Klinger collection*

C&S 913 (E5C Class 2-10-2) on northbound (probably No. 76) freight entering Denver, Colorado, on September 17, 1950. *–Denver Public Library; Western History collection, Otto Perry, OP-7116*

C&S Freight Operations

Like the Santa Fe, the C&S managed to handle World War II traffic with steam power. (See previous chapter for a summary table of C&S freight trains just prior to World War II.) Unlike the Santa Fe, which added a new freight train, the C&S in July 1942 cut two through freight trains, Nos. 72 and 75. At the same time No. 73 cut an hour from its schedule arriving at Pueblo at 5:00 AM instead of 6:00 AM. This allowed the C&S to get through the war without buying any new power unlike the Santa Fe and the Rio Grande, both of which had to buy both new steam and diesel locomotives for their systems. Apparently a midnight departure from Denver did not suit the railroad as in November 1942 it cut No. 73 and added No. 75 back on a schedule similar to the one it had previously. No. 75 left Denver at 10:00 AM and arrived in Pueblo five hours later. The C&S managed to meet its wartime obligations with just two scheduled freight trains, Nos. 75 and 76. If scheduled freights are an indication of a railroad's traffic density, it is unclear why this occurred when other railroads had greatly increased wartime traffic.

The war was over when in November 1945 the C&S reinstated No. 73, giving it three through freight trains on the line. No. 73 basically assumed No. 75's old slot with a 10:00 AM departure from Denver and a 3:30 PM Pueblo arrival, a lengthening of 30 minutes. No. 75 moved to a midnight departure with a 5:00 AM arrival in Pueblo. In June 1946, No. 76 finally got its schedule adjusted departing from Pueblo and arriving in Denver two hours later than previously. The 4:00 AM arrival in Denver still gave switch crews plenty of time to get cars to their destination in Denver in time for the opening of the business day.

During the next three years the C&S adjusted the schedules of all three trains. In June 1947, No. 73 had its Denver departure moved back an hour to 11:00 AM but still made the trip to Pueblo in five hours.

In February 1949 Nos. 75 and 76 were given faster schedules. No. 75 moved from a midnight departure to a 6:00 AM departure. It arrived in Pueblo a very fast 3¾ hours later. It is likely that CB&Q F units pulled this train to make this speedy schedule. No. 76 moved from a 4:00 AM arrival in Denver to an 11:00 PM arrival in Denver 4½ hours after it left Pueblo.

In 1950, the C&S bought its first road freight diesels, three sets of ABBA F7s. Prior to this, CB&Q F units had pulled some C&S freight trains. The C&S also leased a four-unit F3 set from the Q, which it eventually purchased in 1960. These units were initially drawbar-connected then drawbar-connected in an AB configuration. Finally, couplers replaced the drawbars. Also in 1950, 15 minutes were added to No. 75's schedule and it got a 4:45 AM departure from Denver. Early the next year the C&S moved Denver's arrival back another hour to 10:00 PM while still maintaining a five-hour timing on the Joint Line. The road also dropped No. 73 from the schedule leaving just one north- and one southbound through freight train. Later in the year, No. 75 departed Denver and arrived in Pueblo 45 minutes earlier than previously scheduled.

The F units were followed by purchases of ten SD7s in 1953, giving the C&S enough power to eliminate steam on the Joint Line. Also in 1953, No. 73 returned on a 4¾-hour Joint Line schedule and a 2:30 PM Denver departure. The next year No. 75 moved to a 5:00 AM Denver departure while still on a 4-hour timing over the Joint Line. Table 4-17 shows the way the C&S looked in 1955 when freight schedules disappeared from the employee timetables.

Table 4-17

No.	Name	Details
73	*Fast Freight*	Scheduled mid-afternoon from Denver for Ft. Worth on a 4¾-hour schedule
75	*Fast Freight*	Early morning departure from Denver for Pueblo on a 4-hour schedule
76	*Fast Freight*	Ft. Worth to Denver train scheduled for an evening arrival at Denver

C&S 913 (E5C Class 2-10-2) on southbound freight, between Sedalia and Castle Rock, Colorado, January 13, 1951. *–Denver Public Library, Western History collection, Otto Perry, OP-7105*

CB&Q 120 (F3) on southbound freight (probably No. 73) near Palmer Lake, Colorado, on October 20, 1950. C&S used CB&Q F3s prior to buying its own three ABBA sets of F7s in August 1950. Obviously the leased Q units remained for some time after the purchase of the C&S units. *Denver Public Library, Western History collection, Otto Perry, OP-4677*

D&RGW 3700 (L-105 Class 4-6-6-4) on southbound freight south of Castle Rock, Colorado, November 11, 1954. *–Denver Public Library, Western History collection, Otto Perry, OP-10800*

D&RGW Freight Operations

Once World War II started, the Rio Grande experienced an increase in traffic although much of that was on the Moffat Route. On the Joint Line, D&RGW continued to schedule four freight trains, three manifest freight trains and the daily except Sunday *Rocket*. (See previous chapter for a summary chart.) No. 65 primarily handled perishables from team tracks and other businesses in Denver for Pueblo, handing over fruit blocks going east to the Missouri Pacific. No. 66 connected from Missouri Pacific No. 75 at Pueblo and handled MP business for Colorado Springs and Denver. It was scheduled to provide for early morning Denver deliveries and departed

Pueblo at 10:00 PM arriving in Denver at 3:30 AM. No. 68 connected from MP No. 61, departed Pueblo at 1:15 PM and arrived in Denver at 7:00 PM. It also made connections with perishable traffic from the San Luis Valley and connected to D&RGW No. 75 (Denver to Salt Lake City via the Moffat Route) once a week with Nuckolls Packing Company meat for Salt Lake City.

In November 1942 the Rio Grande received its first road diesels in the form of eight 5,400 horsepower, four-unit FT locomotives. The Rio Grande also received five more L-105 Class 4-6-6-4 steam locomotives in 1942 and in 1943 six L-97 Class 4-6-6-4 locomotives, which the War Production Board had diverted from the Union Pacific. The Rio Grande did

not like these foreign locomotives and sold them to the Clinchfield in 1947. In 1944 four additional FTs arrived, one of which was geared for passenger service. The FTs had begun to appear on Joint Line freight trains shortly after their purchase and by 1946, diesels pulled 32.3% of system freight-ton miles.

The M-67 and M-78 4-8-2s were 20 years old in 1943 but were still capable and were still the principal freight locomotives on the Joint Line although they often needed to be double headed. They were supplemented with L-105 Class 4-6-6-4s and L-131 and L-132 Class 2-8-8-2s.

The Rio Grande's freight schedule remained remarkably consistent during the war. In June 1942, the Rio Grande lengthened *The Rocket's* schedule to four hours fifteen minutes and then adjusted the departure from Denver a half hour earlier to 6:00 PM in November. These were the only changes until May 1945 when *The Rocket* made its last run, causing the railroad to adjust the schedules of two of the remaining three trains. No. 65 left an hour and a half earlier at 8:00 PM and arrived in Pueblo six hours later, a 30-minute longer run. No. 66 was put on a reciprocal six-hour schedule arriving in Denver at 2:00 AM, giving switch crews plenty of time to deliver to Denver businesses before they opened.

The Rio Grande must have been happy with the schedules of the three Joint Line trains because they did not make any changes until November 1948 when No. 66 had its schedule moved back to a 3:00 AM arrival in Denver after a six-hour trip. Then in February 1949, No. 65 began leaving Denver an hour later at 9:00 PM. An hour faster schedule still allowed it to arrive in Pueblo at 2:00 AM. Freight traffic increased during the Korean War, but the Rio Grande handled the increase on the Joint Line by running longer trains and using second sections rather than increasing the number of scheduled trains. The Rio Grande made no more changes through 1955 when the freight train schedules were dropped from the employee timetables. It is interesting to note that No. 68 had operated on the same schedule since October 1937, a remarkably long time. Photographic evidence indicates that the Rio Grande continued to run a local freight, probably between Denver and Sedalia. Table 4-18 shows how the freight schedule looked in 1955.

At the end of World War II the Rio Grande had twelve FT drawbar-connected diesel locomotives consisting of 48 1,350 horsepower units. Ten years later in 1955 it had 195 diesel units. For freight service after the FTs came twelve F3s in 1946, 88 F7s from 1949 to 1952, 15 GP7s in 1950 and 1952, five RS3s in 1951, five SD7s in 1953, and twelve GP9s in 1955. The F units originally had three-digit numbers but in 1950 the numbers 1 and 4 were added after

D&RGW 1503, 1513 (both 4-8-2s) on southbound freight at Greenland on January 14, 1950. –*Colorado Railroad Museum collection*

D&RGW 540 (FT) on northbound freight (probably No. 68) at Struby, Colorado, April 27, 1942. –*Denver Public Library, Western History collection, Otto Perry, OP-10829*

Diesels Supplant Steam: World War II to 1955   115

Table 4-18

No.	Name	Details
65	Fast Freight	Evening departure Denver to Pueblo with primarily perishable traffic for the MP on a 5-hour schedule over the Joint Line
66	Fast Freight	Pueblo to Denver for early morning delivery with traffic received off MP at Pueblo on a 6-hour schedule
68	Fast Freight	Pueblo to Denver with traffic from the MP and San Luis Valley on a 5¾-hour schedule with an early evening arrival
(Unscheduled)	Local Freight	Denver-Sedalia turn?

the original three digits for cab units and 2 and 3 were added after the original three digits for booster units, a pattern continued for all subsequent F unit purchases. Thus it is an oddity that the Rio Grande never had F unit numbers ending in 5, 6, 7, 8, 9, or 0.

By 1952, the M-67 and M-78 4-8-2s were virtually gone from Joint Line freight trains and diesels were mostly in charge. But during the late summer and fall rush, steam returned with 4-6-6-4s, 2-8-8-2s and 4-8-4s pulling freight trains. Between 1953 and 1955 diesels pulled freight trains except during the July to December traffic peak when 4-6-6-4s and 2-8-8-2s were also in service. The only movement of steam on the Joint Line in 1956 occurred in August when two 2-8-8-2s ran from Pueblo to Denver to work as helpers on the Moffat Route.

Top-left: D&RGW 3700 (L-105 Class 4-6-6-4) leading southbound freight that just left Littleton, Colorado, on September 18, 1953. –*Denver Public Library, Western History collection, Otto Perry, OP-10798*

Left: D&RGW 3610 (L-132 Class 2-8-8-2) on southbound freight near Palmer Lake, Colorado, September 23, 1955. –*Denver Public Library, Western History collection, Otto Perry, OP-10742*

D&RGW 151 (FM H15-44) leads the Rio Grande local at Sedalia on January 14, 1952. *–Bob Andrews photo, Tom Klinger collection*

D&RGW 5594 (F7) on a southbound freight of 92 cars near Palmer Lake, Colorado, on October 20, 1950. *–Denver Public Library, Western History collection, Otto Perry, OP-10942*

Chapter Five

Passenger Trains Decline as Freight Holds Steady: 1955-1971

BY 1955, EXCEPT FOR STEAM SWITCHERS in Denver on the C&S, the Joint line was completely in charge of diesel locomotives. All three Joint Line railroads could see that passenger traffic was likely to continue to decline due to competition from airplanes and automobiles. Hereafter the efforts were to hold onto as much passenger traffic as possible and to concentrate on building freight traffic. Freight trains were also facing heavy competition from trucks and although they were in absolute terms holding their own or growing business due to the expanding transportation business, freight trains continued to lose market share to trucks.

Passenger Trains

All three railroads on the Joint Line maintained what passenger service they could, but train lengths got shorter and services contracted. The C&S and AT&SF were pro-passenger trains at this time while the D&RGW was not. Yet none of the three actively tried to drive passengers away as some other railroads did. At the same time, the decline was inexorable and gradually train after train disappeared until only the one Santa Fe stub train with a baggage and chair car was left. Then in 1971 Amtrak took over almost all

Opposite: AT&SF 84 (E8m) with a heavy No. 200 near Spruce, Colorado, in October 1967. *–Stuart J. Sutton photo*

AT&SF 33 on Train No. 201 leaving Denver, Colorado, on March 24, 1957. In another year, the Santa Fe would not be running passenger trains on the Joint Line. The C&S would be carrying Santa Fe passenger cars between Denver and Pueblo. *–Denver Public Library, Western History collection, Otto Perry, OP-2165*

passenger service in the U.S. but did not include the Joint Line in its system.

Santa Fe Passenger Trains

Despite facing declining traffic and increasing competition from automobiles and airplanes, the Santa Fe continued to operate Nos. 130 and 141 and

Nos. 101 and 102 until early 1957 when, because of declining business, the two train pairs were consolidated into one Nos. 190/191 and 201/200 connecting to Nos. 19 and 20 *The Chief* at La Junta. Numbers on the Joint Line were 190 and 201. This train pair officially brought all lightweight equipment to the Santa Fe on the Joint Line. No. 201 left Denver just before dinner and arrived in Pueblo around eight in

No. 84 is southbound on No. 191 at the D&RGW depot at Colorado Springs with four cars. –*Steve Patterson photo*

No. 81 on an ATSF passenger train has just arrived at track 11 at Denver Union Terminal. A C&S switch crew will turn the train before it's ready to head south. –*Steve Patterson photo*

the evening making seven stops. No. 190 left Pueblo around five in the morning and arrived in Denver just after breakfast. It made six stops and both trains averaged around 43 miles per hour on the Joint Line. According to photographic evidence Santa Fe warbonnet Fs provided the normal power for Nos. 190 and 201. The initial consist, including a lunch-counter diner serving dinner on No. 201 and breakfast on No. 190 is shown in Table 5-1.

In January 1959 the Santa Fe and C&S combined Santa Fe's 190 and 201 with C&S 27 and 28, *Gulf Coast Special*, north of Pueblo. This caused a major schedule adjustment for Santa Fe passengers as No. 27 left Denver at 8:00 PM instead of before dinner. No. 28 arrived in Denver at 6:05 PM instead of before breakfast. Nos. 27 and 28 then made the stops formerly made by the Santa Fe trains, seven southbound and six northbound. This change allowed the Santa Fe to drop the lunch–counter diner. The combined operation lasted until April 1967 when the C&S abandoned *Gulf Coast Special*. Thus for almost ten years the C&S's stylish E5s pulled Santa Fe trains.

The C&S abandonment of *Gulf Coast Special* meant that the Santa Fe had to reinstate Nos. 191 and 200 north of Pueblo. The numbers were also switched from those of 1957. No. 190 became 200 and No. 201 became No. 191 on the Joint Line. At this time in the employee timetables, these two trains carried the name *The Chief* because of the connection with that train at La Junta. No. 191 left Denver at No. 27's old time of 8:00 PM with eight stops on the Joint Line. No. 200 arrived in Denver at 4:45 PM, an hour and twenty minutes earlier than No. 28 had. With the continued loss of passengers, Nos. 191 and 200 carried one or two chair cars and fairly heavy head end traffic, usually pulled by a single E8m. There were no through passenger carrying cars. Connecting passengers had to get off and re-board at La Junta. Table 5-2 shows the consist at that time.

When the Post Office cancelled most railway

mail contracts in late 1967, Nos. 191 and 200 lost most of their head end cars, with usually only a single baggage car remaining. Depending on traffic, there were one or two chair cars. In June 1968, the Santa Fe published its last employee timetable showing pas-

Table 5-1: 1957 No. 191(190) & 200(201)

Car Type	Route
Express Mail	Kansas City to Denver (191/190 only) off No. 7
Express Mail	La Junta to Denver (191/190 only) Sunday, Monday, Tuesday
Baggage	La Junta to Denver (191/190 only)
Express Mail	Denver to Los Angeles (200/201 only) for No. 123
Baggage Express Mail	Denver to Albuquerque (200/201 only) for No. 123
Lunch-Counter Diner	La Junta and Denver
Chair Car	Chicago and Denver via Nos. 19 and 20
Chair Car	Denver and Los Angeles via Nos. 20 and 19
6-6-4 Sleeping Car	Denver and Los Angeles via Nos. 20 and 19
6-6-4 Sleeping Car	Chicago and Denver via Nos. 19 and 20
Chair Car	La Junta and Denver

Table 5-2: 1967 No. 191(190) & 200(201)

Car Type	Route
Storage Mail	La Junta to Pueblo (201 only) except Sunday
Express Mail	Los Angeles to Denver (201 only) off No. 8 at La Junta
Baggage Express Mail	Kansas City and Denver via Nos. 23 and 8 at La Junta
Express Mail	Denver to Albuquerque (190 only) for No. 23 at La Junta (except Saturday and Sunday)
Express Mail	Denver to Los Angeles (190 only) for No. 23 at La Junta (Saturday and Sunday)
Express Mail	Pueblo to Kansas City (190 only) for No. 8 at La Junta (except Saturday and Sunday)
Express Mail	Pueblo to La Junta (190 only) (Saturday only)
Chair Car	La Junta and Denver

The end is near and the E8s are gone as AT&SF 38 (F7) is on Train No. 191 at Colorado Springs, Colorado, July 21, 1970. The first car is a steam generator car as there is no steam generator in the F7a. *–Denver Public Library, Western History collection, Otto Perry, OP-2173*

Santa Fe E8m No. 84 pulls the usual two-car No. 191 at Bragdon circa 1968. Today's train is unusual because it has a business car tacked on the end. *–Steve Patterson photo*

C&S 9954 on Train 21, *Texas Zephyr*, at Fountain, Colorado, in the early 1960s. The train has the full articulated consist, inherited from the *Denver Zephyr*. –*Denver Public Library, Western History collection, Otto Perry, OP-7181*

senger service on the Joint Line. No. 191 left Denver at 3:30 PM, four and a half hours earlier than previously and arrived in Pueblo at 6:00 PM. No. 200 left Pueblo at 9:50 PM and arrived in Denver at 12:30 AM. After the E8ms were retired in 1970, almost any four-axle unit available at La Junta could be found at the head of the train, which now had to include a steam generator car. In May 1971, Amtrak took over passenger service and the last passenger train on the Joint Line disappeared.

C&S Passenger Trains

The C&S faced the same declining traffic and increased competition that the Santa Fe and Rio Grande did. Like the Santa Fe, the C&S's parent CB&Q was pro passenger and tried to maintain a strong passenger service. The C&S had purchased ten SD7s with steam boilers so they could be used in standby passenger service. In 1956 and 1957, the C&S purchased eleven SD9s, also with steam boilers. Between 1955 and 1961, the C&S purchased seven CB&Q E5s to replace steam and boiler equipped SDs for its passenger trains. These E5s along with the original C&S/FW&D E5s remained on C&S passenger trains to the end. On the Joint Line, *Gulf Coast Special* and *Texas Zephyr* continued their daily trek between Denver and Dallas/Ft. Worth with little change until May 1956 when a 12-roomette, 2 single bedroom, 4 double bedroom sleeping car was added

to *Texas Zephyr*. *Gulf Coast Special* left Denver at 8:00 PM and took a shade over 2½ hours to get to Pueblo. No. 28 arrived back in Denver at 5:48 PM after a 2 hour 41 minute trip from Pueblo. *Texas Zephyr* left Denver at noon and arrived in Denver at 7:00 AM. Both trains made only one intermediate stop, Colorado Springs, on the Joint Line.

In October 1956, *Texas Zephyr* finally became all lightweight. The Burlington transferred the 1936- and 1938-built *Denver Zephyr* cars to the C&S for *Texas Zephyr*. These cars were mostly articulated except for the coach-dinette. Although the cars were older than the previous *Texas Zephyr* lightweight cars, they were more luxurious, so this was considered an upgrade. However, being articulated, the consist was less flexible than a consist of individual cars had been. Table 5-3 shows the initial consist as of October 1956.

In June 1957, *Texas Zephyr's* Denver departure was moved back an hour, and it arrived back in Denver 20 minutes earlier.

As shown above, in January 1959 the C&S and Santa Fe combined Santa Fe cars from Nos. 190 and 201 with Nos. 27 and 28, *Gulf Coast Special*, north of Pueblo. Although *Gulf Coast Special* picked up Santa Fe's four flag stops, No. 27's schedule did not change. However, No 28's did change a bit with a 6:05 PM arrival in Denver. The combined consist is shown in Table 5-4.

In the early 1960s the C&S began using a light-weight sleeping car, either a 6-section, 6-roomette, 4-double bedroom or a 4-section, 7-duplex roomette, 3-double bedroom, 1-compartment car. In April 1963, the Santa Fe dropped its sleeping car and in May 1965 the C&S dropped its sleeping car from

Table 5-3: 1956 Nos. 21 (1) & 22 (2) *Texas Zephyr*

Car Type	Route
Auxiliary Power Baggage-RPO	Denver and Ft. Worth-Dallas
Baggage Mail	Denver and Ft. Worth-Dallas
Baggage Dorm Lounge	Denver and Ft. Worth-Dallas
Coach Dinette (64-seat)	Denver and Ft. Worth-Dallas
Coach (60-seat)	Denver and Ft. Worth-Dallas
Coach (38-seat)	Denver and Ft. Worth-Dallas
Dining Car	Denver and Ft. Worth-Dallas
12-Sec Sleeping Car	Denver and Ft. Worth-Dallas
12-Sec Sleeping Car	Denver and Ft. Worth-Dallas
12-Sec Sleeping Car	Denver and Ft. Worth-Dallas
3-Compartment 1-Drawing Room 6-Bedroom Sleeping Car	Denver and Ft. Worth-Dallas
4-Roomette 4 Duplex Single Room 4 Bedroom 1 Compartment 1 Drawing Room Sleeping Car	Denver and Ft. Worth-Dallas
Parlor Lounge Observation	Denver and Ft. Worth-Dallas

Texas Zephyr across from Louviers in July 1965. The only heavyweight car in the consist is the baggage car. *–Hol Wagner photo, Colorado Railroad Museum collection*

C&S 9950, *Silver Racer*, on Train 22, *Texas Zephyr*, near Palmer Lake, Colorado, circa 1965. There is a heavyweight car, probably a sleeper, in the consist. *–Denver Public Library, Western History collection, Otto Perry, OP-7158*

C&S Train No. 28 northbound departs Pueblo, Colorado, with both C&S and AT&SF passenger cars in April 1965. One track over is No. 1 *Texas Zephyr*, also departing. Both No. 1 and No. 29 were scheduled out of Pueblo at 3:15 PM. *–Hol Wagner photo, Colorado Railroad Museum collection*

Table 5-4: 1959 Nos. 27 & 28 Gulf Coast Special

Car Type	Route
Baggage (C&S)	Denver and Ft. Worth-Dallas
Express Mail (AT&SF)	Los Angeles to Denver (No. 28 only) off No. 191
Express Mail (AT&SF)	Kansas City to Denver (No. 28 only) off No. 191
Baggage Express Mail (AT&SF)	Denver to Los Angeles (No. 27 only) for No. 200
Baggage Express Mail (AT&SF)	Denver to Kansas city (No. 27 only) for No. 200
6-6-4 Sleeping Car (AT&SF)	Denver and Los Angeles via Nos. 191 and 200 at Pueblo, Nos. 20 and 19 at La Junta
Chair Car (AT&SF)	Chicago and Denver via Nos. 191 and 200 at Pueblo, Nos. 20 and 19 at La Junta
Chair Car (AT&SF)	Denver and Los Angeles via Nos. 191 and 200 at Pueblo, Nos. 20 and 19 at La Junta
Chair Car (C&S)	Denver and Ft. Worth-Dallas
Chair Car (C&S)	Denver and Ft. Worth-Dallas
8-Sec. 5-Dbl. Bedroom Sleeping Car (C&S)	Denver and Ft. Worth-Dallas

Nos. 27 and 28. The Santa Fe and C&S continued this arrangement until April 1967 when the C&S dropped Nos. 27 and 28.

Meanwhile *Texas Zephyr* continued to run essentially the same schedule with gradually shrinking consists. By November 1963, the parlor lounge observation was gone and the train was down to only one sleeping car, two chair cars and a dining car. By January 1967 the dining car was eliminated and in September 1967, the C&S dropped all passenger service.

Left: An observation car brings up the rear of northbound No. 22, *Texas Zephyr*, just after leaving Spruce, Colorado, in April 1965. *–Stuart J. Sutton photo*

D&RGW Passenger Trains

Two factors affected the Rio Grande passenger trains on the Joint Line. The Joint Line had been replaced as the primary passenger train route to Salt Lake City by the Moffat Tunnel Route and the Missouri Pacific controlled the fate of *Colorado Eagle*. In 1955 *Royal Gorge* was the only pure Rio Grande passenger train remaining on the Joint Line. No. 1 left Denver around 9:00 AM and No. 2 arrived in Denver around 3:00 PM. Both Nos. 1 and 2 made eight intermediate stops between Denver and Pueblo, the most of any train operating on the Joint Line. As it had since 1951, the train consisted of a couple of head end cars, a chair car, a Vista-Dome chair car, a grill-lounge car and a sleeping car, usually a heavyweight 10-section, 2-compartment, 1-drawing room car. The other Rio Grande train on the route, Missouri Pacific's *Colorado Eagle*, was still a fine train with a dome, chair cars, diner-lounge and sleeping cars. It departed Denver in the late afternoon and arrived in Denver around mid-morning, stopping only in Colorado Springs between Denver and Pueblo.

In October 1956, the Rio Grande, inexplicably, and the CB&Q agreed that *Royal Gorge* would carry four *Denver Zephyr* cars between Denver and Colorado Springs. The Rio Grande got the cars rather than the Q's own subsidiary Colorado and Southern, probably because the *Royal Gorge's* departure and arrival times in Denver were closer to the *Denver Zephyr's* arrival and departure times in Denver. The cars had to be switched from the Rio Grande to the Santa Fe depot to be ready for the trip back north. This agreement ran until January 1, 1967. Thus *Royal Gorge's* consist was as shown in Table 5-5.

Power normally consisted of two Fs but the Rio Grande's classy PAs could also be found on the point of *Royal Gorge*. A study of the consists in the public timetables indicate that the CB&Q chair car ran only in peak times as it is not always listed. In January 1958,

C&S 822, 826 (boiler-equipped SD9s) are on a southbound Boy Scout passenger special north of Bragdon on April 6, 1963. *–Stuart J. Sutton photo*

C&S 9955A (E5) on No. 28 at Pring, Colorado, in July 1965. Note both Burlington and Santa Fe cars as well as an MP baggage car in the consist. *–Stuart J. Sutton photo*

Castle Rock is in the background as D&RGW 5584 (F7AB) leads D&RGW No. 2, *Royal Gorge*, northbound on September 16, 1961. The three cars at the end are the CB&Q cars for the *Denver Zephyr*. –Bob Andrews photo, Tom Klinger collection

D&RGW 5551 (F7) + PA on No. 1 near Fountain, Colorado, in July 1965. The short train has dropped its three CB&Q cars at Colorado Springs. –Stuart J. Sutton photo

Table 5-5: 1957 Nos. 1 & 2 Royal Gorge

Car Type	Route
Head End	
Vista Dome Chair Car	Denver and Salt Lake City via Nos. 7 and 8 at Grand Junction
Grill Lounge	Denver and Grand Junction
10-1-2 Sleeping Car	Denver and Salt Lake City via Nos. 7 and 8 at Grand Junction
Chair Car	Colorado Springs and Chicago via *Denver Zephyr* at Denver
Vista Dome Buffet Lounge	Colorado Springs and Chicago via *Denver Zephyr* at Denver
10-6 Sleeping Car	Colorado Springs and Chicago via *Denver Zephyr* at Denver
24-8 Slumbercoach	Colorado Springs and Chicago via *Denver Zephyr* at Denver

a Rio Grande 8-section 5-double bedroom sleeping car replaced the heavyweight 10-1-2 sleeping car. After this, the Rio Grande sleeping car ran only in the summer. The Rio Grande, after 1958, attempted to prop up sagging revenues on *Royal Gorge* by expanding on the Thrift-T-Sleeper concept initiated by Pullman and the Missouri Pacific. These cars were heavyweight Pullmans of 8-sections 5-double bedrooms, modified with skirting and sheathed roofs to better emulate streamlined cars. The interiors were modernized as well. Later, various Pullmans would be used on this assignment, both heavyweight and lightweight. By May 1962, the Rio Grande sleeping car was gone.

Meanwhile Nos. 3 and 4, *Colorado Eagle*, also suffered declining patronage. No. 3 left Denver around 4:00 PM and No. 4 arrived in Denver around 10:00 AM. While retaining the basic consist of a dome chair, chair cars, diner-lounge and sleeping cars, the number of cars decreased. The Missouri Pacific normally provided power for *Colorado Eagle* on its entire St. Louis to Denver run. By 1955, E7s and E8s had replaced the stylish E6s with which the MP had inaugurated service in 1942. Alco PAs could also be assigned. By 1959, *Colorado Eagle* received a Thrift-T-Sleeping car,

Table 5-6: 1959 Nos. 3 & 4 Colorado Eagle

Car Type	Route
Baggage-RPO (30')	Denver and St. Louis via MP
Baggage	Denver and St. Louis via MP
Vista Dome Chair Car	Denver and St. Louis via MP
Grill Chair Car	Denver and St. Louis via MP
Chair Car	Denver and St. Louis via MP
Diner-Lounge	Denver and St. Louis via MP
8-4 Thrift-T-Sleeping Car	Denver and St. Louis via MP
6-6-4 Sleeping Car	Denver and St. Louis via MP
10-6 Sleeping Car	Denver and St. Louis via MP

MP 8015 (PA, E6, PA) leads No. 4, *Colorado Eagle*, between Sedalia and Acequia on July 30, 1960. The train is still a heavy first class train at this time. *–Bob Andrews photo, Tom Klinger collection*

and the resulting consist is shown in Table 5-6.

The grill-chair did not last long as it was gone by 1961, replaced by another chair car. The 6-6-4 sleeping car was also gone by 1961. By October 1962, *Colorado Eagle* was down to a dome-chair, a single chair car, the diner-lounge, a Thrift-T Sleeping car and a 10-6 sleeping car. By May 1964 the sleeping cars and diner-lounge as well as the name were gone. Nos. 3 and 4 were down to four cars, two head end cars, a dome-chair and a chair car. In 1965 the dome was replaced by a standard chair car and on May 16, 1966, the train ceased operation.

The end was also near for Nos. 1 and 2, *Royal Gorge*. By November 1965 the Rio Grande's Vista Dome and grill-lounge were dropped, leaving only head end cars and a single chair car as the Rio Grande's contribution to the train. The train had also been cut back to Salida as its western terminal. The CB&Q discontinued operation of its cars between Denver and Colorado Springs effective January 1, 1967, leaving only the head end and single chair car. Nos. 1 and 2 ended Rio Grande passenger service on the Joint Line on July 27, 1967.

Freight Trains

Freight train schedules were no longer listed in the employee timetables after 1955, so informa-

A D&RGW PA leads two other units on No. 2 departing Colorado Springs, Colorado, in June 1965. This is the Santa Fe track, which would be taken up in 1970. Trailing the Rio Grande coach are the three Burlington cars for *Denver Zephyr*. *–Stuart J. Sutton photo*

AT&SF 280C (F7ABBB) on northbound freight (No. 36) at Monument, Colorado, in July 1965. Note deadhead baggage car and lone TOFC. –*Stuart J. Sutton photo*

tion on freight trains for the remainder of the book has been gathered from multiple sources, notably Santa Fe System Circular 231, *Freight Train Schedules*, and John Carr's *Santa Fe Freight Train Symbol History 1968 to 1984* being the most important. Information on the Colorado and Southern and the Rio Grande proved to be even more difficult. A few scattered Transportation Plans of the two railroads were available and recollections from employees and knowledgeable observers filled out what little documentary evidence was available. The results are a few snapshots of the freight schedules over the remaining forty years.

AT&SF Freight Trains

By 1956, the Santa Fe preponderance of traffic was eastbound and so the railroad eliminated No. 46 from the schedule leaving two scheduled through freights out of Denver and only one into Denver. No.

Table 5-7

No.	Name	Details
31	Fast Freight	Denver to Pueblo with traffic for No. 32 for east at La Junta. Scheduled for 10:00 AM departure from Denver.
36	Fast Freight	Pueblo to Denver with traffic off No. 35 from the east at La Junta. Scheduled for an evening arrival in Denver.
41	Fast Freight	Denver to Pueblo connecting to No. 42 at Pueblo for Newton. Scheduled for midnight departure from Denver.
97	Local Freight	Denver to Colorado Springs on a 5-hour schedule, Monday, Wednesday and Friday.
98	Local Freight	Colorado Springs to Denver on a 4½-hour schedule Tuesday, Thursday and Saturday.

36 arrived in Denver in the evening, so there was plenty of time to switch cars to industries for the start of the next day's business. Nos. 97 and 98, by now called local freight instead of way freight, continued to run between Denver and Colorado Springs three days a week each way. Power for the through freight trains throughout the 1950s was provided by 100 Class FT locomotives, usually in three- or four-unit consists. GP7s or RSD4 or 5s provided power for the locals. Table 5-7 summarizes Santa Fe freight trains up to about 1960.

Around 1961, the Santa Fe eliminated No. 36 leaving just two through freight trains on the Joint Line. No. 31 was a Denver to Kansas City train leaving Denver around 10:00 AM and arriving in Pueblo four hours later. The train handled all traffic for La Junta and east. No. 36 arrived in Denver from Kansas City around 8:00 PM. It handled loads and billed empties destined Dodge City to Denver. Nos. 97 and 98 continued to provide local freight service three days a week each way between Denver and Colorado Springs.

In February 1965, Nos. 97 and 98 had their schedules lengthened significantly. Now taking over seven hours to accomplish their work, No. 97 left

Denver Monday, Wednesday and Friday at 9:00 AM and arrived in Colorado Springs seven and a half hours later. On Tuesday, Thursday and Saturday, No. 98 left Colorado Springs at 10:15 AM and arrived in Denver at 6:00 PM.

Around 1968, two Santa Fe through freight trains, CWT (Colorado-West Texas) and WCT (West Texas-Colorado) were added to the Joint Line. These trains between Colorado and west Texas via the mid-1930s-built line between Amarillo and Las Animas Junction, formerly had terminated at La Junta, but they now ran all the way to Denver, in direct competition with the Colorado and Southern trains. Train CWT left Denver at midnight and took four hours to make the trip to Pueblo. Train WCT left Pueblo at 4:00 AM and arrived in Denver five hours later.

A year later the Santa Fe changed the symbols of Nos. 31 and 36 to DKC (Denver-Kansas City) and KCD (Kansas City-Denver). This change eliminated the number change at Pueblo for through freight trains. Train KCD operated on an eight-hour schedule (nearly twice No. 36's four hour 40 minute schedule) departing Pueblo at 7:00 AM and arriving in Denver at 3:00 PM handling loads and billed empties destined north of Pueblo. Train DKC ran on the same schedule as that of old No. 31 leaving Denver at 10:00 AM and arriving in Pueblo four hours later.

Train WTC arrived at 9:00 AM (too late for early morning delivery) and train KCD arrived in mid afternoon. Trucks were now handling freight to small local business and railroads were only switching larger industries by this time. Table 5-8 shows Santa Fe freight trains at the end of the 1960s.

In the 1960s, power for Santa Fe through freight trains usually came from the 200 Class F3 and F7 freight locomotives, supplemented by 325 Class dual

Right: AT&SF 177C leads a (probably No. 31 southbound) freight at 8th Avenue, Denver on May 7, 1961. *Bob Andrews photo, Tom Klinger collection*

AT&SF 308 (F7) leads a southbound, probably DKC, train with two TOFC at Sedalia in February 1970. *–Stuart J. Sutton photo*

Passenger Trains Decline as Freight Holds Steady: 1955-1971   129

AT&SF 244 (F7ABBB) on southbound freight (No. 31) at Spruce, Colorado, in July 1965. –*Stuart J. Sutton photo*

Table 5-8

No.	Name	Details
DKC	*Denver-Kansas City*	Denver to Kansas City. Scheduled for 10 AM departure from Denver. Handled all traffic destined to La Junta and east.
KCD	*Kansas City-Denver*	Kansas City to Denver on an 8-hour schedule over the Joint Line. Handled loads and billed empties destined north of Pueblo.
CWT	*Colorado-West Texas*	Denver to Ft. Worth handling all traffic for Pueblo and beyond.
WTC	*West Texas-Colorado*	Ft. Worth to Denver handling all traffic destined for La Junta and beyond.
97	*Local Freight*	Denver to Colorado Springs on a 7½-hour schedule, Monday, Wednesday and Friday.
98	*Local Freight*	Colorado Springs to Denver on a 7¾-hour schedule Tuesday, Thursday and Saturday.

service F7s. Occasionally GP20s and the rare GE U25B, which were normal power east of Kansas City, would make a trip to Denver and back. GP7s and RSD4s and 5s continued to power the local freight trains. In 1969, the Santa Fe bought twenty SD39s and twenty U23Cs, primarily for service over Raton Pass west of La Junta. These locomotives also found their way to Denver over the Joint Line.

Left: AT&SF 330 (F7ABB) on northbound freight train (probably No. 36) at Monument, Colorado in July 1965. –*Stuart J. Sutton photo*

Former passenger unit AT&SF 16 (F3A) + 3 lead a southbound freight (probably DKC) in Sedalia in February 1970. –*Stuart J. Sutton photo*

Nearly new AT&SF 4006, 4007, 4002, FW&D 87 (SD39, SD39, SD39, SD9) on freight south of Colorado Springs circa 1970. –*Author's collection*

Above: C&S 156 (SW1200 lettered for both C&S and AT&SF) switching AT&SF way car at Denver in May 1967. *–Stuart J. Sutton photo*

Left: C&S 839 (SD9) + 7 SDs and Fs on northbound manifest freight (probably No. 72) passes AT&SF 2788 (GP7) + 1 working the hump at Pueblo, Colorado, in December 1969. *–Stuart J. Sutton photo*

C&S Freight Trains

It turned out that the C&S was the most difficult road for which to find freight train schedules. It appears that the C&S continued with the schedules that existed in 1955 for quite a while as shown in Table 5-9. The C&S started the period covered by this chapter with three freight trains, two southbound and one northbound, and ended the period with one each way. No. 73 left the schedule around 1958, leaving Nos. 75 and 76 to carry the loads between Denver and Ft. Worth through around 1966. One interesting train was the C&S ore train. This ran extra about once a week from a load out at Sunrise, Wyoming, on the Colorado and Wyoming, and was interchanged to the C&S at Guernsey, Wyoming. C&S took the train to Colorado Fuel and Iron in Pueblo

using C&S, FW&D, CB&Q (later BN) hopper cars. The empties returned in regular freight trains. This was a regular feature on the Joint Line until the mill closed its blast furnaces in 1980-81.

By 1967, the C&S had added two, as needed, manifest freight trains, Nos. 72 and 73. No. 72 ran to Pueblo from Amarillo with cars for Pueblo and connections and was then switched and left for Denver at 6:15 PM with cars for Colorado Springs and Denver. No. 73 was a Denver to Amarillo train leaving Denver at 3:00 PM with cars for Colorado Springs, Pueblo proper, and connections. It took four and a half hours to make the trip over the Joint Line. By this time, No. 75 was a Denver to Galveston train that connected from C&S No. 78 in Denver and handled Coors beer from Golden as well as cars for Pueblo and connections and points beyond. It departed Denver at 5:00 AM

Table 5-9

No.	Name	Details
73	*Fast Freight*	Scheduled mid-afternoon from Denver for Ft. Worth on a 4¾-hour schedule
75	*Fast Freight*	Early morning departure from Denver for Pueblo on a 4-hour schedule
76	*Fast Freight*	Ft. Worth to Denver scheduled for an evening arrival at Denver

and arrived in Pueblo four fours later. No. 76 was a Houston to Denver train, handling loads and empties for Denver and beyond. It also carried Santa Fe cars from Pueblo to Denver, departing at 8:30 AM and arriving in Denver four hours later. It appears as if this schedule continued up to the end of the period covered by this chapter and is summarized in Table 5-10.

The C&S bought 23 SD9s between 1956 and 1959. The early SD9s were dual-service units and

Table 5-10

No.	Name	Details
72	*Amarillo-Denver Manifest*	As needed. Handled loads and empties for Colorado Springs, Denver and beyond on a 6-hour schedule.
73	*Denver-Amarillo Manifest*	As needed. Handled cars for Colorado Springs, Pueblo proper, and connections and beyond on a 4½-hour schedule.
75	*Denver-Galveston Manifest*	Operated daily. Connects from No. 78. Handled beer from Golden and cars for Pueblo proper and connections.
76	*Houston-Denver Manifest*	Operated daily. Handled loads and empties for Denver and beyond. Handled AT&SF cars Pueblo to Denver.

had steam boilers. The twelve SD9s purchased in 1959 were the first to wear the Burlington Chinese red and gray paint and did not have steam boilers. The Fs and SDs held down C&S freight assignments until 1967 when thirteen SD40s and four U30Cs were purchased in that year and the following one. For a short period of time after the demise of C&S passenger trains, the railroad tried the E5s on freight trains, but the racers proved to be unsuitable to haul freight. In March 1970, the Great Northern (GN), Northern Pacific (NP), Burlington with its subsidiaries, and the Spokane, Portland and Seattle Railway (SP&S) merged to form the Burlington Northern (BN). Shortly after the merger, around 1970, former CB&Q, GN, and NP units started to show up on C&S freight trains.

C&S 9955A + 5 (E5) on southbound freight train (probably No. 73) at Larkspur, Colorado, in October 1967. *–Stuart J. Sutton photo*

Right: C&S 702-A (F7ABBA) on a southbound freight train at Castle Rock, Colorado, in July 1965. *–Stuart J. Sutton photo*

134　　The Joint Line

Above: FW&D 752-D (F7ABBA) on C&S southbound ore train near Sedalia in January 1966. –*Stuart J. Sutton photo*

Opposite, clock-wise from top-left:
C&S 893 (U30C) + 5 lead a southbound freight (probably No. 75) at Larkspur, Colorado, in June 1969. –*Stuart J. Sutton photo*

SP 9803 + 3 (leased to BN) on Burlington Northern northbound manifest train (probably C&S 177) at Palmer Lake, Colorado, May 1970. The merger that created the Burlington Northern had occurred only two months prior. Although the C&S had been included in the merger it retained nominal independence for another ten years. –*Stuart J. Sutton photo*

D&FW 750-D (F7ABBA) leads a southbound freight train (probably No. 75) arriving at Palmer Lake, Colorado, in June 1967. –*Stuart J. Sutton photo*

C&S 822 (SD9) + another SD7 or 9 on southbound manifest freight (probably No. 75) at Spruce, Colorado, in June 1965. –*Stuart J. Sutton photo*

C&S 702-D + 6 (F7AB, 3 SDs, F7AB) on southbound freight train (probably No. 75) at Tomah, Colorado, on March 29, 1968. –*Stuart J. Sutton photo*

CB&Q 151 (U30B) + 4 on C&S southbound manifest freight (probably No. 75) at Palmer Lake, Colorado, in December 1969. –*Stuart J. Sutton photo*

D&RGW 5571 (F7 rebuilt to F9ABB) on southbound (probably No. 67) freight train south of Security, Colorado, in July 1965. –*Stuart J. Sutton photo*

D&RGW Freight Trains

The Rio Grande started the period covered by this chapter with three Denver and Pueblo freight trains and ended it with four, two each way. Table 5-11 summarizes the freight schedules at the beginning of 1956. There were two northbound and one southbound trains. The Rio Grande also continued to provide local service between Denver and Sedalia on an unscheduled, probably as-needed, basis.

By 1958, the Rio Grande had added an additional southbound freight train, No. 67. Departing Denver just after supper, it arrived in Pueblo five hours later with traffic for Pueblo west and southbound Rio Grande connections and eastbound Missouri Pacific No. 68. No. 65 continued on the same five-hour schedule as before, departing Denver at 9:00 PM but the transportation plan noted that it connected to MP No. 62. No. 66 departed Pueblo two hours later than before at 11:00 PM and had its schedule chopped by an hour with a 4:00 AM arrival in Denver. It connected at Pueblo from MP No. 81. No. 68 departed Pueblo 3¾ hours later than before at 5:00 PM and had its schedule lengthened by 45 minutes so it arrived in Denver at 11:30 PM. It connected from MP No. 61.

Rio Grande freight schedules continued pretty much unchanged until around 1968. No. 65 continued on its old schedule, but the other three had minor schedule changes. No. 66 still operated on a five-hour schedule but departed Pueblo an hour earlier. No. 67 departed Denver at 4:00 PM and arrived in Pueblo four and a half hours later. No. 68 still departed Pueblo at 5:00 PM but had its schedule cut by 30 minutes, arriving in Denver at 11:00 PM. Throughout the 1960s the local continued to run between Denver and Sedalia, probably as needed. Table 5-12 shows these changes.

In 1970, the Rio Grande changed the schedule of No. 65 to a 4:00 PM departure from Denver, the same time as No. 67. However No. 65 took eight hours to get to Pueblo, three and a half hours longer than No. 67.

In the mid-1950s, the Rio Grande bought dual-purpose F9s, GP9s and SD9s to supplement the FTs, F7s and road switchers bought earlier. In the 1960s, RS3 5203 was assigned to the Joint Line and often pulled the unscheduled local freight train between

Denver and Sedalia. When the Alco was not on the job, GP7s or 9s handled the local

In the early 1960s the Rio Grande began buying second-generation diesel power. In 1962, the Rio Grande traded in thirteen FTs and bought thirteen GP30s. In 1963 the road added fifteen GP30s, 22 GP35s in 1963-64, 35 GP40s between 1966-69, and finally 26 SD45s between January 1967 and March 1968. Any of these could show up on the Joint Line trains.

Table 5-11

No.	Name	Details
65	Fast Freight	Evening departure Denver to Pueblo with primarily perishable traffic for MP on a 5-hour schedule over the Joint Line
66	Fast Freight	Pueblo to Denver for early morning delivery with traffic received off MP at Pueblo on a 6-hour schedule
68	Fast Freight	Pueblo to Denver with traffic from the MP and San Luis Valley on a 5¾-hour schedule with an early evening arrival
(Unscheduled)	Local Freight	Denver-Sedalia turn

Table 5-12

No.	Name	Details
65	Denver to Pueblo Manifest	Evening departure with primarily perishable traffic for MP No. 62 on a 5-hour schedule over the Joint Line
66	Pueblo to Denver Manifest	For early morning delivery with traffic received off MP No. 81 at Pueblo on a 5-hour schedule
67	Denver to Pueblo Manifest	Traffic for MP No. 68 at Pueblo on a 4½-hour schedule
68	Pueblo to Denver Manifest	Traffic from MP No. 61 and San Luis Valley on a 6-hour schedule
(Unscheduled)	Local Freight	Denver-Sedalia turn

D&RGW 3068 (GP40) + 3 on southbound ore train for CF&I at Louviers, Colorado, in June 1970. About six months a year the UP and D&RGW cooperated to run an ore train from mines in Utah to CF&I. The UP interchanged the train to D&RGW at Denver. The other six months of the year the UP interchanged the train to the D&RGW at Salt Lake City and it ran over Tennessee Pass. (See Chapter 6). *–Stuart J. Sutton photo*

Right: D&RGW 5501 (FT) + 4 on freight near Littleton, Colorado, in the early 1960s. *–Denver Public Library, Western History collection, Otto Perry, OP-10899*

D&RGW 5106 (GP7) + 3 GP9 on southbound freight (could be either 65 or 67 as they both left Denver at 4:00 PM) at Blakeland, a named spur on the D&RGW southbound track between Littleton and Acequia, Colorado, put in after the Plum Creek flood of 1965 in May 1970. –*Stuart J. Sutton photo*

D&RGW 5110 (GP7) on local switching in May 1968.
–*Stuart J. Sutton photo*

D&RGW 5681 + 2 (F7AB, GP30) on southbound freight (probably No. 67) at Tomah, Colorado, in October 1967. –*Stuart J. Sutton photo*

Track maintenance on the Joint Line was always a challenge. In June 1965, Stuart Sutton caught Sperry Rail Service 136 (detector car) inspecting track approaching Castle Rock, Colorado. –*Stuart J. Sutton photo*

Chapter Six

Enter Powder River Coal: 1971-1995

ALL THREE JOINT LINE RAILROADS entered the summer of 1971with no passenger traffic and freight traffic little changed from 1945. Santa Fe's track northward through Colorado Springs was a nuisance to citizens who complained frequently and loudly. Because there was minimal traffic on the line (two to six trains a day from each of the three railroads on the route) in 1971 the Santa Fe and Rio Grande reached an agreement for the Santa Fe to use the Rio Grande track between Kelker and Palmer Lake for all trains in both directions, with Centralized Traffic Control (CTC) being installed. Santa Fe dispatchers won the right to dispatch trains. This conversion was completed and trains were running over the new route by July of 1974 (see track chart on the following page). Then Powder River coal trains hit the Joint Line.

It started with the Burlington Northern merger mentioned in the previous chapter. Shortly thereafter, the Burlington Northern (BN) decided to actively pursue heavy shipments of coal from the Powder River Basin in Wyoming, and by 1972 the BN was building a new railroad into the coalfields. Much of that coal was destined for power plants in Texas, and the entire character of the Joint Line changed as a result. Coal trains began to dominate the Joint Line just

Opposite: AT&SF 3431 + 1 lead a southbound Q train past Castle Rock circa 1987. –Steve Patterson photo

after the passenger trains stopped running. The Colorado and Southern, officially merged into the Burlington Northern on December 31, 1981, became by far the largest user of the Joint Line.

For all three railroads, freight train schedules began to change with far greater rapidity over the final 25 years covered by this book. Where a basic schedule might not change for years in the early half of the century, by 1995, schedules could change monthly or even weekly. As the pace of American life and the pace of change in and character of American business increased and changed due to new and constantly improving technologies, the pace of change in freight schedules increased to keep pace. An example of a railroad response to the changes in freight traffic patterns is the Santa Fe's Big Lift intermodal yard and auto unloading facility that it built in the late 1970s near Denver to expedite the handling of piggy-back and container freight. Although the Santa Fe tried mightily to make Denver an intermodal hub, it met with, at best, mixed results.

Santa Fe

The Santa Fe started the 1970s with the same four through freight trains that it ended the 1960s with: KCD and DKC between Denver and Kansas City as well as CWT and WCT between Denver

and Ft. Worth. On the Joint Line KCD was the slowest, running between Denver and Pueblo in eight hours. The other three were much faster, with WCT on a five-hour schedule and DKC and CWT on four-hour schedules. The local continued to run tri-weekly between Denver and Colorado Springs using over seven hours to get the job done. (See table in previous chapter.)

On January 1, 1971, new, computerized symbols were instituted on the Santa Fe. These new three-digit symbols were designed so that the first digit was the region of origin, "1" for Chicago area up to "9" for northern California. The last digit was for the destination and used the same numerical code. The second digit shows the type of service. Origin and destination codes of interest to this study are "3" for the Kansas City area, "4" for Kansas-Oklahoma-Colorado, "5" for east Texas and "8" for southern California. Second digits 0, 1, 2, 3 were for general merchandise and 4 for trains generally handling perishables. Nine was used for high priority, generally intermodal trains. Local trains used a four-digit number.

The new symbols for the Joint Line trains are shown in Table 6-1 below. The trains, except the Englewood Switcher, operated on the same schedules over the Joint Line as their predecessors.

In January 1975, the Santa Fe completely reworked its Joint Line freight schedules. The prepon-

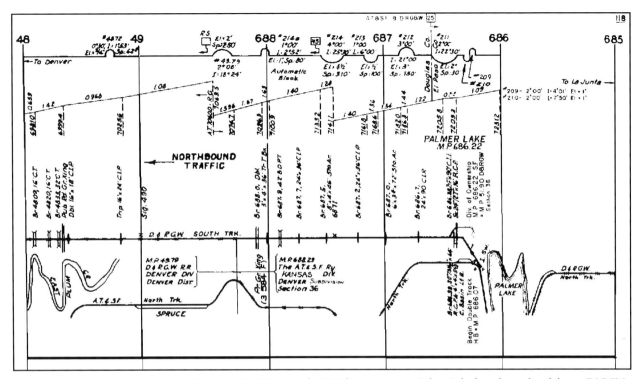

This track chart of Palmer lake shows the D&RGW and AT&SF lines coming into Palmer Lake from the north and the one D&RGW line leaving. –R. L. Crump/Priest Library collection

Table 6-1

No.	Name	Details
413	Denver-Kansas City	Old DKC. Denver to Kansas City. Handled all traffic destined to La Junta and east. Denver to Pueblo in 4 hours.
314	Kansas City-Denver	Old KCD. Kansas City to Denver on an 8-hour schedule over the Joint Line. Handled all traffic destined for Pueblo and beyond.
405	Denver-Ft. Worth	Old CWT. Denver to Ft. Worth handling all traffic for Pueblo and beyond. Midnight Denver departure to Pueblo in 4 hours.
504	Temple-Denver	Old WCT. Temple-Denver. Handled all cars for Amarillo and beyond routed to La Junta or beyond. Pueblo to Denver in 5 hours.
1561	Englewood Switcher	Daily except Sunday road switcher. Replaced Local Nos. 97 and 98.

derance of traffic appeared to now be westbound so one eastbound train (413) was cancelled. Train 114 replaced westbound train 314 because the eastern terminal was changed from Kansas City to Chicago. It left Pueblo at 10:30 AM and arrived in Denver 4½ hours later with general freight. Train pair 405 and 504 became 495 and 594. The Texas terminal for these trains moved to Houston and it is probable that these trains carried significant intermodal traffic as indicated by the "9" middle digit. Train 495 left Denver at 3:00 AM with traffic for Pueblo and beyond. It took only 3¼ hours, making it the fastest train on the Joint Line up to that time. Its northbound counterpart train, 594, handled all cars Amarillo and beyond routed to La Junta or beyond and left Pueblo at 10:00 PM and arrived in Denver at 3:00 AM as 495 was leaving. Apparently the 3¼-hour schedule proved to be a bit too much for the Santa Fe to handle so in October 1976 495's departure from Denver was moved to midnight and

arrival in Pueblo was 4½ hours later.

February 1977 continued additional schedule changes for the westbound trains. The Santa Fe reinstated train 314 replacing 114 on virtually the same schedule. Departure from Pueblo was at 10:20 AM with a 3:00 PM arrival in Denver. The railroad also added another westbound train - 194. This train ran from Chicago to the newly established Big Lift intermodal terminal south of Denver with trailers and automobiles. Yet the schedule was remarkably slow for such a high priority train, a bit over 8½ hours with a 9:25 PM departure from Pueblo and a 6:00 AM arrival at Big Lift. Later the schedule would be shortened by over three hours. At some point after Big Lift opened, the base for the Englewood Switcher was moved to Big Lift and it could go as far south as Colorado Springs.

In November 1977 the Santa Fe added two more trains to the Joint Line. Trains 414 and 464 were both Denver to La Junta trains handling general freight.

Both trains operated on a 6-hour schedule over the Joint Line. Train 414 left Denver at 10:00 AM while train 464 departed Denver at 6:00 PM. A year later these two trains were gone, but the Santa Fe replaced them with a counterpart to 194. Train 491 handling Trailers On Flat Cars (TOFC), departed Big Lift at 6:00 PM, taking 464's slot and arrived in Pueblo 6 hours later.

In April 1979 even more changes came. Apparently 491 did not generate much traffic and it was dropped. In its place train 464 reappeared on a slightly faster schedule, departing at 7:30 PM and arriving in Pueblo at midnight. The Santa Fe added train 444, departing Denver at 6:00 PM and also arriving at Pueblo at midnight. Finally the Santa Fe cut back Train 314's western terminal to Pueblo and ran new Train 434 from Pueblo to Denver on a 6-hour schedule, departing Pueblo at 10:00 AM.

In 1982, the Santa Fe added another Denver to La Junta train, 424. This train departed Denver with traffic off the Burlington Northern for Pueblo and beyond at 7:00 PM and arrived in Pueblo five

SOUTHWARD ↓

JOINT LINE TIME TABLE No. 2 — February 6, 1977

Turn Tables, Wyes & Communications	Mile Post	Capacity of Sidings in Feet	Ruling Grade Ascending (Feet Per Mile)	STATIONS
	*3.6			SOUTH DENVER YL
				3.9
B	*7.5		51.0	ENGLEWOOD YL
				0.7
B	*8.2		52.8	MILITARY JCT. YL
				2.1
C	10.3	2700	52.8	LITTLETON YL
				6.7
B	17.0	4200	52.8	ACEQUIA
				3.7
C	20.7	2300	53.0	LOUVIERS
				3.8
B	24.5	4800	64.5	SEDALIA
				3.3
B	709.5	3900	73.9	ORSA
				4.3
B	705.2	5700	73.9	CASTLE ROCK
				5.0
B	700.2	2900	73.9	TOMAH
				5.3
B	694.9	4000	73.9	LARKSPUR
				5.4
B	691.5	4000	73.9	GREENLAND
				2.7
B	688.8	2800	73.9	SPRUCE
				2.5
B	*52.0		73.9	PALMER LAKE
				5.2
B	*57.2	6900	0	MONUMENT
				8.1
B	*65.3	7200	0	ACADEMY
				9.6
Y C R	*74.9	15300	0	COLORADO SPRINGS
				4.2
B	659.9	5400	0	KELKER
				5.4
	654.4		0	CREWS
				4.0
B	650.5	3900	0	FOUNTAIN
				6.8
B	643.7	3500	0	BUTTES
				5.3
B	638.4	2300	0	HENKEL
				5.7
B	632.7	4000	0	PINON
				2.4
	630.3		0	BRAGDON

(ABS ... TCS ... ABS with DT on right edge)

(104.1)

RULE 251 IN EFFECT: Between South Denver and Palmer Lake.

T.C.S. IN EFFECT: On main track and sidings between Palmer Lake and Crews.

RULE 251 IN EFFECT: Between Crews and Bragdon.

Southward AT&SF and D&RGW trains originating Denver must secure two numbered AT&SF clearance cards Form 902, one of which issued by D&RGW train dispatcher and one by AT&SF train dispatcher, before leaving.

Interlocked junction switch with CRI&P main track at MP 74.3 is off Colorado Springs siding.

*Indicates D&RGW Mile Posts.

NORTHWARD ↑

JOINT LINE TIME TABLE No. 2 — February 6, 1977

STATIONS	Ruling Grade Ascending (Feet Per Mile)	Capacity of Sidings in Feet	Mile Post	Turn Tables, Wyes & Communications
SOUTH DENVER			733.4	
4.0				
ENGLEWOOD YL	0	3100	729.4	C
2.8				
LITTLETON YL	0	2600	726.6	C
13.8				
SEDALIA	0	4900	712.8	B
8.0				
CASTLE ROCK	0	3700	*32.5	B
19.5				
PALMER LAKE	0		*52.0	B
5.2				
MONUMENT	75.0	6900	*57.2	B
8.1				
ACADEMY	75.0	7200	*65.3	B
9.6				
COLORADO SPRINGS	52.8	15300	*74.9	Y C R
4.2				
KELKER	52.8	5400	659.9	B
5.4				
CREWS	52.8		654.4	
3.1				
FOUNTAIN	39.0	4500	*87.9	B
20.6				
BRAGDON	48.0		*108.5	B

(ABS ... TCS ... ABS with DT on right edge)

(104.3)

RULE 251 IN EFFECT: Between Bragdon and Crews.

T.C.S. IN EFFECT: On main track and sidings between Crews and Palmer Lake.

RULE 251 IN EFFECT: Between Palmer Lake and South Denver.

RULE 94 IN EFFECT: Between AT&SF MP 730.1 and South Denver.

Interlocked junction switch with CRI&P main track at MP 74.3 is off Colorado Springs siding.

*Indicates D&RGW Mile Posts.

1977 Timetable for the Joint Line operators. –*John R. Signor collection*

The Atchison, Topeka & Santa Fe Railway Company

The Denver and Rio Grande Western Railroad Company

JOINT LINE

TIME TABLE No. 2

In Effect Sunday, February 6, 1977

At 12:01 A.M. Mountain Standard Time

This Time Table is for the Exclusive Use and Guidance of Employes.

H. J. BRISCOE
General Manager
Topeka, Kansas

A. H. NANCE
General Manager
Denver, Colorado

C. R. ROSE
Assistant Gen'l Mgr.
Topeka, Kansas

D. J. BUTTERS
Chief Transportation Officer
Denver, Colorado

J. K. HASTINGS
Superintendent
La Junta, Colorado

L. R. PARSONS
Superintendent
Denver, Colorado

hours later. By 1983, 434 had been dropped from the schedule and the schedules for 424 and 444 had been lengthened considerably. Train 424 departed Denver at 7:00 PM and arrived in Pueblo 11 hours later. Train 444 departed Denver at 6:00 PM and arrived in Pueblo ten hours later. Train 594 arrived in Denver eight hours later than previously. Train 495 had been cut back to La Junta and no longer appeared on the Joint Line. Table 6-2 shows how the Santa Fe on the Joint Line looked in October 1983.

By spring 1986 the Santa Fe had concluded that Big Lift had failed to develop the intended intermodal traffic and it moved its intermodal traffic to UP's Denver yard. Geography was against the Santa Fe competing for Denver intermodal traffic. UP had a faster route westbound and BN had the better route to the east. That just left Texas-bound traffic and there was not much of that.

This eliminated Train 194, which was replaced by Train 364, a Kansas City to Denver intermodal train terminating in UP's yard. Train 444 had also been eliminated by 1986 and 594 had been replaced by train 534, a Brownwood to Denver manifest freight train. However, by the fall 534 was gone leaving just two numbered Santa Fe trains on the Joint Line: 364 and 424. Train 364 left Pueblo at 3:00 AM for morning arrival in Denver. Train 424 was scheduled to leave Denver at 11:00 AM.

More changes were due because on Labor Day 1986 Santa Fe began the Quality Service Network (QSN), a series of short, fast trains connecting se-

Top-left: AT&SF 287 + 2, BN 507 + 2 (F9A, F7B, F7B, SD9, SD9, SD9) smoke it up as they leave Denver on southbound 314 in February 1971. New designations went into effect Jan. 1, 1971.
–Al Chione collection

Left: AT&SF 6345 (U23B) + 2 on southbound freight (probably 413) at Sedalia, Colorado, in June 1974. The train is stopped in the siding and apparently being inspected by the crew.
–Stuart I. Sutton photo

lected key cities. The railroad could provide this service because an agreement between the railroad and operating unions allowed for reduced crews (three-person) operating over extended districts on trains that carried new business, mainly diverted from the highways. The agreement also eliminated way cars. Denver was one of the key cities and so by the fall, the Joint Line saw two pairs of QSN trains: Q-DVLJ/Q-LJDV which connected Denver and La Junta, and QDVHO/QHODV which connected Denver with Houston, thus reintroducing Denver to Houston service. The two pairs operated twelve hours apart, with Q-DVLJ and Q-DVHO leaving Denver at 9:00 AM and 9:00 PM, respectively. Q-LJDV and Q-HODV left Pueblo at 11:00 AM and 11:00 PM, respectively.

A year later in 1987, the Santa Fe was still running two regular freight trains, 364, the intermodal from Kansas City to Denver and 423 from Denver to Kansas City, which had replaced 424. It was still running two pairs of Q trains, but the connecting terminals to Denver had changed to El Paso and Oklahoma City. The symbols for the Q trains were now Q-DVEP, Q-EPDV, Q-DVOK, and Q-OKDV. By August the two El Paso trains were gone leaving just the Denver to Oklahoma City pair. Table 6-3 sum-

Table 6-2

No.	Name	Details
194	*Chicago–Big Lift*	TOFC and autos on a 5¼-hour schedule, arriving at Big Lift at 4:00 AM.
424	*Denver–La Junta*	General manifest freight carrying BN traffic from Denver to Pueblo and beyond. Operated on an 11-hour schedule, arriving Pueblo at 6:00 AM.
444	*Denver–La Junta*	General manifest train departing Denver's UP yard at 6:00 PM on a 10-hour schedule. Picks up at Big Lift.
594	*Houston–Denver*	Old 504 Houston to Denver. Handled all cars Amarillo and beyond routed to La Junta or beyond.
1561	*Big Lift Switcher*	Worked as far south as Colorado Springs.

AT&SF 3612, 3220, 6612 (GP30-2, GP30, U25B) lead train 194 on July 6, 1977, after sorting out its intermodal traffic at Big Lift, Colorado. *–Gary A. Rich photo*

AT&SF 3225, CN 5132, 5140, C&S 839, 823, 841 (GP30, SD40, SD40, SD9, SD9, SD9) on the point of southbound train 414 at Blakeland, Colorado, on August 13, 1977. Santa Fe, which was short power at this time, leased some CN units and used BN units extensively on the Joint Line. *–Gary A. Rich photo*

AT&SF 3240 (GP30) leads the Santa Fe local 1561 with a BN caboose at Littleton, Colorado, on July 6, 1977. –*Gary A. Rich photo*

AT&SF 6391 (B23-7) + 3 on southbound freight train (probably 424) at Larkspur in May 1985.
–*Stuart J. Sutton photo*

AT&SF 8718 (U36C) + 2 on northbound freight 434 at Fountain, Colorado, on July 8, 1979.
–*Robert R. Harmen photo, author's collection*

marizes the Santa Fe trains at this time.

By July 1990 the Q trains were gone as the concept of reduced crews over longer districts had proved itself and the Santa Fe negotiated new agreements with the unions for reduced way car-less trains operating over longer crew districts. On the Joint Line every train hauled north out of Big Lift lost the Santa Fe money. So when the Santa Fe attempted to raise rates, all the shippers disappeared, and the Q trains with them. Thus the Santa Fe reworked its Joint Line schedules. There were four trains on the line, two pairs of Kansas City and Denver trains. All four performed local work en route. One pair, 304/403, was manifest and one pair, 344/443, was intermodal and manifest. Train 304 left Pueblo at 2:30 PM and arrived in Denver eight hours later. Train 403 left Denver at midnight and arrived in Pueblo seven hours later. Train 344 left Pueblo at 8:30 PM and arrived in Denver seven hours later. Finally, train 443 left Denver at 7:00 PM taking seven hours to make it to Pueblo.

It wasn't until 1993 that the Santa Fe made any significant schedule changes on the Joint Line. At

Table 6-3

No.	Name	Details
364	*Kansas City to Denver Intermodal*	Intermodal train to UP Yard in Denver, arriving in the morning.
423	*Denver to Kansas City*	General manifest freight. Departs Denver at 11:00 AM.
Q-DVEP	*Denver to El Paso Quality*	Departs from Big Lift.
Q-EPDV	*El Paso to Denver Quality*	Arrives at Big Lift.
Q-DVOK	*Denver to Oklahoma City Quality*	Departs from Big Lift.
Q-OKDV	*Oklahoma City to Denver Quality*	Arrives at Big Lift.
1561	*Big Lift Switcher*	Works as far south as Colorado Springs.

AT&SF 7514 (U23C) + 2 on freight meets BN 5815 (U30C) on southbound as crews switch in February 1976. –*Stuart J. Sutton photo*

AT&SF 3520, CNW 818, CN 5132 (GP38, GP30, SD40) lead train 314 coming into Pueblo on August 16, 1977. It will soon head west on the Joint Line. –*Gary A. Rich photo*

AT&SF 5188 + others pull a loaded coal train of BN hopper cars out of Denver circa 1985. –*Steve Patterson photo*

AT&SF 5097, 5169 (SD40-2) gets underway with southbound Q (probably Q-DVEP) train at Palmer Lake, Colorado, in July 1989. –*Stuart J. Sutton photo*

that time, the railroad changed most train symbols from the numerical system to an alphabetic system. The first letter designated the type of service and the next two letters designated the originating point of the train and the last two the terminating point of the train. By September of that year there were still four trains on the line, a Kansas City and Denver pair of manifest trains (Symbol "H" means priority manifest) performing local work en route, the H-KCDV and H-DVKC. The Santa Fe had by this time given up promoting Denver as an intermodal hub and replaced the Kansas City and Denver intermodal and manifest train pair with a pair of Denver and Barstow, California, manifest trains, the H-DVBA and H-BADV. All four of these trains would carry whatever intermodal traffic was offered. Table 6-4 summarizes the Joint Line trains in 1993.

This lineup continued up to the merger with the BN creating BNSF in 1995. The Big Lift switcher continued to work as needed. Its schedule called for it to leave Big Lift around 9:00 AM and arrive in Colorado Springs at 2:00 PM, departing 30 minutes later and arriving back in Big Lift at 9:00 PM. Occasionally there would be so much work that a relief crew would be sent to Colorado Springs.

In March 1970, the Santa Fe had consolidated

Table 6-4

No.	Name	Details
H-KCDV	*Kansas City to Denver Priority Manifest*	Intermodal/manifest train. Performs local work en route.
H-DVKC	*Denver to Kansas City Priority Manifest*	Intermodal/manifest train. Performs local work en route.
H-DVBA	*Denver to Barstow Priority Manifest*	Manifest train. Performs local work en route.
H-BADV	*Barstow to Denver Priority Manifest*	Manifest train. Performs local work en route.
LCA-911	*Big Lift Switcher*	Works as far south as Colorado Springs.

Above: AT&SF 5960 + 3 (F45, SD45-2, F45, GE) on freight at Spruce in October 1986. *–Gordon Bassett photo, author's collection*

all locomotive assignments and had created a centralized power bureau in Chicago. From that time forward, almost any locomotive type could appear on the Joint Line. And in the 24 years between 1971 and 1995, most did at one time or another. Photographic evidence indicates that the Englewood/Big Lift Switcher, work trains and lighter trains such as the early Q trains received medium horsepower four-axle road switchers such as the GP38, GP35u, GP39-2 and the B23-7. Heavier trains received six-axle power such as the SD45, SD40-2, and C30-7. Santa Fe contributions to coal train pools were usually SD40-2s or C30-7s. In the 1990s rebuilt U36Cs, the SF30Cs, were popular especially on the Barstow trains. Red and silver warbonnet liveried C40-8Ws powered coal trains and the manifest trains in the last few years.

A northbound Q train led by AT&SF 3687 passes an empty coal train at Colorado Springs circa 1987. *–Steve Patterson photo*

AT&SF 5046 (SD40-2) + 2 (including an SD45-2B) on a manifest freight train (probably 423) at Palmer Lake in July 1988. –*Stuart J. Sutton photo*

AT&SF 3402, 2347 (GP39-2u, GP38u) + 1 on southbound Q (probably Q-DVOK) train at Palmer Lake, Colorado, in October 1988. –*Stuart J. Sutton photo*

AT&SF 3697 +1 are on a southbound Q train at Academy circa 1987. –*Steve Patterson photo*

Clock-wise from top-right: AT&SF 9514 (SF30C) + 3 on north-bound freight train (probably 304) at Palmer Lake in July 1989. –*Stuart J. Sutton photo*

AT&SF 808, 841, 925 (C40-8W) on southbound (H-DVKC or H-DVBA) at Greenland in August 1994. –*Stuart J. Sutton photo*

AT&SF 609 (C44-9W) + C40-8W lead a northbound manifest freight (H-BADV or H-KCDV) at Palmer Lake in April 1994. –*Stuart J. Sutton photo*

C&S 880 (SD40) leads BN and SP power on northbound SACE, a coal train through Pueblo On October 27, 1977. –*Gary A. Rich photo*

BN 5833 (U30C) + 3 including two C&S locomotives on coal loads for Pueblo's Comanche power plant at Stadium on August 21, 1977. –*Gary A. Rich photo*

Colorado and Southern / Burlington Northern

As long as the C&S was nominally independent it kept the train numbers it had long used. But on December 31, 1981, C&S was absorbed into the BN and thereafter BN three-digit train numbers supplanted the C&S's two-digit system. In 1970, at the time of the BN merger, the C&S was running two pairs of Denver and Fort Worth general manifest trains. The southern terminals had changed from Houston and Galveston back to Dallas and Ft. Worth. Table 6-5 is taken from the April 30, 1970, Rio Grande freight schedules.

No. 75, from Denver for Dallas, departed Pueblo at 9:00 AM, indicating an early morning departure from Denver. Its northbound counterpart arrived in Pueblo at 10:00 PM, probably was reclassified and then ran on to Denver overnight. For the first time, the C&S instituted trains with three-numeral train numbers, Nos. 177 and 178, which replaced the Denver to Houston trains shown in the previous chapter. No. 177, after travelling the Joint Line in the afternoon and following reclassification, departed Pueblo southbound at 6:16 PM. No. 178 arrived in Pueblo at 3:00 AM, was reclassified, then sent on to Denver.

For the 1970s, the C&S, according to the recollections of some employees, probably got by with two or four trains a day, Nos. 75 and 76 and 77 and 78, which replaced 177 and 178. Toward the end of the decade only Nos. 77 and 78 were running. It is interesting to note that C&S trains from here on had odd

Table 6-5

No.	Name	Details
75	*Denver-Dallas Manifest*	Operates daily.
76	*Dallas-Denver Manifest*	Operates daily.
177	*Denver-Dallas Manifest*	Operates daily.
178	*Dallas-Denver Manifest*	Operates daily.

numbers northbound and even southbound. Around 1980 when the C&S had been fully absorbed into the BN, the two manifest trains running between Denver and Dallas became Nos. 151 and 152, running between Denver and Ft. Worth. No. 152 was mostly Coors beer.

By July 1986, the C&S was at its high point in terms of numbers of non-coal trains. The railroad was trying to develop an intermodal market between the northwest and Texas. Accordingly it had instituted trains 91 and 92. No. 91 ran from Ft. Worth to Seattle departing Pueblo for Denver in the mid-morning. Counterpart No. 92 ran from Portland to Houston, departing Denver for Pueblo at 11:00 PM. The railroad also ran a pair of priority manifests between Ft. Worth and Seattle, Nos. 195 and 196. No. 195 usually departed Pueblo for Denver in the early evening and No. 196 departed Denver for Pueblo after reclassification, about 10:00 AM. (The source for the information in this paragraph is two lineups taken from *Colorado's Joint Line: A Guide to Facilities and Operations* by Donald K. Park II.) There were also two pairs of Ft. Worth and Denver manifest trains, Nos. 261/262 and 561/562. Train 262 was on duty at 2:00 AM, but I could not determine approximate scheduled times for the rest of these trains from the limited information available. By the fall of 1986 Nos. 91 and 92 were running between Houston and Spokane and Nos. 561 and 562 were gone. Table 6-6 summarizes the situation in the fall of 1986.

By 1990 BN again had eight freight trains on the line. Nos. 91, 92, 195, 196, 261 and 262 were all still in the lineup, and Nos. 193 and 194 had been added. The latter two trains were manifest trains running between Ft. Worth and probably Denver, although that is not certain. By 1995, at the time of the merger with the Santa Fe, BN had cancelled Nos. 91 and 92, the intermodal trains, as well as 261 and 262, the manifest "Junk" trains. This left Nos. 193 and 194, which probably ran between Ft. Worth and Denver

BN 6322, 6304 (SD40-2) + 2 lead a southbound manifest freight (probably No. 152) downgrade at Palmer Lake, Colorado, in June 1974. –*Stuart J. Sutton photo*

BN 6315, 6331 (SD40-2) on C&S No. 77 at Colorado Springs on June 5, 1977. –*Gary A. Rich photo*

BN 6461, 5370, C&S 904, BN 6626, 5474, + 2 (SD40-2, U30C, SD40-2, F45, U30C, SD45, U30C) on BN train No. 77 at Bragdon, Colorado, in August 1978. –*Gary A. Rich photo*

and 195/196, the Seattle to Ft Worth priority manifest trains.

Power for the manifest trains was quite varied. The C&S/BN used SD40-2 and C30-7 locomotives frequently. These were supplemented by four-axle power such as GP39s, GP38-2s, GP50s after 1980, and leased LMX B39-8s after 1987.

Although the BN had significant manifest traffic on the Joint Line, coal trains predominated. Coal trains were run based on contracts, usually for 15 years, between the railroad and the power plant. As contracts came up for renewal, other railroads bid on them. This, coupled with the fact that coal trains were unscheduled and ran in cycles based on loading and unloading time as well as demand, makes tracking

difficult. The power companies owned most coal carrying cars. Therefore a snapshot of coal traffic must suffice to illustrate the magnitude of the traffic.

By 1986, the BN was running about six loaded coal trains a day south and an equal number of empties north on the Joint Line. The BN provided coal to the Comanche plant in Pueblo and interchanged three coal trains with the Santa Fe in Pueblo. Most of the remaining coal trains ran to power plants in Texas. Additional coal trains ran to plants in Oklahoma, Louisiana, and Arkansas. Table 6-7 shows the BN train symbol (where known), reporting marks of the cars in the train, name of the power company, and any interchange partners.

Additionally at this time, the Santa Fe scheduled

Table 6-6

No.	Name	Details
91	Intermodal	Operated daily from Houston to Spokane
92	Intermodal	Operated daily from Spokane to Houston
195	Priority Manifest	Operated daily from Ft. Worth to Seattle
196	Priority Manifest	Operated daily from Seattle to Ft. Worth
261	Manifest	Formerly No. 151, Ft. Worth to Denver daily "Junk" freight
262	Manifest	Formerly No. 152, Denver to Ft. Worth daily "Junk" freight

two coal trains over the Joint Line which it interchanged with the BN at Denver, the C-DVML (loads) and C-MLDV empties. These were to and from a power plant at Muleshoe, Texas. It is unclear why the interchange point was Denver rather than Pueblo as Santa Fe crews operated both Santa Fe and BN trains.

To provide power for the many coal trains it was operating, the C&S bought six SD45s in 1971, the first units delivered to the C&S in BN cascade green, and 168 SD40-2 locomotives from 1972 to 1980. This was more than twice the total number of diesel locomotives it had bought in all its previous years of existence. The 3,000 horsepower SD40-2 and C30-7 were the power of choice for coal trains until 1986 when the 3,800 horsepower Oakway SD60s began showing up. Four or five 3,000 horsepower locomotives were usually at the head end of southbound loaded coal trains.

Two 3,000 horsepower locomotives, most often SD40-2s, were coupled on the rear either at Denver or at Big Lift to aid in getting the trains over the Palmer Divide. Instructions were that any train over 8,000 tons must have pusher locomotives. The pushers uncoupled at Palmer Lake. The Santa Fe practice was to uncouple the pushers north of the double-to-single track switch. The train would then proceed with the pushers following through the switch where they would stop, throw the switch to the northbound track and then proceed back to Denver. Pushers were rarely needed for northbound trains, but if required they were added at Colorado Springs and ran all the way to Denver.

After testing three 1991-built SD60MACs in pusher service, in 1993 the BN ordered over 300 4,000 (later 4,300) horsepower SD70MACs. By 1995, the BN was well on the way to replacing four- and five-3,000 horsepower unit locomotive consists with three SD70MACs. Two 3,000 horsepower pushers were still required to get the southbound trains up the Palmer Divide.

BN 6749, 6725 (SD40-2) helpers cut off a southbound coal train at Palmer Lake, Colorado, in August 1988. –*Stuart J. Sutton photo*

Table 6-7

Symbol	Reporting Marks	Power company	Location	Interchange
SLE/SLW	UFIX	Houston Light & Power	Smithers Lake, TX	AT&SF at Ft. Worth
AME/AMW	AMAX	TUCO Harrington Plant	Amarillo, TX	
HLE/HLW	WFAX	Western Fuels Ass'n., Sunflower Electric	Holcomb, KS	AT&SF at Pueblo
	SATX	City Public Service Board of San Antonio	San Antonio, TX	MKT at Ft. Worth
	RTPX	TUCO Tolk Plant	Muleshoe, TX	AT&SF at Pueblo
CCE/CCW	PSCX	Public Service Co. of CO Comanche Plant	Pueblo, CO	AT&SF delivery
	LCRX/FPPX	Lower Colorado River Authority	Fayette Power Project, La Grange, TX	MKT at Ft. Worth
	BN	Texas Municipal Power	Gibbons Creek, TX	
AML/AMW	BN	Springerville Station	Springerville, AZ	AT&SF at Amarillo?
		Plains Escalante Generating Station	PEGS, NM	AT&SF at Pueblo
	GNSX	Entergy Gulf States	Mossville, LA	SP at Ft. Worth?
	GNSX	Entergy Arkansas	Redfield, AR	SP at Ft. Worth?

Left: Oakway 9075 + 1 (SD60) are on south-bound BN (probably No. 196, Seattle-Ft. Worth manifest) freight train at Palmer Lake in September 1990. –*Stuart J. Sutton photo*

Bottom-left: BN 3040 (GP40-2) + 3 including two cabless B30-7As have just left Spruce for Palmer Lake on a manifest train in September 1993. –*Stuart J. Sutton photo*

Bottom-right: An all-GE locomotive consist of BN 5544 (C30-7) + 4 (3 C30-7, U30C) on southbound coal loads at Baptist Road in May 1989. Baptist Road is just south of the Monument siding. –*Stuart J. Sutton photo*

BN 8117, 5594, 8085, 5100, 7083 (SD40-2, C30-7, SD40-2, C30-7, SD40-2) on BN northbound (either 261 or 195) at Larkspur, Colorado, on April 11, 1992. –Gary A. Rich photo

BN 7305 6399 (SD40-2, SDP40) + 3 AT&SF units illustrate the mixing of Santa Fe and BN units on a manifest freight at Acequia in August 1993. –Stuart J. Sutton photo

BN 5566 + 1 (C30-7) on a northbound used tie train at Greenland, Colorado, on April 11, 1992. –Gary A. Rich photo

Rear pushers BN 6370 + 1 (both SD40-2) on C-DVML at Orsa, Colorado, on May, 9, 1992. –*Gary A. Rich photo*

BN 7935, 7849 + 2 (SD40-2, SD40-2, C30-7, C30-7) lead a southbound BN ballast train at Palmer Lake on April 11, 1992. –*Gary A. Rich photo*

BN 9221 (SD60) + 3 leads C-DVML coal loads at Orsa, Colorado, on May 9, 1992. –*Gary A. Rich photo*

Oakway 9019 (SD60) + 3 (C30-7) lead a southbound coal train north of Larkspur on April 3, 1992. –*Gary A. Rich photo*

Rio Grande

During the 1970s, the Rio Grande continued to run four Denver and Pueblo freight trains, Nos. 65/66 and 67/68 as seen in Table 6-8.

No. 65 had moved to a new schedule from that noted at the end of Chapter 5 with a 4:00 PM Denver departure, the same time as No. 67, but with a three hour longer schedule. The other three trains maintained the same schedule as they had had at the end of the 1960s. In August 1972, No. 65 moved to a 4:00 AM departure and a five-hour schedule to Pueblo. At the same time, No. 67's time over the road to Pueblo was lengthened by two and a half hours resulting in an 11:00 PM arrival in Pueblo. No. 65 lasted on this schedule for about a month and then returned to 4:00 PM departure and eight hours on the Joint Line.

By 1977, the traditional two pairs of manifest trains, Nos. 65/66, and 67/68 become 165/166 and 167/168. This continued to be the norm through the 1980s. No. 165 was an early morning train out of Denver, handling empty TOFC and auto racks along with general freight. It usually set out at Colorado Springs. No. 166 usually left Pueblo in the early morning, mostly with hot loads off the MP. No. 167 left Denver between 2:00 and 8:00 PM, carrying cars for interchange in Pueblo as well as cars for the San Luis Valley. No. 168 left in the afternoon carrying cars from the San Luis Valley and cars that had arrived in Pueblo after the departure of No. 166.

Occasionally there would be a No. 265, which handled coal for the Drake Power Plant and general freight. It would normally stop in Colorado Springs. By the early 1980s traffic had increased on the Rio Grande so that the railroad added a regular No. 265 to Pueblo and No. 266 north to Denver from Pueblo handling the additional traffic. On some days there would even be a No. 267 and No. 268. The increased traffic was probably due to the Rio Grande's acquir

D&RGW 3008, 3095, 3052 (GP30, GP40-2, GP40) +3 lead train 165 southbound at Academy, Colorado, on August 7, 1977. –Gary A. Rich photo

ing haulage rights over the Union Pacific to Kansas City and St. Louis as a result of the Union Pacific buying the Missouri Pacific in late 1982.

Finally the Rio Grande ran a local from Denver's North Yard to Sedalia and back, trains 553 and 554. The local would work Englewood and Littleton, go to Sedalia and return back north to Denver. Table 6-9 below summarizes the situation on the Rio Grande in the mid-1980s.

Preferred power for the manifest freight trains continued to be four-axle EMD locomotives bought in the 1960s, the GP30, GP35, GP40, and GP 40-2, although six-axle power such as SD45s and SD40T-2s could also be found working the manifest trains.

In 1988, the Rio Grande's owner, Philip Anschutz, purchased the Southern Pacific, resulting in a merger of the two railroads under the SP ban-

Table 6-8

No.	Name	Details
65	Denver to Pueblo Manifest	Afternoon departure running on an 8-hour schedule over the Joint Line for connections at Pueblo
66	Pueblo to Denver Manifest	Traffic for an early morning delivery at Denver on a 5-hour schedule
67	Denver to Pueblo Manifest	Afternoon departure for connections at Pueblo on a 4½-hour schedule
68	Pueblo to Denver Manifest	Traffic from Pueblo with connections for Denver on a 6-hour schedule with late evening arrival
(Unscheduled)	Local Freight	Denver to Sedalia turn

D&RGW 5365 + 2 (SD40T-2) lead train 774 (coal empties) as a southbound BN train recedes in the distance through Colorado Springs, Colorado, on June 17, 1977. –*Gary A. Rich photo*

Table 6-9

No.	Name	Details
165	*Denver to Pueblo Manifest*	Early morning departure with empty TOFC and auto racks and traffic for connections at Pueblo.
166	*Pueblo to Denver Manifest*	Early morning departure from Pueblo with traffic from Pueblo connections, especially hot loads off MP.
167	*Denver to Pueblo Manifest*	Afternoon/evening departure for connections at Pueblo and for San Luis Valley.
168	*Pueblo to Denver Manifest*	Afternoon departure from Pueblo with cars from San Luis Valley and connecting cars for Denver.
265	*Denver to Pueblo Manifest*	Second section of No. 165 often with coal for Drake Power Plant at Colorado Springs. Would often turn back to No. 266 at Colorado Springs.
266	*Pueblo to Denver Manifest*	Second section of No. 166. Often originating at Colorado Springs.
553/554	*Local Freight*	Denver to Sedalia turn.

D&RGW 5374 + 2 (SD40T-2) at Bragdon with No. 775 ore loads on August 8, 1977. This is an ore train from Utah for CF&I in Pueblo. D&RGW would get the train from UP at Denver about 6 months of the year. The other six months it would travel over Tennessee Pass to Pueblo. –*Gary A. Rich photo*

D&RGW 5366 + 4 (SD40T-2) on train 712, southbound coal loads, at Acequia, Colorado, on August 8, 1977, heading to MP at Pueblo. –*Gary A. Rich photo*

D&RGW 5902 (GP9) with the local at Littleton, Colorado, in April 1979. The former Santa Fe depot is in the background to the right of the crewman on the steps of 5902. –*Stuart J. Sutton photo*

D&RGW 3121 (GP40-2) on train 553 (Local) at Blakeland, Colorado, in February 1980. This train ran from Denver to Sedalia and return, switching Englewood and Littleton. –*Gary A. Rich photo*

ner. One consequence of the merger was a change of train numbers to alpha codes. The first two letters indicated a train's origin and the second two indicated a train's destination. The last letter indicated type of service. Thus 167/168 became DVPUM and PUDVM respectively. By this time the SP was running only a single pair of manifest freight trains on the Joint Line although it could and did run multiple sections of DVPUM and PUDVM. This continued up through 1995.

Increased coal trains began to appear on the Rio Grande in the mid-1970s, about the same time as they did on the C&S/BN. The D&RGW, and later the SP, did not operate as many coal trains on the Joint Line as did the BN. Coal trains on the Rio Grande were numbered in the 700-series with even numbers being southbound loads and odd numbers northbound empties. The Rio Grande directly served two Colorado Springs Utilities power plants in the Colorado Springs area, the Nixon Plant near Fountain and the Drake Plant in the city itself. In

D&RGW 3087 (GP40) + 3 on southbound freight (probably SP DVPUM)) at Greenland, Colorado, in October 1988. The first cars are a block of coal loads for the Drake Power Plant in Colorado Springs. –*Stuart J. Sutton photo*

Power-short SP has an EMD loaner and a Family Lines EMD in the power consist led by D&RGW GP 40-2 3094 on northbound PUDVM at Palmer Lake in June 1993. –*Stuart J. Sutton photo*

Table 6-10

Symbol	Reporting Marks	Power company	Location	Interchange
725/726	CELX/MIDX	Celanese Chemical	Kings Mill, TX	AT&SF at Pueblo
709/710	CSUX	Nixon Power Plant	Fountain, CO	
717/718	D&RGW/CSUX	Drake Power Plant	Colorado Springs, CO	
711/712	D&RGW		On C&IM	MP at Pueblo
707/708	CCTX	Central Power & Light Co.	Coleto Creek, TX	AT&SF at Pueblo/SP at Ft. Worth
721/722	KPLX	Kansas Power & Light	Tecumseh/Kansas City	AT&SF at Pueblo
719/720	NORX	Northern Indiana Public Service Co.	Indiana Harbor, IN	MP at Pueblo
713/714	UCEX	Union Electric Co.	2 plants near St. Louis	MP at Pueblo

Pueblo the Rio Grande interchanged three unit coal trains with the Santa Fe and two with the MP. The Rio Grande also supplied coal in D&RGW cars to a power plant in Cañon City and to the cement plant in Portland, Colorado. However these cuts were not large enough for unit coal trains. As with the BN a snapshot of the mid 1980s is provided in Table 6-10 to give an idea of the amount of coal traffic on the Joint Line.

In the mid 1970s D&RGW unit coal trains were 73 cars long. The first 105-car D&RGW train was the 707/708. No. 708 was split at Phippsburg into two sections of 70 and 35 cars, respectively. At Denver it was combined into one 105-car train and a manned helper set was added for the trip to Pueblo. The Rio Grande crews interchanged the train to the Santa Fe in the Santa Fe yard in Pueblo.

In addition, about six months a year, the Rio Grande and the UP cooperated to run a unit iron ore train from mines in Utah to CF&I in Pueblo. The UP handled the train between Utah and Denver and the Rio Grande between Denver and CF&I in Pueblo. The other six months of the year, the UP handed the train over to the Rio Grande in Salt Lake City and the Rio Grande ran it over Tennessee Pass to Pueblo, bypassing the Joint Line. This lasted until the steel mill closed its blast furnaces in 1980-1981 and became a mini-mill.

Preferred power for the Rio Grande coal trains

SP 8494, 7553 (SD40T-2, SD45-2) leads DVPUM at Littleton, Colorado, circa 1991. –*Gary A. Rich photo*

SP 8318 (SD40T-2) + 2 are on a DVPUM with a block of coal loads for the Drake Power Plant in Colorado Springs in August 1994. –*Stuart J. Sutton photo*

were usually SD45s or SD40T-2 units. The Rio Grande had bought 26 SD45s in 1967 and 1968 for general freight service. Like the Southern Pacific, the Rio Grande had had trouble with units overheating in tunnels so they bought the SD40T-2 when coal traffic started to increase in the 1970s. All told, the railroad bought 73 SD40T-2s in five orders between 1974 and 1980.

Like the BN coal trains, the Rio Grande also added power, called helpers, at Denver for the climb up to Palmer Lake. As on the BN, the helpers were usually two 3,000 or 3,600 horsepower units. Most often they were added at the rear of the train but could be added about two-thirds of the way into the train. When this was done they were called swing helpers. At Palmer Lake, the Rio Grande removed the helpers by pulling past the switch where double track became single track. The helpers then could head directly to Denver on the northbound track.

The SP merger did not markedly affect the coal traffic, except that coal trains also received alpha designations with the last letter being C. A typical coal train would be AICLC, which stood for Axle Mine (near Craig, Colorado) to Coleto Creek, Texas, coal loads. The returning empties would be CLAIC.

SP 7562 (SD45) + 5 lead northbound SP PUDVM at Palmer Lake in July 1993. –*Stuart J. Sutton photo*

Left: SP 9690 + 1 (GP60) lead a train of passenger cars at Palmer Lake in June 1995. Although scheduled passenger trains disappeared from the Joint Line in 1971, the three railroads (later two) continued to run passenger specials for company officers and shippers. –*Stuart J. Sutton photo*

Postscript

THE JOINT LINE WAS AND STILL IS a unique piece of railroad. There are other stretches of track where two railroads run, but usually one railroad is either a tenant of the other or just runs on trackage rights. I know of no other stretch of American railroad similar to the Joint Line in which the rails of two railroads are seamlessly merged into a double-track operation. On the Joint Line three railroads both cooperated and competed in the same territory for nearly 100 years. The government's USRA forced parallel railroads to, in effect, merge their two single-line operations into one double-track operation that has continued to work after the removal of government control. Yet despite their merged operations under a single set of rules and timetable, the three railroads were still able to compete with one another. All three provided complementary yet competing passenger services up into the 1960s. Passenger agents sold tickets for whichever railroad was most convenient to the passenger unless the passenger expressed a preference. Both the Santa Fe and the Rio Grande provided local freight service.

I think the reason this worked so well is that the competitive focus of each railroad was different. The Santa Fe's focus was on Denver east through Kansas to Kansas City. The C&S's focus was on Denver south to Dallas/Ft. Worth in Texas. The Rio Grande's focus, before the completion of the Moffat Route, was Denver south over the Joint Line and then west to Salt Lake City and southwest to the San Luis Valley. After the completion of the Moffat Route, the Joint Line became a secondary interest focusing on Denver and interchange with the MP to east and southwest to the San Luis Valley. Thus the competitive focus of all three lines was not on the Joint Line itself but beyond Pueblo in different directions. The Santa Fe did try to take on the C&S directly between Denver and Amarillo, but this was via a long branch line that was not nearly as important to the Santa Fe as was the C&S's main line to Amarillo to itself. It was simply in the interest of all three railroads to cooperate and run a merged operation over the Joint Line.

In 1995, the Santa Fe and the BN merged to form the Burlington Northern Santa Fe, later just BNSF. The merger brings this history of the Joint Line to a close as the two original partners in the Joint Line became part of a single railroad. In 1996 the Union Pacific bought the Southern Pacific and Armour yellow replaced SP scarlet and gray on the Joint Line.

While this chapter of the Joint Line history ends, the story continues. Both railroads still share the track as before, as it is still in the interest of the BNSF and UP to run a merged operation over the Joint Line. Coal traffic dominates traffic on the Joint Line. The single track between Palmer Lake and Kelker is still a bottleneck, but the line continues to evolve. In August 2013, Big Lift will become BNSF's auto loading facility. This facility will be expanded north and rebuilt to handle auto racks with 15,000 foot long unloading tracks. The Joint Line is now, and will be in the future, a wonderful place for rail fans to catch lots of railroad action in strikingly beautiful scenery.

Appendix

Document Summaries

August 1, 1900 Joint Line Contract Between the Santa Fe and the Colorado and Southern

Major provisions of the initial Joint Line Contract:
- Properties that made up the Joint Line included:
  - » Denver terminal properties of each company
  - » Pueblo terminal properties of each company
  - » Santa Fe mainline between Denver Yard Limits and Pueblo Yard Limits
  - » Colorado and Southern mainline between Denver Yard Limits and Pueblo Yard Limits, including the line from Manitou Junction to the Colorado Springs Yard Limits
- Colorado Springs terminal properties of each company
- Each company granted the other the "right to use fully, jointly, and equally the property of the other" that made up the joint Line.
- Neither company could conduct business on the other's line except at Denver, Colorado Springs, or Pueblo.
- Each company had "sole charge of maintenance, supervision and operation" of its own mainline. The Colorado and Southern had "sole charge of the maintenance, supervision and operation" of the Denver terminal for both companies and the Santa Fe had the same for Pueblo and Colorado Springs.
- "All employees in the service of either party shall, while engaged in the maintenance supervision or operation of the property and facilities" covered by the agreement, "be considered as joint employees."
- Traffic of both companies between Denver and Pueblo would be carried on the Santa Fe's mainline. The C&S could carry any traffic originating or destined to stations between Denver and Pueblo Yard Limits on its own line.
- Created a "Joint Expense Account" under the supervision of an auditor appointed by both companies.
- The Santa Fe agreed to improve its line by relocating 10 miles north from Pueblo, rearranging its facilities at Pueblo, fencing its line and replacing the mainline rails with heavier rail. It also agreed to construct a system of block signals on its line between Denver and Pueblo. When necessary the C&S agreed to improve the Denver terminal at its own expense and the Santa Fe agreed to improve the Pueblo terminal at its own expense.
- Any additions or improvements to the Santa Fe mainline, which were necessitated by Santa Fe's own business, were to be done at Santa Fe expense. Any improvements, necessitated by the use of the Santa Fe line by the C&S, were to be charged to the Joint Expense Account.
- The Santa Fe agreed to maintain its line in first class condition at its own expense except that the C&S agreed to pay the Santa Fe $500 per mile for the 110 miles of the Santa Fe line covered under the agreement. The C&S was to maintain its own line at its expense.
- The entire expense of maintaining and operating freight stations and warehouses at Denver, Colorado Springs, and Pueblo, including salaries of employees and supplies was to be charged to the Joint Expense Account and paid by the parties in the proportion of the number of tons of freight handled for each.
- "All taxes, assessments, and other governmental charges for all properties covered by the agreement were to be charged to the Joint Expense Account," and each party agreed to pay one-half.
- All locomotives in service were to be cared for by the C&S at Denver and by the Santa Fe everywhere else, including C&S locomotives used south of Pueblo, except those on the C&S mainline which were to be serviced by the C&S. All passenger cars, including Pullman cars in service were to be

cleaned and inspected at Denver by the C&S and at Colorado Springs and Pueblo by the Santa Fe. Each company was to provide "coal of satisfactory quality" at all coaling stations of "its proper proportion."

- The C&S was to provide switch locomotives at Denver and the Santa Fe at Colorado Springs and Pueblo for the combined business of both railroads. Each railroad was to provide a proportion of the freight and passenger locomotives required to move the combined business of both railroads. The freight proportion was figured on the basis of ton-miles of freight handled the previous month and the passenger proportion was figured on the proportion of passenger-miles handled the previous month. Likewise each party was required to furnish a proportion of the freight and passenger cars on the same basis of freight ton-miles and passenger miles.[9]

- "All time cards, rules, regulations and orders for the care and movement of traffic were to be fair and reasonable and just to each party with no undue preference or discrimination to either party."

- If a dispute between the parties arose, it was to be submitted to arbitration by a board composed of a person appointed by each railroad and a third person chosen by the two railroad appointed arbitrators. If in ten days the two railroad-appointed arbitrators could not agree, the President of the Southern Railroad or if he was unavailable or unable, the President of the New York Central and Hudson River Railroad would appoint the third arbitrator.

Minutes of a Meeting on June 29, 1920, Between Representatives of the Santa Fe and the Rio Grande

The minutes of this meeting constituted the agreement for operation of the line until 1936 when a written agreement was finalized. Main provisions of this agreement included:

- The lines of the AT&SF and D&RG parallel each other, in close proximity, so that joint operation, using the lines of the two companies as double track is feasible and economical.

- The D&RG should ballast their line on the portions not already ballasted.

- D&RG to construct and arrange, jointly with AT&SF, suitable manual block system for safe and economical handling of trains of both lines. AT&SF al-

ready have block system installed and in operation on its tracks. D&RG have already installed partial block service and agree to complete it at an early date.

- All facilities that serve the public such as stock yards, team tracks, station facilities except private industry tracks are to be included in the joint facilities and could be used by either of the companies including the C&S.

- Extend the D&RG passing track at Pinon south 1000 feet and move the Santa Fe depot north to a point opposite the south end of the D&RG passing track and the north end of the Santa Fe passing track--to be used as a joint station and also for block and telegraph office of both lines.

- Move the D&RG Buttes siding from present location to a location opposite Santa Fe, Buttes siding; move D&RG depot from present location, and locate it between the two lines for joint use as a station and block office.

- It was decided that it was desirable to complete arrangements for joint station at Palmer Lake by moving the Santa Fe depot to a point north of the lake, in proximity of the road crossing, and constructing platforms; move water crane on D&RG side to a suitable location to avoid extra stop of passenger trains to take water. Lake track in Santa Fe yard to be made the main line, in order to bring main line next to depot when moved. Santa Fe station building to be used as a joint station, telephone and block office.

- It was decided to arrange for suitable joint station at Sedalia by moving Santa Fe depot south to a point where tracks are close together and north of the bridge. As the difference in elevation of the two lines is considerable, it is thought that suitable platform and stairway can be constructed from D&RG track to the depot to answer the purpose adequately; this station to be used jointly by both companies, for station, telegraph and block office.

- Build a block office with sufficient height and signals so both lines can use it jointly, abandoning Gann and Struby including the AT&SF water station. D&RG have an office at Louviers, opposite Gann, which can be used for the handling of both companies.

- Arrange the platform, etc. at Littleton and continue the joint station. Make the present AT&SF passing track the main line in order to place main line next to joint station.

- Division of expenses for maintenance of roadway, cost of water, telephones, and dispatching trains was in contention; a decision was put off for further consideration.

February 26, 1936, the Santa Fe and Rio Grande Formal Agreement for Operation of the Joint Line

While the minutes were mostly concerned with property and facilities, this

---

9. It apparently was envisioned that passenger and freight trains would be scheduled jointly and that locomotives and cars would be freely intermixed. In fact it did not work out quite as envisioned. Each carrier maintained its own freight and passenger train schedules, but both railroad's schedules, especially passenger schedules, were carried in the public timetables of each for a while. However, it was not uncommon to see locomotives of one railroad on the other railroad's trains. Although not mentioned in the contract, eventually Santa Fe crews manned all C&S trains on the Joint Line.

agreement dealt mostly with operations. The key provisions of the agreement are:

- Effective on January 1, 1936,
- The parties agreed to continue the joint use of facilities for a double-track railroad, except that private industry tracks of either party and industries served by only one party were excluded, as were the facilities of either party at Colorado Springs other than passenger stations, water and fuel stations, sidings and train yard tracks.
- The agreement between the Santa Fe and the Colorado and Southern for joint use of the Santa Fe's facilities continued in effect and for purposes of the agreement between the Santa Fe and the Rio Grande, the C&S locomotives, cars, trains, employees and traffic be deemed to be the locomotives, cars, trains, employees, and traffic of the Santa Fe who assumed all liability for the C&S on the Joint Line.
- The agents and other employees at all stations on the Joint Line were to act as the agents and employees of both parties without preference in the handling of their respective traffic, except at Colorado Springs where each party was to handle its own business. Freight shipments offered to any agent of either party for forwarding except at Colorado Springs, the routing of which was not designated by the shipper, was to be routed as follows:
  » During calendar year 1936, freight offered during the first calendar month was to be shipped under bills of lading issued in behalf to the Rio Grande as its business and during the second calendar month under the Santa Fe's bills of lading and that was to continue to be so alternated during the year.
  » During calendar year 1937 such shipments offered during the first calendar month were to be shipped under the bills of lading issued on behalf of the Santa Fe as its business and during the second calendar month under the Rio Grande's bills of lading as its business and were to be continued to be so alternated during the year.
  » The same rotation by years was to continue during the period of the agreement.
  » When prospective passengers did not designate the route, agents on the Joint Line, including those at the two Colorado Springs passenger stations, will sell tickets over the line of the party whose train was next scheduled to depart, unless the passenger specified a train leaving at another time.
- The Santa Fe had the right, if it wanted to exercise it, to operate its trains over the Rio Grande between the interlocking plant at Bragdon and the interlocking plant at the Santa Fe-Rio Grande-Colorado and Southern crossing at Pueblo Junction.

- Improvements, additions or changes to facilities were to be made by each party at its own expense as were reasonably necessary or desirable for the economical or safe operation for the combined use of the parties.
- Unless otherwise mutually agreed, the Santa Fe would have exclusive direction and control of the dispatching of trains moving on the tracks designated for use by northward trains and the Rio Grande was to have exclusive direction and control of the dispatching of trains moving on the tracks designated for use by southward trains regardless of ownership.
- The Santa Fe was to clear all wrecks, snow, and other obstructions on the northward route and the Rio Grande on the southward route.
- The Rio Grande shall have the charge of and employ necessary forces for the operation and maintenance of the consolidated stations at Littleton, Pinon and Kelker.
- Each party could take coal from coal chutes of the other party on the Joint Line; the party so taking coal shall replace coal taken ton for ton with coal of equal quality.

1940 Updated C&S/AT&SF Joint Line Contract

In 1940, the Santa Fe and Colorado and Southern updated their Joint Line agreement which expired on March 1 of that year but which had been extended by letter of agreement to September 1, 1940. This agreement did not substantially change the agreement of 1915, which had updated the original 1900 agreement. Important provisions that had changed are given below:

- The C&S engine terminal at Denver had been consolidated in 1926 with that of the Burlington and the new agreement so noted.
- Because of the agreement between the Rio Grande and the Santa Fe for joint use of each other's facilities between Bragdon and South Denver, the C&S was prohibited from conducting local business except at Colorado Springs, including Roswell and the Colorado Springs stockyards of the Santa Fe located at Pikeview.
- Each company was to furnish freight locomotive tractive effort each month as was required to move their combined freight business in a ratio based on the aggregate Freight Gross Ton Miles of the second preceding calendar month.
- Each party was to furnish passenger locomotives for its own passenger trains including helpers. If, in an emergency, one party should furnish power for another's passenger trains, the party furnishing the power was to receive $0.32 per mile.
- Each party was to furnish its own passenger and freight cars and cabooses each year in a ratio based on the Freight Gross Ton Miles of the previous year.

Bibliography

Books

Athearn, Robert G. *Rebel of the Rockies*. New Haven, CT: Yale University Press, 1962.

Boyd, Jim. *Trackside Around Pueblo 1955-1970 with Stuart J. Sutton*. Scotch Plains, NJ: Morning Sun Books, 2009.

Bryant, Keith L. Jr. *History of the Atchison, Topeka & Santa Fe Railway*. Lincoln, NE: University of Nebraska Press, 1974.

Carr, John. *Santa Fe Freight Train Symbol History 1968 to 1984*. (self published, 1984).

Conway, Chuck. *Rio Grande: Crest of the Continent*. Kansas City: White River Productions, 2010.

Danneman, Herbert. *A Ticket to Ride the Narrow Gauge*. Golden, CO: Colorado Railroad Museum, 2000.

Farewell, R. C. *Rio Grande: A Last Look Back 1974-2010*. Arvada, CO: Crescent Publications, 2010.

Heimburger, Donald J. *Rio Grande Steam Locomotives*. River Forest, IL: Heimburger House Publishing Co. 1981.

Jones, James R. *Denver & New Orleans: In the Shadow of the Rockies*. Denver: Sundance Publications, 1997.

Locomotives of the Rio Grande. Golden, CO: Colorado Railroad Museum, 1980.

Park, Donald K. II. *Colorado's Joint Line: A Guide to Facilities and Operations*. Ft. Collins, CO: PARKRAIL, 1987.

Pate, J'Nell L. *Livestock Hotels: America's Historic Stockyards*. Ft. Worth: TCU Press, 2005.

Stagner, Lloyd E. *Rio Grande Steam Finale*. David City, NE: South Platte Press, 1999.

Thode, Jackson C. *A Century of Passenger Trains…And Then Some*. Denver: Rocky Mountain Railroad Club, 2001.

Wagner, F. Hol Jr. *The Colorado Road: History, Motive Power, & Equipment of the Colorado and Southern, Fort Worth and Denver Railways*. Denver: Intermountain Chapter National Railway Historical Society, Inc. 1970.

Worley, E. D. *Iron Horses of the Santa Fe Trail*. Dallas: Southwest Railroad Historical Society, 1965

Articles:

Duel, E. W. "Discussion Program, Denver and Rio Grande Western Railroad 1941-1942, the Pueblo Division," October 6, 1941. **http://www.drgw.org/data/trains/duel.htm** accessed on March 22, 2011.

Walz, Robert D. "A Survey of Denver Passenger Service," *The Warbonnet*, Second Quarter, 2010, pp. 6-12.

_____. "Pueblo, a Santa Fe Town," *The Warbonnet*, Second Quarter, 2010, pp. 13-28.

Documents:

Atchison, Topeka & Santa Fe Railway Co. *Colorado Division Employees' Time Table*. 1900-1918.

Atchison, Topeka & Santa Fe Railway Co. *Passenger Consists*. 1914-1970.

Atchison, Topeka & Santa Fe Railway Co. *Passenger Timetables*. 1900-1970.

Atchison, Topeka & Santa Fe Railway Co. *Building Record, Colorado Division*. Corrected to April 11, 1983.

Atchison, Topeka & Santa Fe Railway Co. *Rules and Regulations of the Operating Department*, 1927.

Atchison, Topeka & Santa Fe Railway Co. *System Circular 231 Freight Train Schedules*. Various years 1942-1990.

Atchison, Topeka & Santa Fe Railroad, Denver and Rio Grande Railroad. *Denver Division Employees' Joint Time Table*. 1920-1995.

Burlington Route. *System Timetables*. February 1930, February-April 1953, November 1953,

Colorado & Southern Railway Company. *Passenger Timetables*. 1899-1967.

Denver and Rio Grande Railroad. *Passenger Timetables*. 1918-1967.

Rio Grande Freight Traffic Guide – 1951- Tramway Press. 1983.

United States Railroad Administration. *Atchison, Topeka & Santa Fe Railroad, Denver and Rio Grande Railroad Denver Division Employees' Joint Time Table*. Nos. 1-6, 1918-1919.

United States Railroad Administration. *Passenger Timetables*. 1918-1919.